Pope's Iliad
VOLUME ONE

I0203124

ISBN: 979-8-9863364-3-5
Price: 23.99 USD
Publication: December 2023
Publisher: Nachlebenone

Pope's Iliad

Publisher's Forward

Books are my passion.

But I'm picky about how they are laid out, designed, and printed.

So I have undertaken to publish some of my favorite titles in convenient pocketbook editions, with attractive covers drawn by me, Roland Lifkowitz.

I hope you enjoy them as much as I do!

Respectfully,

Roland Lifkowitz
New York, New York
2023

THE ILIAD.

BOOK I.

THE CONTENTION OF ACHILLES AND AGAMEMNON.

Achilles' wrath, to Greece the direful spring
Of woes unnumber'd, heavenly goddess, sing!
That wrath which hurl'd to Pluto's gloomy reign
The souls of mighty chiefs untimely slain;
Whose limbs unburied on the naked shore,
Devouring dogs and hungry vultures tore.
Since great Achilles and Atrides strove,
Such was the sovereign doom, and such the will of Jove!
Declare, O Muse! in what ill-fated hour
Sprung the fierce strife, from what offended power
Latona's son a dire contagion spread,
And heap'd the camp with mountains of the dead;
The king of men his reverent priest defied,
And for the king's offence the people died.
For Chryses sought with costly gifts to gain
His captive daughter from the victor's chain.
Suppliant the venerable father stands;
Apollo's awful ensigns grace his hands:
By these he begs; and lowly bending down,
Extends the sceptre and the laurel crown.
He sued to all, but chief implored for grace
The brother-kings, of Atreus' royal race
"Ye kings and warriors! may your vows be crown'd,
And Troy's proud walls lie level with the ground.
May Jove restore you when your toils are o'er
Safe to the pleasures of your native shore.
But, oh! relieve a wretched parent's pain,
And give Chryseïs to these arms again;
If mercy fail, yet let my presents move,
And dread avenging Phœbus, son of Jove."
The Greeks in shouts their joint assent declare,
The priest to reverence, and release the fair.
Not so Atrides; he, with kingly pride,
Repulsed the sacred sire, and thus replied:
"Hence on thy life, and fly these hostile plains,
Nor ask, presumptuous, what the king detains:
Hence, with thy laurel crown, and golden rod,
Nor trust too far those ensigns of thy god.
Mine is thy daughter, priest, and shall remain;
And prayers, and tears, and bribes, shall plead in vain;

Till time shall rifle every youthful grace,
And age dismiss her from my cold embrace,
In daily labours of the loom employ'd,
Or doom'd to deck the bed she once enjoy'd.
Hence then; to Argos shall the maid retire,
Far from her native soil and weeping sire."
The trembling priest along the shore return'd,
And in the anguish of a father mourn'd.
Disconsolate, not daring to complain,
Silent he wander'd by the sounding main;
Till, safe at distance, to his god he prays,
The god who darts around the world his rays.
"O Smintheus! sprung from fair Latona's line,
Thou guardian power of Cilla the divine,
Thou source of light! whom Tenedos adores,
And whose bright presence gilds thy Chrysa's shores.
If e'er with wreaths I hung thy sacred fane,
Or fed the flames with fat of oxen slain;
God of the silver bow! thy shafts employ,
Avenge thy servant, and the Greeks destroy."
Thus Chryses pray'd:—the favouring power attends,
And from Olympus' lofty tops descends.
Bent was his bow, the Grecian hearts to wound;
Fierce as he moved, his silver shafts resound.
Breathing revenge, a sudden night he spread,
And gloomy darkness roll'd about his head.
The fleet in view, he twang'd his deadly bow,
And hissing fly the feather'd fates below.
On mules and dogs the infection first began;
And last, the vengeful arrows fix'd in man.
For nine long nights, through all the dusky air,
The pyres, thick-flaming, shot a dismal glare.
But ere the tenth revolving day was run,
Inspired by Juno, Thetis' godlike son
Convened to council all the Grecian train;
For much the goddess mourn'd her heroes slain.
The assembly seated, rising o'er the rest,
Achilles thus the king of men address'd:
"Why leave we not the fatal Trojan shore,
And measure back the seas we cross'd before?
The plague destroying whom the sword would spare,
'Tis time to save the few remains of war.
But let some prophet, or some sacred sage,
Explore the cause of great Apollo's rage;
Or learn the wasteful vengeance to remove
By mystic dreams, for dreams descend from Jove.

If broken vows this heavy curse have laid,
Let altars smoke, and hecatombs be paid.
So Heaven, atoned, shall dying Greece restore,
And Phœbus dart his burning shafts no more."
He said, and sat: when Chalcas thus replied;
Chalcas the wise, the Grecian priest and guide,
That sacred seer, whose comprehensive view,
The past, the present, and the future knew:
Uprising slow, the venerable sage
Thus spoke the prudence and the fears of age:
"Beloved of Jove, Achilles! would'st thou know
Why angry Phœbus bends his fatal bow?
First give thy faith, and plight a prince's word
Of sure protection, by thy power and sword:
For I must speak what wisdom would conceal,
And truths, invidious to the great, reveal,
Bold is the task, when subjects, grown too wise,
Instruct a monarch where his error lies;
For though we deem the short-lived fury past,
'Tis sure the mighty will revenge at last."
To whom Pelides:— "From thy inmost soul
Speak what thou know'st, and speak without control.
E'en by that god I swear who rules the day,
To whom thy hands the vows of Greece convey.
And whose bless'd oracles thy lips declare;
Long as Achilles breathes this vital air,
No daring Greek, of all the numerous band,
Against his priest shall lift an impious hand;
Not e'en the chief by whom our hosts are led,
The king of kings, shall touch that sacred head."
Encouraged thus, the blameless man replies:
"Nor vows unpaid, nor slighted sacrifice,
But he, our chief, provoked the raging pest,
Apollo's vengeance for his injured priest.
Nor will the god's awaken'd fury cease,
But plagues shall spread, and funeral fires increase,
Till the great king, without a ransom paid,
To her own Chrysa send the black-eyed maid.
Perhaps, with added sacrifice and prayer,
The priest may pardon, and the god may spare."
The prophet spoke: when with a gloomy frown
The monarch started from his shining throne;
Black choler fill'd his breast that boil'd with ire,
And from his eye-balls flash'd the living fire:
"Augur accursed! denouncing mischief still,
Prophet of plagues, for ever boding ill!

Still must that tongue some wounding message bring,
And still thy priestly pride provoke thy king?
For this are Phœbus' oracles explored,
To teach the Greeks to murmur at their lord?
For this with falsehood is my honour stain'd,
Is heaven offended, and a priest profaned;
Because my prize, my beauteous maid, I hold,
And heavenly charms prefer to proffer'd gold?
A maid, unmatch'd in manners as in face,
Skill'd in each art, and crown'd with every grace;
Not half so dear were Clytæmnestra's charms,
When first her blooming beauties bless'd my arms.
Yet, if the gods demand her, let her sail;
Our cares are only for the public weal:
Let me be deem'd the hateful cause of all,
And suffer, rather than my people fall.
The prize, the beauteous prize, I will resign,
So dearly valued, and so justly mine.
But since for common good I yield the fair,
My private loss let grateful Greece repair;
Nor unrewarded let your prince complain,
That he alone has fought and bled in vain."
"Insatiate king (Achilles thus replies),
Fond of the power, but fonder of the prize!
Would'st thou the Greeks their lawful prey should yield,
The due reward of many a well-fought field?
The spoils of cities razed and warriors slain,
We share with justice, as with toil we gain;
But to resume whate'er thy avarice craves
(That trick of tyrants) may be borne by slaves.
Yet if our chief for plunder only fight,
The spoils of Ilion shall thy loss requite,
Whene'er, by Jove's decree, our conquering powers
Shall humble to the dust her lofty towers."
Then thus the king: "Shall I my prize resign
With tame content, and thou possess'd of thine?
Great as thou art, and like a god in fight,
Think not to rob me of a soldier's right.
At thy demand shall I restore the maid?
First let the just equivalent be paid;
Such as a king might ask; and let it be
A treasure worthy her, and worthy me.
Or grant me this, or with a monarch's claim
This hand shall seize some other captive dame.
The mighty Ajax shall his prize resign;
Ulysses' spoils, or even thy own, be mine.

The man who suffers, loudly may complain;
And rage he may, but he shall rage in vain.
But this when time requires.—It now remains
We launch a bark to plough the watery plains,
And waft the sacrifice to Chrysa's shores,
With chosen pilots, and with labouring oars.
Soon shall the fair the sable ship ascend,
And some deputed prince the charge attend:
This Creta's king, or Ajax shall fulfil,
Or wise Ulysses see perform'd our will;
Or, if our royal pleasure shall ordain,
Achilles' self conduct her o'er the main;
Let fierce Achilles, dreadful in his rage,
The god propitiate, and the pest assuage."

At this, Pelides, frowning stern, replied:
"O tyrant, arm'd with insolence and pride!
Inglorious slave to interest, ever join'd
With fraud, unworthy of a royal mind!
What generous Greek, obedient to thy word,
Shall form an ambush, or shall lift the sword?
What cause have I to war at thy decree?
The distant Trojans never injured me;
To Phthia's realms no hostile troops they led:
Safe in her vales my warlike coursers fed;
Far hence removed, the hoarse-resounding main,
And walls of rocks, secure my native reign,
Whose fruitful soil luxuriant harvests grace,
Rich in her fruits, and in her martial race.
Hither we sail'd, a voluntary throng,
To avenge a private, not a public wrong:
What else to Troy the assembled nations draws,
But thine, ungrateful, and thy brother's cause?
Is this the pay our blood and toils deserve;
Disgraced and injured by the man we serve?
And darest thou threat to snatch my prize away,
Due to the deeds of many a dreadful day?
A prize as small, O tyrant! match'd with thine,
As thy own actions if compared to mine.
Thine in each conquest is the wealthy prey,
Though mine the sweat and danger of the day.
Some trivial present to my ships I bear:
Or barren praises pay the wounds of war.
But know, proud monarch, I'm thy slave no more;
My fleet shall waft me to Thessalia's shore:
Left by Achilles on the Trojan plain,

What spoils, what conquests, shall Atrides gain?"
To this the king: "Fly, mighty warrior! fly;
Thy aid we need not, and thy threats defy.
There want not chiefs in such a cause to fight,
And Jove himself shall guard a monarch's right.
Of all the kings (the god's distinguish'd care)
To power superior none such hatred bear:
Strife and debate thy restless soul employ,
And wars and horrors are thy savage joy,
If thou hast strength, 'twas Heaven that strength bestow'd;
For know, vain man! thy valour is from God.
Haste, launch thy vessels, fly with speed away;
Rule thy own realms with arbitrary sway;
I heed thee not, but prize at equal rate
Thy short-lived friendship, and thy groundless hate.
Go, threat thy earth-born Myrmidons:—but here
'Tis mine to threaten, prince, and thine to fear.
Know, if the god the beauteous dame demand,
My bark shall waft her to her native land;
But then prepare, imperious prince! prepare,
Fierce as thou art, to yield thy captive fair:
Even in thy tent I'll seize the blooming prize,
Thy loved Briseïs with the radiant eyes.
Hence shalt thou prove my might, and curse the hour
Thou stood'st a rival of imperial power;
And hence, to all our hosts it shall be known,
That kings are subject to the gods alone."
Achilles heard, with grief and rage oppress'd,
His heart swell'd high, and labour'd in his breast;
Distracting thoughts by turns his bosom ruled;
Now fired by wrath, and now by reason cool'd:
That prompts his hand to draw the deadly sword,
Force through the Greeks, and pierce their haughty lord;
This whispers soft his vengeance to control,
And calm the rising tempest of his soul.
Just as in anguish of suspense he stay'd,
While half unsheathed appear'd the glittering blade,
Minerva swift descended from above,
Sent by the sister and the wife of Jove
(For both the princes claim'd her equal care);
Behind she stood, and by the golden hair
Achilles seized; to him alone confess'd;
A sable cloud conceal'd her from the rest.
He sees, and sudden to the goddess cries,
Known by the flames that sparkle from her eyes:
"Descends Minerva, in her guardian care,

A heavenly witness of the wrongs I bear
From Atreus' son?—Then let those eyes that view
The daring crime, behold the vengeance too."
"Forbear (the progeny of Jove replies)
To calm thy fury I forsake the skies:
Let great Achilles, to the gods resign'd,
To reason yield the empire o'er his mind.
By awful Juno this command is given;
The king and you are both the care of heaven.
The force of keen reproaches let him feel;
But sheathe, obedient, thy revenging steel.
For I pronounce (and trust a heavenly power)
Thy injured honour has its fated hour,
When the proud monarch shall thy arms implore,
And bribe thy friendship with a boundless store.
Then let revenge no longer bear the sway;
Command thy passions, and the gods obey."
To her Pelides:—"With regardful ear,
'Tis just, O goddess! I thy dictates hear.
Hard as it is, my vengeance I suppress:
Those who revere the gods the gods will bless."
He said, observant of the blue-eyed maid;
Then in the sheath return'd the shining blade.
The goddess swift to high Olympus flies,
And joins the sacred senate of the skies.
Nor yet the rage his boiling breast forsook,
Which thus redoubling on Atrides broke:
"O monster! mix'd of insolence and fear,
Thou dog in forehead, but in heart a deer!
When wert thou known in ambush'd fights to dare,
Or nobly face the horrid front of war?
'Tis ours, the chance of fighting fields to try;
Thine to look on, and bid the valiant die:
So much 'tis safer through the camp to go,
And rob a subject, than despoil a foe.
Scourge of thy people, violent and base!
Sent in Jove's anger on a slavish race;
Who, lost to sense of generous freedom past,
Are tamed to wrongs;—or this had been thy last.
Now by this sacred sceptre hear me swear,
Which never more shall leaves or blossoms bear,
Which sever'd from the trunk (as I from thee)
On the bare mountains left its parent tree;
This sceptre, form'd by temper'd steel to prove
An ensign of the delegates of Jove,
From whom the power of laws and justice springs

(Tremendous oath! inviolate to kings);
By this I swear:—when bleeding Greece again
Shall call Achilles, she shall call in vain.
When, flush'd with slaughter, Hector comes to spread
The purpled shore with mountains of the dead,
Then shalt thou mourn the affront thy madness gave,
Forced to deplore when impotent to save:
Then rage in bitterness of soul to know
This act has made the bravest Greek thy foe."
He spoke; and furious hurl'd against the ground
His sceptre starr'd with golden studs around:
Then sternly silent sat. With like disdain
The raging king return'd his frowns again.
To calm their passion with the words of age,
Slow from his seat arose the Pylian sage,
Experienced Nestor, in persuasion skill'd;
Words, sweet as honey, from his lips distill'd:
Two generations now had pass'd away,
Wise by his rules, and happy by his sway;
Two ages o'er his native realm he reign'd,
And now the example of the third remain'd.
All view'd with awe the venerable man;
Who thus with mild benevolence began:—
"What shame, what woe is this to Greece! what joy
To Troy's proud monarch, and the friends of Troy!
That adverse gods commit to stern debate
The best, the bravest, of the Grecian state.
Young as ye are, this youthful heat restrain,
Nor think your Nestor's years and wisdom vain.
A godlike race of heroes once I knew,
Such as no more these aged eyes shall view!
Lives there a chief to match Pirithous' fame,
Dryas the bold, or Ceneus' deathless name;
Theseus, endued with more than mortal might,
Or Polyphemus, like the gods in fight?
With these of old, to toils of battle bred,
In early youth my hardy days I led;
Fired with the thirst which virtuous envy breeds,
And smit with love of honourable deeds,
Strongest of men, they pierced the mountain boar,
Ranged the wild deserts red with monsters' gore,
And from their hills the shaggy Centaurs tore:
Yet these with soft persuasive arts I sway'd;
When Nestor spoke, they listen'd and obey'd.
If in my youth, even these esteem'd me wise;
Do you, young warriors, hear my age advise.

Atrides, seize not on the beauteous slave;
That prize the Greeks by common suffrage gave:
Nor thou, Achilles, treat our prince with pride;
Let kings be just, and sovereign power preside.
Thee, the first honours of the war adorn,
Like gods in strength, and of a goddess born;
Him, awful majesty exalts above
The powers of earth, and sceptred sons of Jove.
Let both unite with well-consenting mind,
So shall authority with strength be join'd.
Leave me, O king! to calm Achilles' rage;
Rule thou thyself, as more advanced in age.
Forbid it, gods! Achilles should be lost,
The pride of Greece, and bulwark of our host."
This said, he ceased. The king of men replies:
"Thy years are awful, and thy words are wise.
But that imperious, that unconquer'd soul,
No laws can limit, no respect control.
Before his pride must his superiors fall;
His word the law, and he the lord of all?
Him must our hosts, our chiefs, ourself obey?
What king can bear a rival in his sway?
Grant that the gods his matchless force have given;
Has foul reproach a privilege from heaven?"
Here on the monarch's speech Achilles broke,
And furious, thus, and interrupting spoke:
"Tyrant, I well deserved thy galling chain,
To live thy slave, and still to serve in vain,
Should I submit to each unjust decree:—
Command thy vassals, but command not me.
Seize on Briseïs, whom the Grecians doom'd
My prize of war, yet tamely see resumed;
And seize secure; no more Achilles draws
His conquering sword in any woman's cause.
The gods command me to forgive the past:
But let this first invasion be the last:
For know, thy blood, when next thou darest invade,
Shall stream in vengeance on my reeking blade."
At this they ceased: the stern debate expired:
The chiefs in sullen majesty retired.
Achilles with Patroclus took his way
Where near his tents his hollow vessels lay.
Meantime Atrides launch'd with numerous oars
A well-rigg'd ship for Chrysa's sacred shores:
High on the deck was fair Chryseïs placed,
And sage Ulysses with the conduct graced:

Safe in her sides the hecatomb they stow'd,
Then swiftly sailing, cut the liquid road.
The host to expiate next the king prepares,
With pure lustrations, and with solemn prayers.
Wash'd by the briny wave, the pious train
Are cleansed; and cast the ablutions in the main.
Along the shore whole hecatombs were laid,
And bulls and goats to Phœbus' altars paid;
The sable fumes in curling spires arise,
And waft their grateful odours to the skies.
The army thus in sacred rites engaged,
Atrides still with deep resentment raged.
To wait his will two sacred heralds stood,
Talthybius and Eurybates the good.
"Haste to the fierce Achilles' tent (he cries),
Thence bear Briseïs as our royal prize:
Submit he must; or if they will not part,
Ourself in arms shall tear her from his heart."
The unwilling heralds act their lord's commands;
Pensive they walk along the barren sands:
Arrived, the hero in his tent they find,
With gloomy aspect on his arm reclined.
At awful distance long they silent stand,
Loth to advance, and speak their hard command;
Decent confusion! This the godlike man
Perceived, and thus with accent mild began:
"With leave and honour enter our abodes,
Ye sacred ministers of men and gods!
I know your message; by constraint you came;
Not you, but your imperious lord I blame.
Patroclus, haste, the fair Briseïs bring;
Conduct my captive to the haughty king.
But witness, heralds, and proclaim my vow,
Witness to gods above, and men below!
But first, and loudest, to your prince declare
(That lawless tyrant whose commands you bear),
Unmoved as death Achilles shall remain,
Though prostrate Greece shall bleed at every vein:
The raging chief in frantic passion lost,
Blind to himself, and useless to his host,
Unskill'd to judge the future by the past,
In blood and slaughter shall repent at last."

Patroclus now the unwilling beauty brought;
She, in soft sorrows, and in pensive thought,
Pass'd silent, as the heralds held her hand,

And oft look'd back, slow-moving o'er the strand.
Not so his loss the fierce Achilles bore;
But sad, retiring to the sounding shore,
O'er the wild margin of the deep he hung,
That kindred deep from whence his mother sprung:
There bathed in tears of anger and disdain,
Thus loud lamented to the stormy main:
"O parent goddess! since in early bloom
Thy son must fall, by too severe a doom;
Sure to so short a race of glory born,
Great Jove in justice should this span adorn:
Honour and fame at least the thunderer owed;
And ill he pays the promise of a god,
If yon proud monarch thus thy son defies,
Obscures my glories, and resumes my prize."
Far from the deep recesses of the main,
Where aged Ocean holds his watery reign,
The goddess-mother heard. The waves divide;
And like a mist she rose above the tide;
Beheld him mourning on the naked shores,
And thus the sorrows of his soul explores.
"Why grieves my son? Thy anguish let me share;
Reveal the cause, and trust a parent's care."
He deeply sighing said: "To tell my woe
Is but to mention what too well you know.
From Thebé, sacred to Apollo's name
(Aëtion's realm), our conquering army came,
With treasure loaded and triumphant spoils,
Whose just division crown'd the soldier's toils;
But bright Chryseïs, heavenly prize! was led,
By vote selected, to the general's bed.
The priest of Phœbus sought by gifts to gain
His beauteous daughter from the victor's chain;
The fleet he reach'd, and, lowly bending down,
Held forth the sceptre and the laurel crown,
Intreating all; but chief implored for grace
The brother-kings of Atreus' royal race:
The generous Greeks their joint consent declare,
The priest to reverence, and release the fair;
Not so Atrides: he, with wonted pride,
The sire insulted, and his gifts denied:
The insulted sire (his god's peculiar care)
To Phœbus pray'd, and Phœbus heard the prayer:
A dreadful plague ensues: the avenging darts
Incessant fly, and pierce the Grecian hearts.
A prophet then, inspired by heaven, arose,

And points the crime, and thence derives the woes:
Myself the first the assembled chiefs incline
To avert the vengeance of the power divine;
Then rising in his wrath, the monarch storm'd;
Incensed he threaten'd, and his threats perform'd:
The fair Chryseïs to her sire was sent,
With offer'd gifts to make the god relent;
But now he seized Briseïs' heavenly charms,
And of my valour's prize defrauds my arms,
Defrauds the votes of all the Grecian train;
And service, faith, and justice, plead in vain.
But, goddess! thou thy suppliant son attend.
To high Olympus' shining court ascend,
Urge all the ties to former service owed,
And sue for vengeance to the thundering god.
Oft hast thou triumph'd in the glorious boast,
That thou stood'st forth of all the ethereal host,
When bold rebellion shook the realms above,
The undaunted guard of cloud-compelling Jove:
When the bright partner of his awful reign,
The warlike maid, and monarch of the main,
The traitor-gods, by mad ambition driven,
Durst threat with chains the omnipotence of Heaven.
Then, call'd by thee, the monster Titan came
(Whom gods Briareus, men Ægeon name),
Through wondering skies enormous stalk'd along;
Not he that shakes the solid earth so strong:
With giant-pride at Jove's high throne he stands,
And brandish'd round him all his hundred hands:
The affrighted gods confess'd their awful lord,
They dropp'd the fetters, trembled, and adored.
This, goddess, this to his remembrance call,
Embrace his knees, at his tribunal fall;
Conjure him far to drive the Grecian train,
To hurl them headlong to their fleet and main,
To heap the shores with copious death, and bring
The Greeks to know the curse of such a king.
Let Agamemnon lift his haughty head
O'er all his wide dominion of the dead,
And mourn in blood that e'er he durst disgrace
The boldest warrior of the Grecian race."
"Unhappy son! (fair Thetis thus replies,
While tears celestial trickle from her eyes)
Why have I borne thee with a mother's throes,
To Fates averse, and nursed for future woes?
So short a space the light of heaven to view!

So short a space! and fill'd with sorrow too!
O might a parent's careful wish prevail,
Far, far from Ilion should thy vessels sail,
And thou, from camps remote, the danger shun
Which now, alas! too nearly threats my son.
Yet (what I can) to move thy suit I'll go
To great Olympus crown'd with fleecy snow.
Meantime, secure within thy ships, from far
Behold the field, not mingle in the war.
The sire of gods and all the ethereal train,
On the warm limits of the farthest main,
Now mix with mortals, nor disdain to grace
The feasts of Æthiopia's blameless race,
Twelve days the powers indulge the genial rite,
Returning with the twelfth revolving light.
Then will I mount the brazen dome, and move
The high tribunal of immortal Jove."
The goddess spoke: the rolling waves unclose;
Then down the steep she plunged from whence she rose,
And left him sorrowing on the lonely coast,
In wild resentment for the fair he lost.
In Chrysa's port now sage Ulysses rode;
Beneath the deck the destined victims stow'd:
The sails they furl'd, they lash the mast aside,
And dropp'd their anchors, and the pinnace tied.
Next on the shore their hecatomb they land;
Chryseïs last descending on the strand.
Her, thus returning from the furrow'd main,
Ulysses led to Phœbus' sacred fane;
Where at his solemn altar, as the maid
He gave to Chryses, thus the hero said:
"Hail, reverend priest! to Phœbus' awful dome
A suppliant I from great Atrides come:
Unransom'd, here receive the spotless fair;
Accept the hecatomb the Greeks prepare;
And may thy god who scatters darts around,
Atoned by sacrifice, desist to wound."
At this, the sire embraced the maid again,
So sadly lost, so lately sought in vain.
Then near the altar of the darting king,
Disposed in rank their hecatomb they bring;
With water purify their hands, and take
The sacred offering of the salted cake;
While thus with arms devoutly raised in air,
And solemn voice, the priest directs his prayer:
"God of the silver bow, thy ear incline,

Whose power incircles Cilla the divine;
Whose sacred eye thy Tenedos surveys,
And gilds fair Chrysa with distinguish'd rays!
If, fired to vengeance at thy priest's request,
Thy direful darts inflict the raging pest:
Once more attend! avert the wasteful woe,
And smile propitious, and unbend thy bow."
So Chryses pray'd. Apollo heard his prayer:
And now the Greeks their hecatomb prepare;
Between their horns the salted barley threw,
And, with their heads to heaven, the victims slew:
The limbs they sever from the inclosing hide;
The thighs, selected to the gods, divide:
On these, in double cauls involved with art,
The choicest morsels lay from every part.
The priest himself before his altar stands,
And burns the offering with his holy hands.
Pours the black wine, and sees the flames aspire;
The youth with instruments surround the fire:
The thighs thus sacrificed, and entrails dress'd,
The assistants part, transfix, and roast the rest:
Then spread the tables, the repast prepare;
Each takes his seat, and each receives his share.
When now the rage of hunger was repress'd,
With pure libations they conclude the feast;
The youths with wine the copious goblets crown'd,
And, pleased, dispense the flowing bowls around
With hymns divine the joyous banquet ends,
The pæans lengthen'd till the sun descends:
The Greeks, restored, the grateful notes prolong;
Apollo listens, and approves the song.
'Twas night; the chiefs beside their vessel lie,
Till rosy morn had purpled o'er the sky:
Then launch, and hoist the mast: indulgent gales,
Supplied by Phœbus, fill the swelling sails;
The milk-white canvas bellying as they blow,
The parted ocean foams and roars below:
Above the bounding billows swift they flew,
Till now the Grecian camp appear'd in view.
Far on the beach they haul their bark to land,
(The crooked keel divides the yellow sand,)
Then part, where stretch'd along the winding bay,
The ships and tents in mingled prospect lay.
But raging still, amidst his navy sat
The stern Achilles, stedfast in his hate;
Nor mix'd in combat, nor in council join'd;

But wasting cares lay heavy on his mind:
In his black thoughts revenge and slaughter roll,
And scenes of blood rise dreadful in his soul.
Twelve days were past, and now the dawning light
The gods had summon'd to the Olympian height:
Jove, first ascending from the watery bowers,
Leads the long order of ethereal powers.
When, like the morning-mist in early day,
Rose from the flood the daughter of the sea:
And to the seats divine her flight address'd.
There, far apart, and high above the rest,
The thunderer sat; where old Olympus shrouds
His hundred heads in heaven, and props the clouds.
Suppliant the goddess stood: one hand she placed
Beneath his beard, and one his knees embraced.
"If e'er, O father of the gods! (she said)
My words could please thee, or my actions aid,
Some marks of honour on my son bestow,
And pay in glory what in life you owe.
Fame is at least by heavenly promise due
To life so short, and now dishonour'd too.
Avenge this wrong, O ever just and wise!
Let Greece be humbled, and the Trojans rise;
Till the proud king and all the Achaian race
Shall heap with honours him they now disgrace."
Thus Thetis spoke; but Jove in silence held
The sacred counsels of his breast conceal'd.
Not so repulsed, the goddess closer press'd,
Still grasp'd his knees, and urged the dear request.
"O sire of gods and men! thy suppliant hear;
Refuse, or grant; for what has Jove to fear?
Or oh! declare, of all the powers above,
Is wretched Thetis least the care of Jove?"
She said; and, sighing, thus the god replies,
Who rolls the thunder o'er the vaulted skies:
"What hast thou ask'd? ah, why should Jove engage
In foreign contests and domestic rage,
The gods' complaints, and Juno's fierce alarms,
While I, too partial, aid the Trojan arms?
Go, lest the haughty partner of my sway
With jealous eyes thy close access survey;
But part in peace, secure thy prayer is sped:
Witness the sacred honours of our head,
The nod that ratifies the will divine,
The faithful, fix'd, irrevocable sign;
This seals thy suit, and this fulfils thy vows—"

He spoke, and awful bends his sable brows,
Shakes his ambrosial curls, and gives the nod,
The stamp of fate and sanction of the god:
High heaven with trembling the dread signal took,
And all Olympus to the centre shook.
Swift to the seas profound the goddess flies,
Jove to his starry mansions in the skies.
The shining synod of the immortals wait
The coming god, and from their thrones of state
Arising silent, wrapp'd in holy fear,
Before the majesty of heaven appear.
Trembling they stand, while Jove assumes the throne,
All, but the god's imperious queen alone:
Late had she view'd the silver-footed dame,
And all her passions kindled into flame.
"Say, artful manager of heaven (she cries),
Who now partakes the secrets of the skies?
Thy Juno knows not the decrees of fate,
In vain the partner of imperial state.
What favourite goddess then those cares divides,
Which Jove in prudence from his consort hides?"
To this the thunderer: "Seek not thou to find
The sacred counsels of almighty mind:
Involved in darkness lies the great decree,
Nor can the depths of fate be pierced by thee.
What fits thy knowledge, thou the first shalt know;
The first of gods above, and men below;
But thou, nor they, shall search the thoughts that roll
Deep in the close recesses of my soul."
Full on the sire the goddess of the skies
Roll'd the large orbs of her majestic eyes,
And thus return'd:— "Austere Saturnius, say,
From whence this wrath, or who controls thy sway?
Thy boundless will, for me, remains in force,
And all thy counsels take the destined course.
But 'tis for Greece I fear: for late was seen,
In close consult, the silver-footed queen.
Jove to his Thetis nothing could deny,
Nor was the signal vain that shook the sky.
What fatal favour has the goddess won,
To grace her fierce, inexorable son?
Perhaps in Grecian blood to drench the plain,
And glut his vengeance with my people slain."
Then thus the god: "O restless fate of pride,
That strives to learn what heaven resolves to hide;
Vain is the search, presumptuous and abhorr'd,

Anxious to thee, and odious to thy lord.
Let this suffice: the immutable decree
No force can shake: what is, that ought to be.
Goddess, submit; nor dare our will withstand,
But dread the power of this avenging hand:
The united strength of all the gods above
In vain resists the omnipotence of Jove."

The thunderer spoke, nor durst the queen reply;
A reverent horror silenced all the sky.
The feast disturb'd, with sorrow Vulcan saw
His mother menaced, and the gods in awe;
Peace at his heart, and pleasure his design,
Thus interposed the architect divine:
"The wretched quarrels of the mortal state
Are far unworthy, gods! of your debate:
Let men their days in senseless strife employ,
We, in eternal peace and constant joy.
Thou, goddess-mother, with our sire comply,
Nor break the sacred union of the sky:
Lest, roused to rage, he shake the bless'd abodes,
Launch the red lightning, and dethrone the gods.
If you submit, the thunderer stands appeased;
The gracious power is willing to be pleased."
Thus Vulcan spoke: and rising with a bound,
The double bowl with sparkling nectar crown'd,
Which held to Juno in a cheerful way,
"Goddess (he cried), be patient and obey.
Dear as you are, if Jove his arm extend,
I can but grieve, unable to defend.
What god so daring in your aid to move,
Or lift his hand against the force of Jove?
Once in your cause I felt his matchless might,
Hurl'd headlong down from the ethereal height;
Toss'd all the day in rapid circles round,
Nor till the sun descended touch'd the ground.
Breathless I fell, in giddy motion lost;
The Sinthians raised me on the Lemnian coast;
He said, and to her hands the goblet heaved,
Which, with a smile, the white-arm'd queen received
Then, to the rest he fill'd; and in his turn,
Each to his lips applied the nectar'd urn,
Vulcan with awkward grace his office plies,
And unextinguish'd laughter shakes the skies.
Thus the blest gods the genial day prolong,
In feasts ambrosial, and celestial song.

Apollo tuned the lyre; the Muses round
With voice alternate aid the silver sound.
Meantime the radiant sun to mortal sight
Descending swift, roll'd down the rapid light:
Then to their starry domes the gods depart,
The shining monuments of Vulcan's art:
Jove on his couch reclined his awful head,
And Juno slumber'd on the golden bed.

BOOK II.

THE TRIAL OF THE ARMY, AND CATALOGUE OF THE FORCES.

Now pleasing sleep had seal'd each mortal eye,
Stretch'd in the tents the Grecian leaders lie:
The immortals slumber'd on their thrones above;
All, but the ever-wakeful eyes of Jove.
To honour Thetis' son he bends his care,
And plunge the Greeks in all the woes of war:
Then bids an empty phantom rise to sight,
And thus commands the vision of the night.
"Fly hence, deluding Dream! and light as air,
To Agamemnon's ample tent repair.
Bid him in arms draw forth the embattled train,
Lead all his Grecians to the dusty plain.
Declare, e'en now 'tis given him to destroy
The lofty towers of wide-extended Troy.
For now no more the gods with fate contend,
At Juno's suit the heavenly factions end.
Destruction hangs o'er yon devoted wall,
And nodding Ilion waits the impending fall."
Swift as the word the vain illusion fled,
Descends, and hovers o'er Atrides' head;
Clothed in the figure of the Pylian sage,
Renown'd for wisdom, and revered for age:
Around his temples spreads his golden wing,
And thus the flattering dream deceives the king.

"Canst thou, with all a monarch's cares oppress'd,
O Atreus' son! canst thou indulge thy rest?
Ill fits a chief who mighty nations guides,
Directs in council, and in war presides,
To whom its safety a whole people owes,
To waste long nights in indolent repose.
Monarch, awake! 'tis Jove's command I bear;
Thou, and thy glory, claim his heavenly care.
In just array draw forth the embattled train,
Lead all thy Grecians to the dusty plain;
E'en now, O king! 'tis given thee to destroy
The lofty towers of wide-extended Troy.
For now no more the gods with fate contend,
At Juno's suit the heavenly factions end.
Destruction hangs o'er yon devoted wall,
And nodding Ilion waits the impending fall.
Awake, but waking this advice approve,
And trust the vision that descends from Jove."
The phantom said; then vanish'd from his sight,
Resolves to air, and mixes with the night.
A thousand schemes the monarch's mind employ;
Elate in thought he sacks untaken Troy:
Vain as he was, and to the future blind,
Nor saw what Jove and secret fate design'd,
What mighty toils to either host remain,
What scenes of grief, and numbers of the slain!
Eager he rises, and in fancy hears
The voice celestial murmuring in his ears.
First on his limbs a slender vest he drew,
Around him next the regal mantle threw,
The embroider'd sandals on his feet were tied;
The starry falchion glitter'd at his side;
And last, his arm the massy sceptre loads,
Unstain'd, immortal, and the gift of gods.
Now rosy Morn ascends the court of Jove,
Lifts up her light, and opens day above.
The king despatch'd his heralds with commands
To range the camp and summon all the bands:
The gathering hosts the monarch's word obey;
While to the fleet Atrides bends his way.
In his black ship the Pylian prince he found;
There calls a senate of the peers around:
The assembly placed, the king of men express'd
The counsels labouring in his artful breast.
"Friends and confederates! with attentive ear
Receive my words, and credit what you hear.

Late as I slumber'd in the shades of night,
A dream divine appear'd before my sight;
Whose visionary form like Nestor came,
The same in habit, and in mien the same.
The heavenly phantom hover'd o'er my head,
'And, dost thou sleep, O Atreus' son? (he said)
Ill fits a chief who mighty nations guides,
Directs in council, and in war presides;
To whom its safety a whole people owes,
To waste long nights in indolent repose.
Monarch, awake! 'tis Jove's command I bear,
Thou and thy glory claim his heavenly care.
In just array draw forth the embattled train,
And lead the Grecians to the dusty plain;
E'en now, O king! 'tis given thee to destroy
The lofty towers of wide-extended Troy.
For now no more the gods with fate contend,
At Juno's suit the heavenly factions end.
Destruction hangs o'er yon devoted wall,
And nodding Ilion waits the impending fall.
This hear observant, and the gods obey!'
The vision spoke, and pass'd in air away.
Now, valiant chiefs! since heaven itself alarms,
Unite, and rouse the sons of Greece to arms.
But first, with caution, try what yet they dare,
Worn with nine years of unsuccessful war.
To move the troops to measure back the main,
Be mine; and yours the province to detain."
He spoke, and sat: when Nestor, rising said,
(Nestor, whom Pylos' sandy realms obey'd,)
"Princes of Greece, your faithful ears incline,
Nor doubt the vision of the powers divine;
Sent by great Jove to him who rules the host,
Forbid it, heaven! this warning should be lost!
Then let us haste, obey the god's alarms,
And join to rouse the sons of Greece to arms."
Thus spoke the sage: the kings without delay
Dissolve the council, and their chief obey:
The sceptred rulers lead; the following host,
Pour'd forth by thousands, darkens all the coast.
As from some rocky cleft the shepherd sees
Clustering in heaps on heaps the driving bees,
Rolling and blackening, swarms succeeding swarms,
With deeper murmurs and more hoarse alarms;
Dusky they spread, a close embodied crowd,
And o'er the vale descends the living cloud.

So, from the tents and ships, a lengthen'd train
Spreads all the beach, and wide o'ershades the plain:
Along the region runs a deafening sound;
Beneath their footsteps groans the trembling ground.
Fame flies before the messenger of Jove,
And shining soars, and claps her wings above.
Nine sacred heralds now, proclaiming loud
The monarch's will, suspend the listening crowd.
Soon as the throngs in order ranged appear,
And fainter murmurs died upon the ear,
The king of kings his awful figure raised:
High in his hand the golden sceptre blazed;
The golden sceptre, of celestial flame,
By Vulcan form'd, from Jove to Hermes came.
To Pelops he the immortal gift resign'd;
The immortal gift great Pelops left behind,
In Atreus' hand, which not with Atreus ends,
To rich Thyestes next the prize descends;
And now the mark of Agamemnon's reign,
Subjects all Argos, and controls the main.
On this bright sceptre now the king reclined,
And artful thus pronounced the speech design'd:
"Ye sons of Mars, partake your leader's care,
Heroes of Greece, and brothers of the war!
Of partial Jove with justice I complain,
And heavenly oracles believed in vain
A safe return was promised to our toils,
Renown'd, triumphant, and enrich'd with spoils.
Now shameful flight alone can save the host,
Our blood, our treasure, and our glory lost.
So Jove decrees, resistless lord of all!
At whose command whole empires rise or fall:
He shakes the feeble props of human trust,
And towns and armies humbles to the dust.
What shame to Greece a fruitful war to wage,
Oh, lasting shame in every future age!
Once great in arms, the common scorn we grow,
Repulsed and baffled by a feeble foe.
So small their number, that if wars were ceased,
And Greece triumphant held a general feast,
All rank'd by tens, whole decades when they dine
Must want a Trojan slave to pour the wine.
But other forces have our hopes o'erthrown,
And Troy prevails by armies not her own.
Now nine long years of mighty Jove are run,
Since first the labours of this war begun:

Our cordage torn, decay'd our vessels lie,
And scarce insure the wretched power to fly.
Haste, then, for ever leave the Trojan wall!
Our weeping wives, our tender children call:
Love, duty, safety, summon us away,
'Tis nature's voice, and nature we obey.
Our shatter'd barks may yet transport us o'er,
Safe and inglorious, to our native shore.
Fly, Grecians, fly, your sails and oars employ,
And dream no more of heaven-defended Troy."
His deep design unknown, the hosts approve
Atrides' speech. The mighty numbers move.
So roll the billows to the Icarian shore,
From east and south when winds begin to roar,
Burst their dark mansions in the clouds, and sweep
The whitening surface of the ruffled deep.
And as on corn when western gusts descend,
Before the blast the lofty harvests bend:
Thus o'er the field the moving host appears,
With nodding plumes and groves of waving spears.
The gathering murmur spreads, their trampling feet
Beat the loose sands, and thicken to the fleet;
With long-resounding cries they urge the train
To fit the ships, and launch into the main.
They toil, they sweat, thick clouds of dust arise,
The doubling clamours echo to the skies.
E'en then the Greeks had left the hostile plain,
And fate decreed the fall of Troy in vain;
But Jove's imperial queen their flight survey'd,
And sighing thus bespoke the blue-eyed maid:
"Shall then the Grecians fly! O dire disgrace!
And leave unpunish'd this perfidious race?
Shall Troy, shall Priam, and the adulterous spouse,
In peace enjoy the fruits of broken vows?
And bravest chiefs, in Helen's quarrel slain,
Lie unrevenged on yon detested plain?
No: let my Greeks, unmoved by vain alarms,
Once more refulgent shine in brazen arms.
Haste, goddess, haste! the flying host detain,
Nor let one sail be hoisted on the main."
Pallas obeys, and from Olympus' height
Swift to the ships precipitates her flight.
Ulysses, first in public cares, she found,
For prudent counsel like the gods renown'd:
Oppress'd with generous grief the hero stood,
Nor drew his sable vessels to the flood.

"And is it thus, divine Laertes' son,
Thus fly the Greeks (the martial maid begun),
Thus to their country bear their own disgrace,
And fame eternal leave to Priam's race?
Shall beauteous Helen still remain unfreed,
Still unrevenged, a thousand heroes bleed!
Haste, generous Ithacus! prevent the shame,
Recall your armies, and your chiefs reclaim.
Your own resistless eloquence employ,
And to the immortals trust the fall of Troy."
The voice divine confess'd the warlike maid,
Ulysses heard, nor uninspired obey'd:
Then meeting first Atrides, from his hand
Received the imperial sceptre of command.
Thus graced, attention and respect to gain,
He runs, he flies through all the Grecian train;
Each prince of name, or chief in arms approved,
He fired with praise, or with persuasion moved.
"Warriors like you, with strength and wisdom bless'd,
By brave examples should confirm the rest.
The monarch's will not yet reveal'd appears;
He tries our courage, but resents our fears.
The unwary Greeks his fury may provoke;
Not thus the king in secret council spoke.
Jove loves our chief, from Jove his honour springs,
Beware! for dreadful is the wrath of kings."
But if a clamorous vile plebeian rose,
Him with reproof he check'd or tamed with blows.
"Be still, thou slave, and to thy betters yield;
Unknown alike in council and in field!
Ye gods, what dastards would our host command!
Swept to the war, the lumber of a land.
Be silent, wretch, and think not here allow'd
That worst of tyrants, an usurping crowd.
To one sole monarch Jove commits the sway;
His are the laws, and him let all obey."
With words like these the troops Ulysses ruled,
The loudest silenced, and the fiercest cool'd.
Back to the assembly roll the thronging train,
Desert the ships, and pour upon the plain.
Murmuring they move, as when old ocean roars,
And heaves huge surges to the trembling shores;
The groaning banks are burst with bellowing sound,
The rocks remurmur and the deeps rebound.
At length the tumult sinks, the noises cease,
And a still silence lulls the camp to peace.

Thersites only clamour'd in the throng,
Loquacious, loud, and turbulent of tongue:
Awed by no shame, by no respect controll'd,
In scandal busy, in reproaches bold:
With witty malice studious to defame,
Scorn all his joy, and laughter all his aim:—
But chief he gloried with licentious style
To lash the great, and monarchs to revile.
His figure such as might his soul proclaim;
One eye was blinking, and one leg was lame:
His mountain shoulders half his breast o'erspread,
Thin hairs bestrew'd his long misshapen head.
Spleen to mankind his envious heart possess'd,
And much he hated all, but most the best:
Ulysses or Achilles still his theme;
But royal scandal his delight supreme,
Long had he lived the scorn of every Greek,
Vex'd when he spoke, yet still they heard him speak.
Sharp was his voice; which in the shrillest tone,
Thus with injurious taunts attack'd the throne.
"Amidst the glories of so bright a reign,
What moves the great Atrides to complain?
'Tis thine whate'er the warrior's breast inflames,
The golden spoil, and thine the lovely dames.
With all the wealth our wars and blood bestow,
Thy tents are crowded and thy chests o'erflow.
Thus at full ease in heaps of riches roll'd,
What grieves the monarch? Is it thirst of gold?
Say, shall we march with our unconquer'd powers
(The Greeks and I) to Ilion's hostile towers,
And bring the race of royal bastards here,
For Troy to ransom at a price too dear?
But safer plunder thy own host supplies;
Say, wouldst thou seize some valiant leader's prize?
Or, if thy heart to generous love be led,
Some captive fair, to bless thy kingly bed?
Whate'er our master craves submit we must,
Plagued with his pride, or punish'd for his lust.
Oh women of Achaia; men no more!
Hence let us fly, and let him waste his store
In loves and pleasures on the Phrygian shore.
We may be wanted on some busy day,
When Hector comes: so great Achilles may:
From him he forced the prize we jointly gave,
From him, the fierce, the fearless, and the brave:
And durst he, as he ought, resent that wrong,

This mighty tyrant were no tyrant long."
Fierce from his seat at this Ulysses springs,
In generous vengeance of the king of kings.
With indignation sparkling in his eyes,
He views the wretch, and sternly thus replies:
"Peace, factious monster, born to vex the state,
With wrangling talents form'd for foul debate:
Curb that impetuous tongue, nor rashly vain,
And singly mad, asperse the sovereign reign.
Have we not known thee, slave! of all our host,
The man who acts the least, upbraids the most?
Think not the Greeks to shameful flight to bring,
Nor let those lips profane the name of king.
For our return we trust the heavenly powers;
Be that their care; to fight like men be ours.
But grant the host with wealth the general load,
Except detraction, what hast thou bestow'd?
Suppose some hero should his spoils resign,
Art thou that hero, could those spoils be thine?
Gods! let me perish on this hateful shore,
And let these eyes behold my son no more;
If, on thy next offence, this hand forbear
To strip those arms thou ill deserv'st to wear,
Expel the council where our princes meet,
And send thee scourged and howling through the fleet."
He said, and cowering as the dastard bends,
The weighty sceptre on his back descends.
On the round bunch the bloody tumours rise:
The tears spring starting from his haggard eyes;
Trembling he sat, and shrunk in abject fears,
From his vile visage wiped the scalding tears;
While to his neighbour each express'd his thought:
"Ye gods! what wonders has Ulysses wrought!
What fruits his conduct and his courage yield!
Great in the council, glorious in the field.
Generous he rises in the crown's defence,
To curb the factious tongue of insolence,
Such just examples on offenders shown,
Sedition silence, and assert the throne."
'Twas thus the general voice the hero praised,
Who, rising, high the imperial sceptre raised:
The blue-eyed Pallas, his celestial friend,
(In form a herald,) bade the crowds attend.
The expecting crowds in still attention hung,
To hear the wisdom of his heavenly tongue.
Then deeply thoughtful, pausing ere he spoke,

His silence thus the prudent hero broke:
"Unhappy monarch! whom the Grecian race
With shame deserting, heap with vile disgrace.
Not such at Argos was their generous vow:
Once all their voice, but ah! forgotten now:
Ne'er to return, was then the common cry,
Till Troy's proud structures should in ashes lie.
Behold them weeping for their native shore;
What could their wives or helpless children more?
What heart but melts to leave the tender train,
And, one short month, endure the wintry main?
Few leagues removed, we wish our peaceful seat,
When the ship tosses, and the tempests beat:
Then well may this long stay provoke their tears,
The tedious length of nine revolving years.
Not for their grief the Grecian host I blame;
But vanquish'd! baffled! oh, eternal shame!
Expect the time to Troy's destruction given.
And try the faith of Chalcas and of heaven.
What pass'd at Aulis, Greece can witness bear,
And all who live to breathe this Phrygian air.
Beside a fountain's sacred brink we raised
Our verdant altars, and the victims blazed:
'Twas where the plane-tree spread its shades around,
The altars heaved; and from the crumbling ground
A mighty dragon shot, of dire portent;
From Jove himself the dreadful sign was sent.
Straight to the tree his sanguine spires he roll'd,
And curl'd around in many a winding fold;
The topmost branch a mother-bird possess'd;
Eight callow infants fill'd the mossy nest;
Herself the ninth; the serpent, as he hung,
Stretch'd his black jaws and crush'd the crying young;
While hovering near, with miserable moan,
The drooping mother wail'd her children gone.
The mother last, as round the nest she flew,
Seized by the beating wing, the monster slew;
Nor long survived: to marble turn'd, he stands
A lasting prodigy on Aulis' sands.
Such was the will of Jove; and hence we dare
Trust in his omen, and support the war.
For while around we gazed with wondering eyes,
And trembling sought the powers with sacrifice,
Full of his god, the reverend Chalcas cried,
'Ye Grecian warriors! lay your fears aside.
This wondrous signal Jove himself displays,

Of long, long labours, but eternal praise.
As many birds as by the snake were slain,
So many years the toils of Greece remain;
But wait the tenth, for Ilion's fall decreed:'
Thus spoke the prophet, thus the Fates succeed.
Obey, ye Grecians! with submission wait,
Nor let your flight avert the Trojan fate."
He said: the shores with loud applauses sound,
The hollow ships each deafening shout rebound.
Then Nestor thus— "These vain debates forbear,
Ye talk like children, not like heroes dare.
Where now are all your high resolves at last?
Your leagues concluded, your engagements past?
Vow'd with libations and with victims then,
Now vanish'd like their smoke: the faith of men!
While useless words consume the unactive hours,
No wonder Troy so long resists our powers.
Rise, great Atrides! and with courage sway;
We march to war, if thou direct the way.
But leave the few that dare resist thy laws,
The mean deserters of the Grecian cause,
To grudge the conquests mighty Jove prepares,
And view with envy our successful wars.
On that great day, when first the martial train,
Big with the fate of Ilion, plough'd the main,
Jove, on the right, a prosperous signal sent,
And thunder rolling shook the firmament.
Encouraged hence, maintain the glorious strife,
Till every soldier grasp a Phrygian wife,
Till Helen's woes at full revenged appear,
And Troy's proud matrons render tear for tear.
Before that day, if any Greek invite
His country's troops to base, inglorious flight,
Stand forth that Greek! and hoist his sail to fly,
And die the dastard first, who dreads to die.
But now, O monarch! all thy chiefs advise:
Nor what they offer, thou thyself despise.
Among those counsels, let not mine be vain;
In tribes and nations to divide thy train:
His separate troops let every leader call,
Each strengthen each, and all encourage all.
What chief, or soldier, of the numerous band,
Or bravely fights, or ill obeys command,
When thus distinct they war, shall soon be known
And what the cause of Ilion not o'erthrown;
If fate resists, or if our arms are slow,

If gods above prevent, or men below."
To him the king: "How much thy years excel
In arts of counsel, and in speaking well!
O would the gods, in love to Greece, decree
But ten such sages as they grant in thee;
Such wisdom soon should Priam's force destroy,
And soon should fall the haughty towers of Troy!
But Jove forbids, who plunges those he hates
In fierce contention and in vain debates:
Now great Achilles from our aid withdraws,
By me provoked; a captive maid the cause:
If e'er as friends we join, the Trojan wall
Must shake, and heavy will the vengeance fall!
But now, ye warriors, take a short repast;
And, well refresh'd, to bloody conflict haste.
His sharpen'd spear let every Grecian wield,
And every Grecian fix his brazen shield,
Let all excite the fiery steeds of war,
And all for combat fit the rattling car.
This day, this dreadful day, let each contend;
No rest, no respite, till the shades descend;
Till darkness, or till death, shall cover all:
Let the war bleed, and let the mighty fall;
Till bathed in sweat be every manly breast,
With the huge shield each brawny arm depress'd,
Each aching nerve refuse the lance to throw,
And each spent courser at the chariot blow.
Who dares, inglorious, in his ships to stay,
Who dares to tremble on this signal day;
That wretch, too mean to fall by martial power,
The birds shall mangle, and the dogs devour."
The monarch spoke; and straight a murmur rose,
Loud as the surges when the tempest blows,
That dash'd on broken rocks tumultuous roar,
And foam and thunder on the stony shore.
Straight to the tents the troops dispersing bend,
The fires are kindled, and the smokes ascend;
With hasty feasts they sacrifice, and pray,
To avert the dangers of the doubtful day.
A steer of five years' age, large limb'd, and fed,
To Jove's high altars Agamemnon led:
There bade the noblest of the Grecian peers;
And Nestor first, as most advanced in years.
Next came Idomeneus, and Tydeus' son,
Ajax the less, and Ajax Telamon;
Then wise Ulysses in his rank was placed;

And Menelaus came, unbid, the last.
The chiefs surround the destined beast, and take
The sacred offering of the salted cake:
When thus the king prefers his solemn prayer;
"O thou! whose thunder rends the clouded air,
Who in the heaven of heavens hast fixed thy throne,
Supreme of gods! unbounded, and alone!
Hear! and before the burning sun descends,
Before the night her gloomy veil extends,
Low in the dust be laid yon hostile spires,
Be Priam's palace sunk in Grecian fires.
In Hector's breast be plunged this shining sword,
And slaughter'd heroes groan around their lord!"
Thus prayed the chief: his unavailing prayer
Great Jove refused, and toss'd in empty air:
The God averse, while yet the fumes arose,
Prepared new toils, and doubled woes on woes.
Their prayers perform'd the chiefs the rite pursue,
The barley sprinkled, and the victim slew.
The limbs they sever from the inclosing hide,
The thighs, selected to the gods, divide.
On these, in double cauls involved with art,
The choicest morsels lie from every part,
From the cleft wood the crackling flames aspire
While the fat victims feed the sacred fire.
The thighs thus sacrificed, and entrails dress'd
The assistants part, transfix, and roast the rest;
Then spread the tables, the repast prepare,
Each takes his seat, and each receives his share.
Soon as the rage of hunger was suppress'd,
The generous Nestor thus the prince address'd.
"Now bid thy heralds sound the loud alarms,
And call the squadrons sheathed in brazen arms;
Now seize the occasion, now the troops survey,
And lead to war when heaven directs the way."
He said; the monarch issued his commands;
Straight the loud heralds call the gathering bands;
The chiefs inclose their king; the hosts divide,
In tribes and nations rank'd on either side.
High in the midst the blue-eyed virgin flies;
From rank to rank she darts her ardent eyes;
The dreadful ægis, Jove's immortal shield,
Blazed on her arm, and lighten'd all the field:
Round the vast orb a hundred serpents roll'd,
Form'd the bright fringe, and seem'd to burn in gold,
With this each Grecian's manly breast she warms,

Swells their bold hearts, and strings their nervous arms,
No more they sigh, inglorious, to return,
But breathe revenge, and for the combat burn.
As on some mountain, through the lofty grove,
The crackling flames ascend, and blaze above;
The fires expanding, as the winds arise,
Shoot their long beams, and kindle half the skies:
So from the polish'd arms, and brazen shields,
A gleamy splendour flash'd along the fields.
Not less their number than the embodied cranes,
Or milk-white swans in Asius' watery plains.
That, o'er the windings of Cayster's springs,
Stretch their long necks, and clap their rustling wings,
Now tower aloft, and course in airy rounds,
Now light with noise; with noise the field resounds.
Thus numerous and confused, extending wide,
The legions crowd Scamander's flowery side;
With rushing troops the plains are cover'd o'er,
And thundering footsteps shake the sounding shore.
Along the river's level meads they stand,
Thick as in spring the flowers adorn the land,
Or leaves the trees; or thick as insects play,
The wandering nation of a summer's day:
That, drawn by milky steams, at evening hours,
In gather'd swarms surround the rural bowers;
From pail to pail with busy murmur run
The gilded legions, glittering in the sun.
So throng'd, so close, the Grecian squadrons stood
In radiant arms, and thirst for Trojan blood.
Each leader now his scatter'd force conjoins
In close array, and forms the deepening lines.
Not with more ease the skilful shepherd-swain
Collects his flocks from thousands on the plain.
The king of kings, majestically tall,
Towers o'er his armies, and outshines them all;
Like some proud bull, that round the pastures leads
His subject herds, the monarch of the meads,
Great as the gods, the exalted chief was seen,
His strength like Neptune, and like Mars his mien;
Jove o'er his eyes celestial glories spread,
And dawning conquest played around his head.
Say, virgins, seated round the throne divine,
All-knowing goddesses! immortal nine!
Since earth's wide regions, heaven's umneasur'd height,
And hell's abyss, hide nothing from your sight,
(We, wretched mortals! lost in doubts below,

But guess by rumour, and but boast we know,)
O say what heroes, fired by thirst of fame,
Or urged by wrongs, to Troy's destruction came.
To count them all, demands a thousand tongues,
A throat of brass, and adamantine lungs.
Daughters of Jove, assist! inspired by you
The mighty labour dauntless I pursue;
What crowded armies, from what climes they bring,
Their names, their numbers, and their chiefs I sing.

The hardy warriors whom Bœotia bred,
Penelius, Leitus, Prothoënor, led:
With these Arcesilaus and Clonius stand,
Equal in arms, and equal in command.
These head the troops that rocky Aulis yields,
And Eteon's hills, and Hyrie's watery fields,
And Schoenos, Scholos, Græa near the main,
And Mycalessia's ample piny plain;
Those who in Peteon or Ilesion dwell,
Or Harma where Apollo's prophet fell;
Heleon and Hylè, which the springs o'erflow;
And Medeon lofty, and Ocalea low;
Or in the meads of Haliartus stray,
Or Thespia sacred to the god of day:
Onchestus, Neptune's celebrated groves;
Copæ, and Thisbè, famed for silver doves;
For flocks Erythræ, Glissa for the vine;
Platea green, and Nysa the divine;
And they whom Thebé's well-built walls inclose,
Where Mydè, Eutresis, Coronè, rose;
And Arnè rich, with purple harvests crown'd;
And Anthedon, Bœotia's utmost bound.
Full fifty ships they send, and each conveys
Twice sixty warriors through the foaming seas.
To these succeed Aspledon's martial train,
Who plough the spacious Orchomenian plain.
Two valiant brothers rule the undaunted throng,
Iälmen and Ascalaphus the strong:
Sons of Astyochè, the heavenly fair,
Whose virgin charms subdued the god of war:
(In Actor's court as she retired to rest,
The strength of Mars the blushing maid compress'd)
Their troops in thirty sable vessels sweep,
With equal oars, the hoarse-resounding deep.
The Phocians next in forty barks repair;
Epistrophus and Schedius head the war:

From those rich regions where Cephisus leads
His silver current through the flowery meads;
From Panopëa, Chrysa the divine,
Where Anemoria's stately turrets shine,
Where Pytho, Daulis, Cyparissus stood,
And fair Lilæ views the rising flood.
These, ranged in order on the floating tide,
Close, on the left, the bold Bœotians' side.
Fierce Ajax led the Locrian squadrons on,
Ajax the less, Oïleus' valiant son;
Skill'd to direct the flying dart aright;
Swift in pursuit, and active in the fight.
Him, as their chief, the chosen troops attend,
Which Bessa, Thronus, and rich Cynos send;
Opus, Calliarus, and Scarphe's bands;
And those who dwell where pleasing Augia stands,
And where Boägrius floats the lowly lands,
Or in fair Tarphe's sylvan seats reside:
In forty vessels cut the yielding tide.
Eubœa next her martial sons prepares,
And sends the brave Abantes to the wars:
Breathing revenge, in arms they take their way
From Chalcis' walls, and strong Eretria;
The Isteian fields for generous vines renown'd,
The fair Caristos, and the Styrian ground;
Where Dios from her towers o'erlooks the plain,
And high Cerinthus views the neighbouring main.
Down their broad shoulders falls a length of hair;
Their hands dismiss not the long lance in air;
But with protended spears in fighting fields
Pierce the tough corslets and the brazen shields.
Twice twenty ships transport the warlike bands,
Which bold Elphenor, fierce in arms, commands.
Full fifty more from Athens stem the main,
Led by Menestheus through the liquid plain.
(Athens the fair, where great Erectheus sway'd,
That owed his nurture to the blue-eyed maid,
But from the teeming furrow took his birth,
The mighty offspring of the foodful earth.
Him Pallas placed amidst her wealthy fane,
Adored with sacrifice and oxen slain;
Where, as the years revolve, her altars blaze,
And all the tribes resound the goddess' praise.)
No chief like thee, Menestheus! Greece could yield,
To marshal armies in the dusty field,
The extended wings of battle to display,

Or close the embodied host in firm array.
Nestor alone, improved by length of days,
For martial conduct bore an equal praise.
With these appear the Salaminian bands,
Whom the gigantic Telamon commands;
In twelve black ships to Troy they steer their course,
And with the great Athenians join their force.
Next move to war the generous Argive train,
From high Trœzenè, and Maseta's plain,
And fair Ægina circled by the main:
Whom strong Tyrinthe's lofty walls surround,
And Epidaure with viny harvests crown'd:
And where fair Asinen and Hermoin show
Their cliffs above, and ample bay below.
These by the brave Euryalus were led,
Great Sthenelus, and greater Diomed;
But chief Tydides bore the sovereign sway:
In fourscore barks they plough the watery way.
The proud Mycenè arms her martial powers,
Cleonè, Corinth, with imperial towers,
Fair Aræthyrea, Ornia's fruitful plain,
And Ægion, and Adrastus' ancient reign;
And those who dwell along the sandy shore,
And where Pellenè yields her fleecy store,
Where Helicè and Hyperesia lie,
And Gonoëssa's spires salute the sky.
Great Agamemnon rules the numerous band,
A hundred vessels in long order stand,
And crowded nations wait his dread command.
High on the deck the king of men appears,
And his refulgent arms in triumph wears;
Proud of his host, unrivall'd in his reign,
In silent pomp he moves along the main.
His brother follows, and to vengeance warms
The hardy Spartans, exercised in arms:
Phares and Brysia's valiant troops, and those
Whom Lacedæmon's lofty hills inclose;
Or Messé's towers for silver doves renown'd,
Amyclæ, Laäs, Augia's happy ground,
And those whom Œtylos' low walls contain,
And Helos, on the margin of the main.
These, o'er the bending ocean, Helen's cause,
In sixty ships with Menelaus draws:
Eager and loud from man to man he flies,
Revenge and fury flaming in his eyes;
While vainly fond, in fancy oft he hears

The fair one's grief, and sees her falling tears.
In ninety sail, from Pylos' sandy coast,
Nestor the sage conducts his chosen host:
From Amphigenia's ever-fruitful land,
Where Æpy high, and little Pteleon stand;
Where beauteous Arene her structures shows,
And Thryon's walls Alpheus' streams inclose:
And Dorion, famed for Thamyris' disgrace,
Superior once of all the tuneful race,
Till, vain of mortals' empty praise, he strove
To match the seed of cloud-compelling Jove!
Too daring bard! whose unsuccessful pride
The immortal Muses in their art defied.
The avenging Muses of the light of day
Deprived his eyes, and snatch'd his voice away;
No more his heavenly voice was heard to sing,
His hand no more awaked the silver string.
Where under high Cyllenè, crown'd with wood,
The shaded tomb of old Æpytus stood;
From Ripè, Stratie, Tegea's bordering towns,
The Phenean fields, and Orchomenian downs,
Where the fat herds in plenteous pasture rove;
And Stymphelus with her surrounding grove;
Parrhasia, on her snowy cliffs reclined,
And high Enispè shook by wintry wind,
And fair Mantinea's ever-pleasing site;
In sixty sail the Arcadian bands unite.
Bold Agapenor, glorious at their head,
(Ancæus' son) the mighty squadron led.
Their ships, supplied by Agamemnon's care,
Through roaring seas the wondering warriors bear;
The first to battle on the appointed plain,
But new to all the dangers of the main.
Those, where fair Elis and Buprasium join;
Whom Hyrmin, here, and Myrsinus confine,
And bounded there, where o'er the valleys rose
The Olenian rock; and where Alisium flows;
Beneath four chiefs (a numerous army) came:
The strength and glory of the Epean name.
In separate squadrons these their train divide,
Each leads ten vessels through the yielding tide.
One was Amphimachus, and Thalpius one;
(Eurytus' this, and that Teätus' son;)
Diores sprung from Amarynceus' line;
And great Polyxenus, of force divine.
But those who view fair Elis o'er the seas

From the blest islands of the Echinades,
In forty vessels under Meges move,
Begot by Phyleus, the beloved of Jove:
To strong Dulichium from his sire he fled,
And thence to Troy his hardy warriors led.
Ulysses follow'd through the watery road,
A chief, in wisdom equal to a god.
With those whom Cephalenia's line inclosed,
Or till their fields along the coast opposed;
Or where fair Ithaca o'erlooks the floods,
Where high Neritos shakes his waving woods,
Where Ægilipa's rugged sides are seen,
Crocylia rocky, and Zacynthus green.
These in twelve galleys with vermilion prores,
Beneath his conduct sought the Phrygian shores.
Thoas came next, Andræmon's valiant son,
From Pleuron's walls, and chalky Calydon,
And rough Pylene, and the Olenian steep,
And Chalcis, beaten by the rolling deep.
He led the warriors from the Ætolian shore,
For now the sons of Œneus were no more!
The glories of the mighty race were fled!
Œneus himself, and Meleager dead!
To Thoas' care now trust the martial train,
His forty vessels follow through the main.
Next, eighty barks the Cretan king commands,
Of Gnossus, Lyctus, and Gortyna's bands;
And those who dwell where Rhytion's domes arise,
Or white Lycastus glitters to the skies,
Or where by Phæstus silver Jardan runs;
Crete's hundred cities pour forth all her sons.
These march'd, Idomeneus, beneath thy care,
And Merion, dreadful as the god of war.
Tlepolemus, the son of Hercules,
Led nine swift vessels through the foamy seas,
From Rhodes, with everlasting sunshine bright,
Jalyssus, Lindus, and Camirus white.
His captive mother fierce Alcides bore
From Ephyr's walls and Sellè's winding shore,
Where mighty towns in ruins spread the plain,
And saw their blooming warriors early slain.
The hero, when to manly years he grew,
Alcides' uncle, old Licymnius, slew;
For this, constrain'd to quit his native place,
And shun the vengeance of the Herculean race,
A fleet he built, and with a numerous train

Of willing exiles wander'd o'er the main;
Where, many seas and many sufferings past,
On happy Rhodes the chief arrived at last:
There in three tribes divides his native band,
And rules them peaceful in a foreign land;
Increased and prosper'd in their new abodes
By mighty Jove, the sire of men and gods;
With joy they saw the growing empire rise,
And showers of wealth descending from the skies.
Three ships with Nireus sought the Trojan shore,
Nireus, whom Agäle to Charopus bore,
Nireus, in faultless shape and blooming grace,
The loveliest youth of all the Grecian race;
Pelides only match'd his early charms;
But few his troops, and small his strength in arms.
Next thirty galleys cleave the liquid plain,
Of those Calydnæ's sea-girt isles contain;
With them the youth of Nisyrus repair,
Casus the strong, and Crapathus the fair;
Cos, where Eurypylus possess'd the sway,
Till great Alcides made the realms obey:
These Antiphus and bold Phidippus bring,
Sprung from the god by Thessalus the king.
Now, Muse, recount Pelasgic Argos' powers,
From Alos, Alopé, and Trechin's towers:
From Phthia's spacious vales; and Hella, bless'd
With female beauty far beyond the rest.
Full fifty ships beneath Achilles' care,
The Achaians, Myrmidons, Hellenians bear;
Thessalians all, though various in their name;
The same their nation, and their chief the same.
But now inglorious, stretch'd along the shore,
They hear the brazen voice of war no more;
No more the foe they face in dire array:
Close in his fleet the angry leader lay;
Since fair Briseïs from his arms was torn,
The noblest spoil from sack'd Lyrnessus borne,
Then, when the chief the Theban walls o'erthrew,
And the bold sons of great Evenus slew.
There mourn'd Achilles, plunged in depth of care,
But soon to rise in slaughter, blood, and war.
To these the youth of Phylacè succeed,
Itona, famous for her fleecy breed,
And grassy Pteleon deck'd with cheerful greens,
The bowers of Ceres, and the sylvan scenes.
Sweet Pyrrhasus, with blooming flowerets crown'd,

And Antron's watery dens, and cavern'd ground.
These own'd, as chief, Protesilas the brave,
Who now lay silent in the gloomy grave:
The first who boldly touch'd the Trojan shore,
And dyed a Phrygian lance with Grecian gore;
There lies, far distant from his native plain;
Unfinish'd his proud palaces remain,
And his sad consort beats her breast in vain.
His troops in forty ships Podarces led,
Iphiclus' son, and brother to the dead;
Nor he unworthy to command the host;
Yet still they mourn'd their ancient leader lost.
The men who Glaphyra's fair soil partake,
Where hills incircle Bœbe's lowly lake,
Where Phære hears the neighbouring waters fall,
Or proud Iölcus lifts her airy wall,
In ten black ships embark'd for Ilion's shore,
With bold Eumelus, whom Alcestè bore:
All Pelias' race Alcestè far outshined,
The grace and glory of the beauteous kind,
The troops Methonè or Thaumacia yields,
Olizon's rocks, or Melibœa's fields,
With Philoctetes sail'd whose matchless art
From the tough bow directs the feather'd dart.
Seven were his ships; each vessel fifty row,
Skill'd in his science of the dart and bow.
But he lay raging on the Lemnian ground,
A poisonous hydra gave the burning wound;
There groan'd the chief in agonizing pain,
Whom Greece at length shall wish, nor wish in vain.
His forces Medon led from Lemnos' shore,
Oïleus' son, whom beauteous Rhena bore.
The Œchalian race, in those high towers contain'd
Where once Eurytus in proud triumph reign'd,
Or where her humbler turrets Tricca rears,
Or where Ithome, rough with rocks, appears,
In thirty sail the sparkling waves divide,
Which Podalirius and Machaon guide.
To these his skill their parent-god imparts,
Divine professors of the healing arts.
The bold Ormenian and Asterian bands
In forty barks Eurypylus commands.
Where Titan hides his hoary head in snow,
And where Hyperia's silver fountains flow.
Thy troops, Argissa, Polypœtes leads,
And Eleon, shelter'd by Olympus' shades,

Gyrtonè's warriors; and where Orthè lies,
And Oloösson's chalky cliffs arise.
Sprung from Pirithous of immortal race,
The fruit of fair Hippodame's embrace,
(That day, when hurl'd from Pelion's cloudy head,
To distant dens the shaggy Centaurs fled)
With Polypœtes join'd in equal sway
Leonteus leads, and forty ships obey.
In twenty sail the bold Perrhæbians came
From Cyphus, Guneus was their leader's name.
With these the Enians join'd, and those who freeze
Where cold Dodona lifts her holy trees;
Or where the pleasing Titaresius glides,
And into Peneus rolls his easy tides;
Yet o'er the silvery surface pure they flow,
The sacred stream unmix'd with streams below,
Sacred and awful! from the dark abodes
Styx pours them forth, the dreadful oath of gods!
Last, under Prothous the Magnesians stood,
(Prothous the swift, of old Tenthredon's blood;)
Who dwell where Pelion, crown'd with piny boughs,
Obscures the glade, and nods his shaggy brows;
Or where through flowery Tempe Peneus stray'd:
(The region stretch'd beneath his mighty shade:)
In forty sable barks they stemm'd the main;
Such were the chiefs, and such the Grecian train.
Say next, O Muse! of all Achaia breeds,
Who bravest fought, or rein'd the noblest steeds?
Eumelus' mares were foremost in the chase,
As eagles fleet, and of Pheretian race;
Bred where Pieria's fruitful fountains flow,
And train'd by him who bears the silver bow.
Fierce in the fight their nostrils breathed a flame,
Their height, their colour, and their age the same;
O'er fields of death they whirl the rapid car,
And break the ranks, and thunder through the war.
Ajax in arms the first renown acquired,
While stern Achilles in his wrath retired:
(His was the strength that mortal might exceeds,
And his the unrivall'd race of heavenly steeds:)
But Thetis' son now shines in arms no more;
His troops, neglected on the sandy shore.
In empty air their sportive javelins throw,
Or whirl the disk, or bend an idle bow:
Unstain'd with blood his cover'd chariots stand;
The immortal coursers graze along the strand;

But the brave chiefs the inglorious life deplored,
And, wandering o'er the camp, required their lord.
Now, like a deluge, covering all around,
The shining armies sweep along the ground;
Swift as a flood of fire, when storms arise,
Floats the wild field, and blazes to the skies.
Earth groan'd beneath them; as when angry Jove
Hurls down the forky lightning from above,
On Arimé when he the thunder throws,
And fires Typhœus with redoubled blows,
Where Typhon, press'd beneath the burning load,
Still feels the fury of the avenging god.
But various Iris, Jove's commands to bear,
Speeds on the wings of winds through liquid air;
In Priam's porch the Trojan chiefs she found,
The old consulting, and the youths around.
Polites' shape, the monarch's son, she chose,
Who from Æsetes' tomb observed the foes,
High on the mound; from whence in prospect lay
The fields, the tents, the navy, and the bay.
In this dissembled form, she hastes to bring
The unwelcome message to the Phrygian king.
"Cease to consult, the time for action calls;
War, horrid war, approaches to your walls!
Assembled armies oft have I beheld;
But ne'er till now such numbers charged a field:
Thick as autumnal leaves or driving sand,
The moving squadrons blacken all the strand.
Thou, godlike Hector! all thy force employ,
Assemble all the united bands of Troy;
In just array let every leader call
The foreign troops: this day demands them all!"
The voice divine the mighty chief alarms;
The council breaks, the warriors rush to arms.
The gates unfolding pour forth all their train,
Nations on nations fill the dusky plain,
Men, steeds, and chariots, shake the trembling ground:
The tumult thickens, and the skies resound.
Amidst the plain, in sight of Ilion, stands
A rising mount, the work of human hands;
(This for Myrinne's tomb the immortals know,
Though call'd Bateïa in the world below;)
Beneath their chiefs in martial order here,
The auxiliar troops and Trojan hosts appear.
The godlike Hector, high above the rest,
Shakes his huge spear, and nods his plumy crest:

In throngs around his native bands repair,
And groves of lances glitter in the air.
Divine Æneas brings the Dardan race,
Anchises' son, by Venus' stolen embrace,
Born in the shades of Ida's secret grove;
(A mortal mixing with the queen of love;)
Archilochus and Acamas divide
The warrior's toils, and combat by his side.
Who fair Zeleia's wealthy valleys till,
Fast by the foot of Ida's sacred hill,
Or drink, Æsepus, of thy sable flood,
Were led by Pandarus, of royal blood;
To whom his art Apollo deign'd to show,
Graced with the presents of his shafts and bow.
From rich Apæsus and Adrestia's towers,
High Teree's summits, and Pityea's bowers;
From these the congregated troops obey
Young Amphius and Adrastus' equal sway;
Old Merops' sons; whom, skill'd in fates to come,
The sire forewarn'd, and prophesied their doom:
Fate urged them on! the sire forewarn'd in vain,
They rush'd to war, and perish'd on the plain.
From Practius' stream, Percotè's pasture lands,
And Sestos and Abydos' neighbouring strands,
From great Arisba's walls and Sellè's coast,
Asius Hyrtacides conducts his host:
High on his car he shakes the flowing reins,
His fiery coursers thunder o'er the plains.
The fierce Pelasgi next, in war renown'd,
March from Larissa's ever-fertile ground:
In equal arms their brother leaders shine,
Hippothous bold, and Pyleus the divine.
Next Acamas and Pyrous lead their hosts,
In dread array, from Thracia's wintry coasts;
Round the bleak realms where Hellespontus roars,
And Boreas beats the hoarse-resounding shores.
With great Euphemus the Ciconians move,
Sprung from Trœzenian Ceüs, loved by Jove.
Pyræchmes the Pæonian troops attend,
Skill'd in the fight their crooked bows to bend;
From Axius' ample bed he leads them on,
Axius, that laves the distant Amydon,
Axius, that swells with all his neighbouring rills,
And wide around the floating region fills.
The Paphlagonians Pylæmenes rules,
Where rich Henetia breeds her savage mules,

Where Erythinus' rising cliffs are seen,
Thy groves of box, Cytorus! ever green,
And where Ægialus and Cromna lie,
And lofty Sesamus invades the sky,
And where Parthenius, roll'd through banks of flowers,
Reflects her bordering palaces and bowers.
Here march'd in arms the Halizonian band,
Whom Odius and Epistrophus command,
From those far regions where the sun refines
The ripening silver in Alybean mines.
There mighty Chromis led the Mysian train,
And augur Ennomus, inspired in vain;
For stern Achilles lopp'd his sacred head,
Roll'd down Scamander with the vulgar dead.
Phorcys and brave Ascanius here unite
The Ascanian Phrygians, eager for the fight.
Of those who round Mæonia's realms reside,
Or whom the vales in shades of Tmolus hide,
Mestles and Antiphus the charge partake,
Born on the banks of Gyges' silent lake.
There, from the fields where wild Mæander flows,
High Mycale, and Latmos' shady brows,
And proud Miletus, came the Carian throngs,
With mingled clamours and with barbarous tongues.
Amphimachus and Naustes guide the train,
Naustes the bold, Amphimachus the vain,
Who, trick'd with gold, and glittering on his car,
Rode like a woman to the field of war.
Fool that he was! by fierce Achilles slain,
The river swept him to the briny main:
There whelm'd with waves the gaudy warrior lies
The valiant victor seized the golden prize.
The forces last in fair array succeed,
Which blameless Glaucus and Sarpedon lead
The warlike bands that distant Lycia yields,
Where gulfy Xanthus foams along the fields.

BOOK III.

THE DUEL OF MENELAUS AND PARIS.

Thus by their leaders' care each martial band
Moves into ranks, and stretches o'er the land.

With shouts the Trojans, rushing from afar,
Proclaim their motions, and provoke the war.
So when inclement winters vex the plain
With piercing frosts, or thick-descending rain,
To warmer seas the cranes embodied fly,
With noise, and order, through the midway sky;
To pigmy nations wounds and death they bring,
And all the war descends upon the wing,
But silent, breathing rage, resolved and skill'd
By mutual aids to fix a doubtful field,
Swift march the Greeks: the rapid dust around
Darkening arises from the labour'd ground.
Thus from his flaggy wings when Notus sheds
A night of vapours round the mountain heads,
Swift-gliding mists the dusky fields invade,
To thieves more grateful than the midnight shade;
While scarce the swains their feeding flocks survey,
Lost and confused amidst the thicken'd day:
So wrapp'd in gathering dust, the Grecian train,
A moving cloud, swept on, and hid the plain.
Now front to front the hostile armies stand,
Eager of fight, and only wait command;
When, to the van, before the sons of fame
Whom Troy sent forth, the beauteous Paris came:
In form a god! the panther's speckled hide
Flow'd o'er his armour with an easy pride:
His bended bow across his shoulders flung,
His sword beside him negligently hung;
Two pointed spears he shook with gallant grace,
And dared the bravest of the Grecian race.
As thus, with glorious air and proud disdain,
He boldly stalk'd, the foremost on the plain,
Him Menelaus, loved of Mars, espies,
With heart elated, and with joyful eyes:
So joys a lion, if the branching deer,
Or mountain goat, his bulky prize, appear;
Eager he seizes and devours the slain,
Press'd by bold youths and baying dogs in vain.
Thus fond of vengeance, with a furious bound,
In clanging arms he leaps upon the ground
From his high chariot: him, approaching near,
The beauteous champion views with marks of fear,
Smit with a conscious sense, retires behind,
And shuns the fate he well deserved to find.
As when some shepherd, from the rustling trees
Shot forth to view, a scaly serpent sees,

Trembling and pale, he starts with wild affright
And all confused precipitates his flight:
So from the king the shining warrior flies,
And plunged amid the thickest Trojans lies.
As godlike Hector sees the prince retreat,
He thus upbraids him with a generous heat:
"Unhappy Paris! but to women brave!
So fairly form'd, and only to deceive!
Oh, hadst thou died when first thou saw'st the light,
Or died at least before thy nuptial rite!
A better fate than vainly thus to boast,
And fly, the scandal of thy Trojan host.
Gods! how the scornful Greeks exult to see
Their fears of danger undeceived in thee!
Thy figure promised with a martial air,
But ill thy soul supplies a form so fair.
In former days, in all thy gallant pride,
When thy tall ships triumphant stemm'd the tide,
When Greece beheld thy painted canvas flow,
And crowds stood wondering at the passing show,
Say, was it thus, with such a baffled mien,
You met the approaches of the Spartan queen,
Thus from her realm convey'd the beauteous prize,
And both her warlike lords outshined in Helen's eyes?
This deed, thy foes' delight, thy own disgrace,
Thy father's grief, and ruin of thy race;
This deed recalls thee to the proffer'd fight;
Or hast thou injured whom thou dar'st not right?
Soon to thy cost the field would make thee know
Thou keep'st the consort of a braver foe.
Thy graceful form instilling soft desire,
Thy curling tresses, and thy silver lyre,
Beauty and youth; in vain to these you trust,
When youth and beauty shall be laid in dust:
Troy yet may wake, and one avenging blow
Crush the dire author of his country's woe."
His silence here, with blushes, Paris breaks:
"'Tis just, my brother, what your anger speaks:
But who like thee can boast a soul sedate,
So firmly proof to all the shocks of fate?
Thy force, like steel, a temper'd hardness shows,
Still edged to wound, and still untired with blows,
Like steel, uplifted by some strenuous swain,
With falling woods to strew the wasted plain.
Thy gifts I praise; nor thou despise the charms
With which a lover golden Venus arms;

Soft moving speech, and pleasing outward show,
No wish can gain them, but the gods bestow.
Yet, would'st thou have the proffer'd combat stand,
The Greeks and Trojans seat on either hand;
Then let a midway space our hosts divide,
And, on that stage of war, the cause be tried:
By Paris there the Spartan king be fought,
For beauteous Helen and the wealth she brought;
And who his rival can in arms subdue,
His be the fair, and his the treasure too.
Thus with a lasting league your toils may cease,
And Troy possess her fertile fields in peace;
Thus may the Greeks review their native shore,
Much famed for generous steeds, for beauty more."
He said. The challenge Hector heard with joy,
Then with his spear restrain'd the youth of Troy,
Held by the midst, athwart; and near the foe
Advanced with steps majestically slow:
While round his dauntless head the Grecians pour
Their stones and arrows in a mingled shower.
Then thus the monarch, great Atrides, cried:
"Forbear, ye warriors! lay the darts aside:
A parley Hector asks, a message bears;
We know him by the various plume he wears."
Awed by his high command the Greeks attend,
The tumult silence, and the fight suspend.
While from the centre Hector rolls his eyes
On either host, and thus to both applies:
"Hear, all ye Trojan, all ye Grecian bands,
What Paris, author of the war, demands.
Your shining swords within the sheath restrain,
And pitch your lances in the yielding plain.
Here in the midst, in either army's sight,
He dares the Spartan king to single fight;
And wills that Helen and the ravish'd spoil,
That caused the contest, shall reward the toil.
Let these the brave triumphant victor grace,
And different nations part in leagues of peace."
He spoke: in still suspense on either side
Each army stood: the Spartan chief replied:
"Me too, ye warriors, hear, whose fatal right
A world engages in the toils of fight.
To me the labour of the field resign;
Me Paris injured; all the war be mine.
Fall he that must, beneath his rival's arms;
And live the rest, secure of future harms.

Two lambs, devoted by your country's rite,
To earth a sable, to the sun a white,
Prepare, ye Trojans! while a third we bring
Select to Jove, the inviolable king.
Let reverend Priam in the truce engage,
And add the sanction of considerate age;
His sons are faithless, headlong in debate,
And youth itself an empty wavering state;
Cool age advances, venerably wise,
Turns on all hands its deep-discerning eyes;
Sees what befell, and what may yet befall,
Concludes from both, and best provides for all.
The nations hear with rising hopes possess'd,
And peaceful prospects dawn in every breast.
Within the lines they drew their steeds around,
And from their chariots issued on the ground;
Next, all unbuckling the rich mail they wore,
Laid their bright arms along the sable shore.
On either side the meeting hosts are seen
With lances fix'd, and close the space between.
Two heralds now, despatch'd to Troy, invite
The Phrygian monarch to the peaceful rite.
Talthybius hastens to the fleet, to bring
The lamb for Jove, the inviolable king.
Meantime to beauteous Helen, from the skies
The various goddess of the rainbow flies:
(Like fair Laodice in form and face,
The loveliest nymph of Priam's royal race:)
Her in the palace, at her loom she found;
The golden web her own sad story crown'd,
The Trojan wars she weaved (herself the prize)
And the dire triumphs of her fatal eyes.
To whom the goddess of the painted bow:
"Approach, and view the wondrous scene below!
Each hardy Greek, and valiant Trojan knight,
So dreadful late, and furious for the fight,
Now rest their spears, or lean upon their shields;
Ceased is the war, and silent all the fields.
Paris alone and Sparta's king advance,
In single fight to toss the beamy lance;
Each met in arms, the fate of combat tries,
Thy love the motive, and thy charms the prize."
This said, the many-coloured maid inspires
Her husband's love, and wakes her former fires;
Her country, parents, all that once were dear,
Rush to her thought, and force a tender tear,

O'er her fair face a snowy veil she threw,
And, softly sighing, from the loom withdrew.
Her handmaids, Clymene and Æthra, wait
Her silent footsteps to the Scæan gate.
There sat the seniors of the Trojan race:
(Old Priam's chiefs, and most in Priam's grace,)
The king the first; Thymœtes at his side;
Lampus and Clytius, long in council tried;
Panthus, and Hicetaon, once the strong;
And next, the wisest of the reverend throng,
Antenor grave, and sage Ucalegon,
Lean'd on the walls and bask'd before the sun:
Chiefs, who no more in bloody fights engage,
But wise through time, and narrative with age,
In summer days, like grasshoppers rejoice,
A bloodless race, that send a feeble voice.
These, when the Spartan queen approach'd the tower,
In secret own'd resistless beauty's power:
They cried, "No wonder such celestial charms
For nine long years have set the world in arms;
What winning graces! what majestic mien!
She moves a goddess, and she looks a queen!
Yet hence, O Heaven, convey that fatal face,
And from destruction save the Trojan race."
The good old Priam welcomed her, and cried,
"Approach, my child, and grace thy father's side.
See on the plain thy Grecian spouse appears,
The friends and kindred of thy former years.
No crime of thine our present sufferings draws,
Not thou, but Heaven's disposing will, the cause
The gods these armies and this force employ,
The hostile gods conspire the fate of Troy.
But lift thy eyes, and say, what Greek is he
(Far as from hence these aged orbs can see)
Around whose brow such martial graces shine,
So tall, so awful, and almost divine!
Though some of larger stature tread the green,
None match his grandeur and exalted mien:
He seems a monarch, and his country's pride."
Thus ceased the king, and thus the fair replied:
"Before thy presence, father, I appear,
With conscious shame and reverential fear.
Ah! had I died, ere to these walls I fled,
False to my country, and my nuptial bed;
My brothers, friends, and daughter left behind,
False to them all, to Paris only kind!

For this I mourn, till grief or dire disease
Shall waste the form whose fault it was to please!
The king of kings, Atrides, you survey,
Great in the war, and great in arts of sway:
My brother once, before my days of shame!
And oh! that still he bore a brother's name!"
With wonder Priam view'd the godlike man,
Extoll'd the happy prince, and thus began:
"O bless'd Atrides! born to prosperous fate,
Successful monarch of a mighty state!
How vast thy empire! Of your matchless train
What numbers lost, what numbers yet remain!
In Phrygia once were gallant armies known,
In ancient time, when Otreus fill'd the throne,
When godlike Mygdon led their troops of horse,
And I, to join them, raised the Trojan force:
Against the manlike Amazons we stood,
And Sangar's stream ran purple with their blood.
But far inferior those, in martial grace,
And strength of numbers, to this Grecian race."
This said, once more he view'd the warrior train;
"What's he, whose arms lie scatter'd on the plain?
Broad is his breast, his shoulders larger spread,
Though great Atrides overtops his head.
Nor yet appear his care and conduct small;
From rank to rank he moves, and orders all.
The stately ram thus measures o'er the ground,
And, master of the flock, surveys them round."
Then Helen thus: "Whom your discerning eyes
Have singled out, is Ithacus the wise;
A barren island boasts his glorious birth;
His fame for wisdom fills the spacious earth."
Antenor took the word, and thus began:
"Myself, O king! have seen that wondrous man
When, trusting Jove and hospitable laws,
To Troy he came, to plead the Grecian cause;
(Great Menelaus urged the same request;)
My house was honour'd with each royal guest:
I knew their persons, and admired their parts,
Both brave in arms, and both approved in arts.
Erect, the Spartan most engaged our view;
Ulysses seated, greater reverence drew.
When Atreus' son harangued the listening train,
Just was his sense, and his expression plain,
His words succinct, yet full, without a fault;
He spoke no more than just the thing he ought.

But when Ulysses rose, in thought profound,
His modest eyes he fix'd upon the ground;
As one unskill'd or dumb, he seem'd to stand,
Nor raised his head, nor stretch'd his sceptred hand;
But, when he speaks, what elocution flows!
Soft as the fleeces of descending snows,
The copious accents fall, with easy art;
Melting they fall, and sink into the heart!
Wondering we hear, and fix'd in deep surprise,
Our ears refute the censure of our eyes."
The king then ask'd (as yet the camp he view'd)
"What chief is that, with giant strength endued,
Whose brawny shoulders, and whose swelling chest,
And lofty stature, far exceed the rest?
"Ajax the great, (the beauteous queen replied,)
Himself a host: the Grecian strength and pride.
See! bold Idomeneus superior towers
Amid yon circle of his Cretan powers,
Great as a god! I saw him once before,
With Menelaus on the Spartan shore.
The rest I know, and could in order name;
All valiant chiefs, and men of mighty fame.
Yet two are wanting of the numerous train,
Whom long my eyes have sought, but sought in vain:
Castor and Pollux, first in martial force,
One bold on foot, and one renown'd for horse.
My brothers these; the same our native shore,
One house contain'd us, as one mother bore.
Perhaps the chiefs, from warlike toils at ease,
For distant Troy refused to sail the seas;
Perhaps their swords some nobler quarrel draws,
Ashamed to combat in their sister's cause."
So spoke the fair, nor knew her brothers' doom;
Wrapt in the cold embraces of the tomb;
Adorn'd with honours in their native shore,
Silent they slept, and heard of wars no more.
Meantime the heralds, through the crowded town,
Bring the rich wine and destined victims down.
Idæus' arms the golden goblets press'd,
Who thus the venerable king address'd:
"Arise, O father of the Trojan state!
The nations call, thy joyful people wait
To seal the truce, and end the dire debate.
Paris, thy son, and Sparta's king advance,
In measured lists to toss the weighty lance;
And who his rival shall in arms subdue,

His be the dame, and his the treasure too.
Thus with a lasting league our toils may cease,
And Troy possess her fertile fields in peace:
So shall the Greeks review their native shore,
Much famed for generous steeds, for beauty more."
With grief he heard, and bade the chiefs prepare
To join his milk-white coursers to the car;
He mounts the seat, Antenor at his side;
The gentle steeds through Scæa's gates they guide:
Next from the car descending on the plain,
Amid the Grecian host and Trojan train,
Slow they proceed: the sage Ulysses then
Arose, and with him rose the king of men.
On either side a sacred herald stands,
The wine they mix, and on each monarch's hands
Pour the full urn; then draws the Grecian lord
His cutlass sheathed beside his ponderous sword;
From the sign'd victims crops the curling hair;
The heralds part it, and the princes share;
Then loudly thus before the attentive bands
He calls the gods, and spreads his lifted hands:
"O first and greatest power! whom all obey,
Who high on Ida's holy mountain sway,
Eternal Jove! and you bright orb that roll
From east to west, and view from pole to pole!
Thou mother Earth! and all ye living floods!
Infernal furies, and Tartarean gods,
Who rule the dead, and horrid woes prepare
For perjured kings, and all who falsely swear!
Hear, and be witness. If, by Paris slain,
Great Menelaus press the fatal plain;
The dame and treasures let the Trojan keep,
And Greece returning plough the watery deep.
If by my brother's lance the Trojan bleed,
Be his the wealth and beauteous dame decreed:
The appointed fine let Ilion justly pay,
And every age record the signal day.
This if the Phrygians shall refuse to yield,
Arms must revenge, and Mars decide the field."
With that the chief the tender victims slew,
And in the dust their bleeding bodies threw;
The vital spirit issued at the wound,
And left the members quivering on the ground.
From the same urn they drink the mingled wine,
And add libations to the powers divine.
While thus their prayers united mount the sky,

"Hear, mighty Jove! and hear, ye gods on high!
And may their blood, who first the league confound,
Shed like this wine, disdain the thirsty ground;
May all their consorts serve promiscuous lust,
And all their lust be scatter'd as the dust!"
Thus either host their imprecations join'd,
Which Jove refused, and mingled with the wind.
The rites now finish'd, reverend Priam rose,
And thus express'd a heart o'ercharged with woes:
"Ye Greeks and Trojans, let the chiefs engage,
But spare the weakness of my feeble age:
In yonder walls that object let me shun,
Nor view the danger of so dear a son.
Whose arms shall conquer and what prince shall fall,
Heaven only knows; for heaven disposes all."
This said, the hoary king no longer stay'd,
But on his car the slaughter'd victims laid:
Then seized the reins his gentle steeds to guide,
And drove to Troy, Antenor at his side.
Bold Hector and Ulysses now dispose
The lists of combat, and the ground inclose:
Next to decide, by sacred lots prepare,
Who first shall launch his pointed spear in air.
The people pray with elevated hands,
And words like these are heard through all the bands:
"Immortal Jove, high Heaven's superior lord,
On lofty Ida's holy mount adored!
Whoe'er involved us in this dire debate,
O give that author of the war to fate
And shades eternal! let division cease,
And joyful nations join in leagues of peace."
With eyes averted Hector hastes to turn
The lots of fight and shakes the brazen urn.
Then, Paris, thine leap'd forth; by fatal chance
Ordain'd the first to whirl the weighty lance.
Both armies sat the combat to survey.
Beside each chief his azure armour lay,
And round the lists the generous coursers neigh.
The beauteous warrior now arrays for fight,
In gilded arms magnificently bright:
The purple cuishes clasp his thighs around,
With flowers adorn'd, with silver buckles bound:
Lycaon's corslet his fair body dress'd,
Braced in and fitted to his softer breast;
A radiant baldric, o'er his shoulder tied,
Sustain'd the sword that glitter'd at his side:

His youthful face a polish'd helm o'erspread;
The waving horse-hair nodded on his head:
His figured shield, a shining orb, he takes,
And in his hand a pointed javelin shakes.
With equal speed and fired by equal charms,
The Spartan hero sheathes his limbs in arms.
Now round the lists the admiring armies stand,
With javelins fix'd, the Greek and Trojan band.
Amidst the dreadful vale, the chiefs advance,
All pale with rage, and shake the threatening lance.
The Trojan first his shining javelin threw;
Full on Atrides' ringing shield it flew,
Nor pierced the brazen orb, but with a bound
Leap'd from the buckler, blunted, on the ground.
Atrides then his massy lance prepares,
In act to throw, but first prefers his prayers:
"Give me, great Jove! to punish lawless lust,
And lay the Trojan gasping in the dust:
Destroy the aggressor, aid my righteous cause,
Avenge the breach of hospitable laws!
Let this example future times reclaim,
And guard from wrong fair friendship's holy name,"
He said, and poised in air the javelin sent,
Through Paris' shield the forceful weapon went,
His corslet pierces, and his garment rends,
And glancing downward, near his flank descends.
The wary Trojan, bending from the blow,
Eludes the death, and disappoints his foe:
But fierce Atrides waved his sword, and strook
Full on his casque: the crested helmet shook;
The brittle steel, unfaithful to his hand,
Broke short: the fragments glitter'd on the sand.
The raging warrior to the spacious skies
Raised his upbraiding voice and angry eyes:
"Then is it vain in Jove himself to trust?
And is it thus the gods assist the just?
When crimes provoke us, Heaven success denies;
The dart falls harmless, and the falchion flies."
Furious he said, and towards the Grecian crew
(Seized by the crest) the unhappy warrior drew;
Struggling he followed, while the embroider'd thong
That tied his helmet, dragg'd the chief along.
Then had his ruin crown'd Atrides' joy,
But Venus trembled for the prince of Troy:
Unseen she came, and burst the golden band;
And left an empty helmet in his hand.

The casque, enraged, amidst the Greeks he threw;
The Greeks with smiles the polish'd trophy view.
Then, as once more he lifts the deadly dart,
In thirst of vengeance, at his rival's heart;
The queen of love her favour'd champion shrouds
(For gods can all things) in a veil of clouds.
Raised from the field the panting youth she led,
And gently laid him on the bridal bed,
With pleasing sweets his fainting sense renews,
And all the dome perfumes with heavenly dews.
Meantime the brightest of the female kind,
The matchless Helen, o'er the walls reclined;
To her, beset with Trojan beauties, came,
In borrow'd form, the laughter-loving dame.
(She seem'd an ancient maid, well-skill'd to cull
The snowy fleece, and wind the twisted wool.)
The goddess softly shook her silken vest,
That shed perfumes, and whispering thus address'd:

"Haste, happy nymph! for thee thy Paris calls,
Safe from the fight, in yonder lofty walls,
Fair as a god; with odours round him spread,
He lies, and waits thee on the well-known bed;
Not like a warrior parted from the foe,
But some gay dancer in the public show."
She spoke, and Helen's secret soul was moved;
She scorn'd the champion, but the man she loved.
Fair Venus' neck, her eyes that sparkled fire,
And breast, reveal'd the queen of soft desire.
Struck with her presence, straight the lively red
Forsook her cheek; and trembling, thus she said:
"Then is it still thy pleasure to deceive?
And woman's frailty always to believe!
Say, to new nations must I cross the main,
Or carry wars to some soft Asian plain?
For whom must Helen break her second vow?
What other Paris is thy darling now?
Left to Atrides, (victor in the strife,)
An odious conquest and a captive wife,
Hence let me sail; and if thy Paris bear
My absence ill, let Venus ease his care.
A handmaid goddess at his side to wait,
Renounce the glories of thy heavenly state,
Be fix'd for ever to the Trojan shore,
His spouse, or slave; and mount the skies no more.
For me, to lawless love no longer led,

I scorn the coward, and detest his bed;
Else should I merit everlasting shame,
And keen reproach, from every Phrygian dame:
Ill suits it now the joys of love to know,
Too deep my anguish, and too wild my woe."

Then thus incensed, the Paphian queen replies:
"Obey the power from whom thy glories rise:
Should Venus leave thee, every charm must fly,
Fade from thy cheek, and languish in thy eye.
Cease to provoke me, lest I make thee more
The world's aversion, than their love before;
Now the bright prize for which mankind engage,
Than, the sad victim, of the public rage."
At this, the fairest of her sex obey'd,
And veil'd her blushes in a silken shade;
Unseen, and silent, from the train she moves,
Led by the goddess of the Smiles and Loves.
Arrived, and enter'd at the palace gate,
The maids officious round their mistress wait;
Then, all dispersing, various tasks attend;
The queen and goddess to the prince ascend.
Full in her Paris' sight, the queen of love
Had placed the beauteous progeny of Jove;
Where, as he view'd her charms, she turn'd away
Her glowing eyes, and thus began to say:
"Is this the chief, who, lost to sense of shame,
Late fled the field, and yet survives his fame?
O hadst thou died beneath the righteous sword
Of that brave man whom once I call'd my lord!
The boaster Paris oft desired the day
With Sparta's king to meet in single fray:
Go now, once more thy rival's rage excite,
Provoke Atrides, and renew the fight:
Yet Helen bids thee stay, lest thou unskill'd
Shouldst fall an easy conquest on the field."
The prince replies: "Ah cease, divinely fair,
Nor add reproaches to the wounds I bear;
This day the foe prevail'd by Pallas' power:
We yet may vanquish in a happier hour:
There want not gods to favour us above;
But let the business of our life be love:
These softer moments let delights employ,
And kind embraces snatch the hasty joy.
Not thus I loved thee, when from Sparta's shore
My forced, my willing heavenly prize I bore,

When first entranced in Cranae's isle I lay,
Mix'd with thy soul, and all dissolved away!"
Thus having spoke, the enamour'd Phrygian boy
Rush'd to the bed, impatient for the joy.
Him Helen follow'd slow with bashful charms,
And clasp'd the blooming hero in her arms.
While these to love's delicious rapture yield,
The stern Atrides rages round the field:
So some fell lion whom the woods obey,
Roars through the desert, and demands his prey.
Paris he seeks, impatient to destroy,
But seeks in vain along the troops of Troy;
Even those had yielded to a foe so brave
The recreant warrior, hateful as the grave.
Then speaking thus, the king of kings arose,
"Ye Trojans, Dardans, all our generous foes!
Hear and attest! from Heaven with conquest crown'd,
Our brother's arms the just success have found:
Be therefore now the Spartan wealth restor'd,
Let Argive Helen own her lawful lord;
The appointed fine let Ilion justly pay,
And age to age record this signal day."
He ceased; his army's loud applauses rise,
And the long shout runs echoing through the skies.

BOOK IV.

THE BREACH OF THE TRUCE, AND THE FIRST BATTLE.

And now Olympus' shining gates unfold;
The gods, with Jove, assume their thrones of gold:
Immortal Hebe, fresh with bloom divine,
The golden goblet crowns with purple wine:
While the full bowls flow round, the powers employ
Their careful eyes on long-contended Troy.
When Jove, disposed to tempt Saturnia's spleen,
Thus waked the fury of his partial queen,
"Two powers divine the son of Atreus aid,
Imperial Juno, and the martial maid;

But high in heaven they sit, and gaze from far,
The tame spectators of his deeds of war.
Not thus fair Venus helps her favour'd knight,
The queen of pleasures shares the toils of fight,
Each danger wards, and constant in her care,
Saves in the moment of the last despair.
Her act has rescued Paris' forfeit life,
Though great Atrides gain'd the glorious strife.
Then say, ye powers! what signal issue waits
To crown this deed, and finish all the fates!
Shall Heaven by peace the bleeding kingdoms spare,
Or rouse the furies, and awake the war?
Yet, would the gods for human good provide,
Atrides soon might gain his beauteous bride,
Still Priam's walls in peaceful honours grow,
And through his gates the crowding nations flow."
Thus while he spoke, the queen of heaven, enraged,
And queen of war, in close consult engaged:
Apart they sit, their deep designs employ,
And meditate the future woes of Troy.
Though secret anger swell'd Minerva's breast,
The prudent goddess yet her wrath suppress'd;
But Juno, impotent of passion, broke
Her sullen silence, and with fury spoke:

"Shall then, O tyrant of the ethereal reign!
My schemes, my labours, and my hopes be vain?
Have I, for this, shook Ilion with alarms,
Assembled nations, set two worlds in arms?
To spread the war, I flew from shore to shore;
The immortal coursers scarce the labour bore.
At length ripe vengeance o'er their heads impends,
But Jove himself the faithless race defends.
Loth as thou art to punish lawless lust,
Not all the gods are partial and unjust."
The sire whose thunder shakes the cloudy skies,
Sighs from his inmost soul, and thus replies:
"Oh lasting rancour! oh insatiate hate
To Phrygia's monarch, and the Phrygian state!
What high offence has fired the wife of Jove?
Can wretched mortals harm the powers above,
That Troy, and Troy's whole race thou wouldst confound,
And yon fair structures level with the ground!
Haste, leave the skies, fulfil thy stern desire,
Burst all her gates, and wrap her walls in fire!
Let Priam bleed! if yet you thirst for more,

Bleed all his sons, and Ilion float with gore:
To boundless vengeance the wide realm be given,
Till vast destruction glut the queen of heaven!
So let it be, and Jove his peace enjoy,
When heaven no longer hears the name of Troy.
But should this arm prepare to wreak our hate
On thy loved realms, whose guilt demands their fate;
Presume not thou the lifted bolt to stay,
Remember Troy, and give the vengeance way.
For know, of all the numerous towns that rise
Beneath the rolling sun and starry skies,
Which gods have raised, or earth-born men enjoy,
None stands so dear to Jove as sacred Troy.
No mortals merit more distinguish'd grace
Than godlike Priam, or than Priam's race.
Still to our name their hecatombs expire,
And altars blaze with unextinguish'd fire."
At this the goddess rolled her radiant eyes,
Then on the Thunderer fix'd them, and replies:
"Three towns are Juno's on the Grecian plains,
More dear than all the extended earth contains,
Mycenæ, Argos, and the Spartan wall;
These thou mayst raze, nor I forbid their fall:
'Tis not in me the vengeance to remove;
The crime's sufficient that they share my love.
Of power superior why should I complain?
Resent I may, but must resent in vain.
Yet some distinction Juno might require,
Sprung with thyself from one celestial sire,
A goddess born, to share the realms above,
And styled the consort of the thundering Jove;
Nor thou a wife and sister's right deny;
Let both consent, and both by terms comply;
So shall the gods our joint decrees obey,
And heaven shall act as we direct the way.
See ready Pallas waits thy high commands
To raise in arms the Greek and Phrygian bands;
Their sudden friendship by her arts may cease,
And the proud Trojans first infringe the peace."
The sire of men and monarch of the sky
The advice approved, and bade Minerva fly,
Dissolve the league, and all her arts employ
To make the breach the faithless act of Troy.
Fired with the charge, she headlong urged her flight,
And shot like lightning from Olympus' height.
As the red comet, from Saturnius sent

To fright the nations with a dire portent,
(A fatal sign to armies on the plain,
Or trembling sailors on the wintry main,)
With sweeping glories glides along in air,
And shakes the sparkles from its blazing hair:
Between both armies thus, in open sight
Shot the bright goddess in a trail of light,
With eyes erect the gazing hosts admire
The power descending, and the heavens on fire!
"The gods (they cried), the gods this signal sent,
And fate now labours with some vast event:
Jove seals the league, or bloodier scenes prepares;
Jove, the great arbiter of peace and wars."
They said, while Pallas through the Trojan throng,
(In shape a mortal,) pass'd disguised along.
Like bold Laodocus, her course she bent,
Who from Antenor traced his high descent.
Amidst the ranks Lycaon's son she found,
The warlike Pandarus, for strength renown'd;
Whose squadrons, led from black Æsepus' flood,
With flaming shields in martial circle stood.
To him the goddess: "Phrygian! canst thou hear
A well-timed counsel with a willing ear?
What praise were thine, couldst thou direct thy dart,
Amidst his triumph, to the Spartan's heart?
What gifts from Troy, from Paris wouldst thou gain,
Thy country's foe, the Grecian glory slain?
Then seize the occasion, dare the mighty deed,
Aim at his breast, and may that aim succeed!
But first, to speed the shaft, address thy vow
To Lycian Phœbus with the silver bow,
And swear the firstlings of thy flock to pay,
On Zelia's altars, to the god of day."
He heard, and madly at the motion pleased,
His polish'd bow with hasty rashness seized.
'Twas form'd of horn, and smooth'd with artful toil:
A mountain goat resign'd the shining spoil.
Who pierced long since beneath his arrows bled;
The stately quarry on the cliffs lay dead,
And sixteen palms his brow's large honours spread:
The workmen join'd, and shaped the bended horns,
And beaten gold each taper point adorns.
This, by the Greeks unseen, the warrior bends,
Screen'd by the shields of his surrounding friends:
There meditates the mark; and couching low,
Fits the sharp arrow to the well-strung bow.

One from a hundred feather'd deaths he chose,
Fated to wound, and cause of future woes;
Then offers vows with hecatombs to crown
Apollo's altars in his native town.
Now with full force the yielding horn he bends,
Drawn to an arch, and joins the doubling ends;
Close to his breast he strains the nerve below,
Till the barb'd points approach the circling bow;
The impatient weapon whizzes on the wing;
Sounds the tough horn, and twangs the quivering string.
But thee, Atrides! in that dangerous hour
The gods forget not, nor thy guardian power,
Pallas assists, and (weakened in its force)
Diverts the weapon from its destined course:
So from her babe, when slumber seals his eye,
The watchful mother wafts the envenom'd fly.
Just where his belt with golden buckles join'd,
Where linen folds the double corslet lined,
She turn'd the shaft, which, hissing from above,
Pass'd the broad belt, and through the corslet drove;
The folds it pierced, the plaited linen tore,
And razed the skin, and drew the purple gore.
As when some stately trappings are decreed
To grace a monarch on his bounding steed,
A nymph in Caria or Mæonia bred,
Stains the pure ivory with a lively red;
With equal lustre various colours vie,
The shining whiteness, and the Tyrian dye:
So great Atrides! show'd thy sacred blood,
As down thy snowy thigh distill'd the streaming flood.
With horror seized, the king of men descried
The shaft infix'd, and saw the gushing tide:
Nor less the Spartan fear'd, before he found
The shining barb appear above the wound,
Then, with a sigh, that heaved his manly breast,
The royal brother thus his grief express'd,
And grasp'd his hand; while all the Greeks around
With answering sighs return'd the plaintive sound.
"Oh, dear as life! did I for this agree
The solemn truce, a fatal truce to thee!
Wert thou exposed to all the hostile train,
To fight for Greece, and conquer, to be slain!
The race of Trojans in thy ruin join,
And faith is scorn'd by all the perjured line.
Not thus our vows, confirm'd with wine and gore,
Those hands we plighted, and those oaths we swore,

Shall all be vain: when Heaven's revenge is slow,
Jove but prepares to strike the fiercer blow.
The day shall come, that great avenging day,
When Troy's proud glories in the dust shall lay,
When Priam's powers and Priam's self shall fall,
And one prodigious ruin swallow all.
I see the god, already, from the pole
Bare his red arm, and bid the thunder roll;
I see the Eternal all his fury shed,
And shake his ægis o'er their guilty head.
Such mighty woes on perjured princes wait;
But thou, alas! deserv'st a happier fate.
Still must I mourn the period of thy days,
And only mourn, without my share of praise?
Deprived of thee, the heartless Greeks no more
Shall dream of conquests on the hostile shore;
Troy seized of Helen, and our glory lost,
Thy bones shall moulder on a foreign coast;
While some proud Trojan thus insulting cries,
(And spurns the dust where Menelaus lies,)
'Such are the trophies Greece from Ilion brings,
And such the conquest of her king of kings!
Lo his proud vessels scatter'd o'er the main,
And unrevenged, his mighty brother slain.'
Oh! ere that dire disgrace shall blast my fame,
O'erwhelm me, earth! and hide a monarch's shame."
He said: a leader's and a brother's fears
Possess his soul, which thus the Spartan cheers:
"Let not thy words the warmth of Greece abate;
The feeble dart is guiltless of my fate:
Stiff with the rich embroider'd work around,
My varied belt repell'd the flying wound."
To whom the king: "My brother and my friend,
Thus, always thus, may Heaven thy life defend!
Now seek some skilful hand, whose powerful art
May stanch the effusion, and extract the dart.
Herald, be swift, and bid Machaon bring
His speedy succour to the Spartan king;
Pierced with a winged shaft (the deed of Troy),
The Grecian's sorrow, and the Dardan's joy."
With hasty zeal the swift Talthybius flies;
Through the thick files he darts his searching eyes,
And finds Machaon, where sublime he stands
In arms incircled with his native bands.
Then thus: "Machaon, to the king repair,
His wounded brother claims thy timely care;

Pierced by some Lycian or Dardanian bow,
A grief to us, a triumph to the foe."
The heavy tidings grieved the godlike man:
Swift to his succour through the ranks he ran.
The dauntless king yet standing firm he found,
And all the chiefs in deep concern around.
Where to the steely point the reed was join'd,
The shaft he drew, but left the head behind.
Straight the broad belt with gay embroidery graced,
He loosed; the corslet from his breast unbraced;
Then suck'd the blood, and sovereign balm infused,
Which Chiron gave, and Æsculapius used.
While round the prince the Greeks employ their care,
The Trojans rush tumultuous to the war;
Once more they glitter in refulgent arms,
Once more the fields are fill'd with dire alarms.
Nor had you seen the king of men appear
Confused, unactive, or surprised with fear;
But fond of glory, with severe delight,
His beating bosom claim'd the rising fight.
No longer with his warlike steeds he stay'd,
Or press'd the car with polish'd brass inlaid
But left Eurymedon the reins to guide;
The fiery coursers snorted at his side.
On foot through all the martial ranks he moves
And these encourages, and those reproves.
"Brave men!" he cries, (to such who boldly dare
Urge their swift steeds to face the coming war),
"Your ancient valour on the foes approve;
Jove is with Greece, and let us trust in Jove.
'Tis not for us, but guilty Troy, to dread,
Whose crimes sit heavy on her perjured head;
Her sons and matrons Greece shall lead in chains,
And her dead warriors strew the mournful plains."
Thus with new ardour he the brave inspires;
Or thus the fearful with reproaches fires:
"Shame to your country, scandal of your kind;
Born to the fate ye well deserve to find!
Why stand ye gazing round the dreadful plain,
Prepared for flight, but doom'd to fly in vain?
Confused and panting thus, the hunted deer
Falls as he flies, a victim to his fear.
Still must ye wait the foes, and still retire,
Till yon tall vessels blaze with Trojan fire?
Or trust ye, Jove a valiant foe shall chase,
To save a trembling, heartless, dastard race?"

This said, he stalk'd with ample strides along,
To Crete's brave monarch and his martial throng;
High at their head he saw the chief appear,
And bold Meriones excite the rear.
At this the king his generous joy express'd,
And clasp'd the warrior to his armed breast.
"Divine Idomeneus! what thanks we owe
To worth like thine! what praise shall we bestow?
To thee the foremost honours are decreed,
First in the fight and every graceful deed.
For this, in banquets, when the generous bowls
Restore our blood, and raise the warriors' souls,
Though all the rest with stated rules we bound,
Unmix'd, unmeasured, are thy goblets crown'd.
Be still thyself, in arms a mighty name;
Maintain thy honours, and enlarge thy fame."
To whom the Cretan thus his speech address'd:
"Secure of me, O king! exhort the rest.
Fix'd to thy side, in every toil I share,
Thy firm associate in the day of war.
But let the signal be this moment given;
To mix in fight is all I ask of Heaven.
The field shall prove how perjuries succeed,
And chains or death avenge the impious deed."
Charm'd with this heat, the king his course pursues,
And next the troops of either Ajax views:
In one firm orb the bands were ranged around,
A cloud of heroes blacken'd all the ground.
Thus from the lofty promontory's brow
A swain surveys the gathering storm below;
Slow from the main the heavy vapours rise,
Spread in dim streams, and sail along the skies,
Till black as night the swelling tempest shows,
The cloud condensing as the west-wind blows:
He dreads the impending storm, and drives his flock
To the close covert of an arching rock.
Such, and so thick, the embattled squadrons stood,
With spears erect, a moving iron wood:
A shady light was shot from glimmering shields,
And their brown arms obscured the dusky fields.
"O heroes! worthy such a dauntless train,
Whose godlike virtue we but urge in vain,
(Exclaim'd the king), who raise your eager bands
With great examples, more than loud commands.
Ah! would the gods but breathe in all the rest
Such souls as burn in your exalted breast,

Soon should our arms with just success be crown'd,
And Troy's proud walls lie smoking on the ground."
Then to the next the general bends his course;
(His heart exults, and glories in his force);
There reverend Nestor ranks his Pylian bands,
And with inspiring eloquence commands;
With strictest order sets his train in arms,
The chiefs advises, and the soldiers warms.
Alastor, Chromius, Haemon, round him wait,
Bias the good, and Pelagon the great.
The horse and chariots to the front assign'd,
The foot (the strength of war) he ranged behind;
The middle space suspected troops supply,
Inclosed by both, nor left the power to fly;
He gives command to "curb the fiery steed,
Nor cause confusion, nor the ranks exceed:
Before the rest let none too rashly ride;
No strength nor skill, but just in time, be tried:
The charge once made, no warrior turn the rein,
But fight, or fall; a firm embodied train.
He whom the fortune of the field shall cast
From forth his chariot, mount the next in haste;
Nor seek unpractised to direct the car,
Content with javelins to provoke the war.
Our great forefathers held this prudent course,
Thus ruled their ardour, thus preserved their force;
By laws like these immortal conquests made,
And earth's proud tyrants low in ashes laid."
So spoke the master of the martial art,
And touch'd with transport great Atrides' heart.
"Oh! hadst thou strength to match thy brave desires,
And nerves to second what thy soul inspires!
But wasting years, that wither human race,
Exhaust thy spirits, and thy arms unbrace.
What once thou wert, oh ever mightst thou be!
And age the lot of any chief but thee."
Thus to the experienced prince Atrides cried;
He shook his hoary locks, and thus replied:
"Well might I wish, could mortal wish renew
That strength which once in boiling youth I knew;
Such as I was, when Ereuthalion, slain
Beneath this arm, fell prostrate on the plain.
But heaven its gifts not all at once bestows,
These years with wisdom crowns, with action those:
The field of combat fits the young and bold,
The solemn council best becomes the old:

To you the glorious conflict I resign,
Let sage advice, the palm of age, be mine."
He said. With joy the monarch march'd before,
And found Menestheus on the dusty shore,
With whom the firm Athenian phalanx stands;
And next Ulysses, with his subject bands.
Remote their forces lay, nor knew so far
The peace infringed, nor heard the sounds of war;
The tumult late begun, they stood intent
To watch the motion, dubious of the event.
The king, who saw their squadrons yet unmoved,
With hasty ardour thus the chiefs reproved:
"Can Peleus' son forget a warrior's part.
And fears Ulysses, skill'd in every art?
Why stand you distant, and the rest expect
To mix in combat which yourselves neglect?
From you 'twas hoped among the first to dare
The shock of armies, and commence the war;
For this your names are call'd before the rest,
To share the pleasures of the genial feast:
And can you, chiefs! without a blush survey
Whole troops before you labouring in the fray?
Say, is it thus those honours you requite?
The first in banquets, but the last in fight."
Ulysses heard: the hero's warmth o'erspread
His cheek with blushes: and severe, he said:
"Take back the unjust reproach! Behold we stand
Sheathed in bright arms, and but expect command.
If glorious deeds afford thy soul delight,
Behold me plunging in the thickest fight.
Then give thy warrior-chief a warrior's due,
Who dares to act whate'er thou dar'st to view."
Struck with his generous wrath, the king replies:
"O great in action, and in council wise!
With ours, thy care and ardour are the same,
Nor need I to commend, nor aught to blame.
Sage as thou art, and learn'd in human kind,
Forgive the transport of a martial mind.
Haste to the fight, secure of just amends;
The gods that make, shall keep the worthy, friends."
He said, and pass'd where great Tydides lay,
His steeds and chariots wedged in firm array;
(The warlike Sthenelus attends his side;)
To whom with stern reproach the monarch cried:
"O son of Tydeus! (he, whose strength could tame
The bounding steed, in arms a mighty name)

Canst thou, remote, the mingling hosts descry,
With hands unactive, and a careless eye?
Not thus thy sire the fierce encounter fear'd;
Still first in front the matchless prince appear'd:
What glorious toils, what wonders they recite,
Who view'd him labouring through the ranks of fight?
I saw him once, when gathering martial powers,
A peaceful guest, he sought Mycenæ's towers;
Armies he ask'd, and armies had been given,
Not we denied, but Jove forbade from heaven;
While dreadful comets glaring from afar,
Forewarn'd the horrors of the Theban war.
Next, sent by Greece from where Asopus flows,
A fearless envoy, he approach'd the foes;
Thebes' hostile walls unguarded and alone,
Dauntless he enters, and demands the throne.
The tyrant feasting with his chiefs he found,
And dared to combat all those chiefs around:
Dared, and subdued before their haughty lord;
For Pallas strung his arm and edged his sword.
Stung with the shame, within the winding way,
To bar his passage fifty warriors lay;
Two heroes led the secret squadron on,
Mason the fierce, and hardy Lycophon;
Those fifty slaughter'd in the gloomy vale.
He spared but one to bear the dreadful tale,
Such Tydeus was, and such his martial fire;
Gods! how the son degenerates from the sire!"
No words the godlike Diomed return'd,
But heard respectful, and in secret burn'd:
Not so fierce Capaneus' undaunted son;
Stern as his sire, the boaster thus begun:
"What needs, O monarch! this invidious praise,
Ourselves to lessen, while our sire you raise?
Dare to be just, Atrides! and confess
Our value equal, though our fury less.
With fewer troops we storm'd the Theban wall,
And happier saw the sevenfold city fall,
In impious acts the guilty father died;
The sons subdued, for Heaven was on their side.
Far more than heirs of all our parents' fame,
Our glories darken their diminish'd name."
To him Tydides thus: "My friend, forbear;
Suppress thy passion, and the king revere:
His high concern may well excuse this rage,
Whose cause we follow, and whose war we wage:

His the first praise, were Ilion's towers o'erthrown,
And, if we fail, the chief disgrace his own.
Let him the Greeks to hardy toils excite,
'Tis ours to labour in the glorious fight."
He spoke, and ardent, on the trembling ground
Sprung from his car: his ringing arms resound.
Dire was the clang, and dreadful from afar,
Of arm'd Tydides rushing to the war.
As when the winds, ascending by degrees,
First move the whitening surface of the seas,
The billows float in order to the shore,
The wave behind rolls on the wave before;
Till, with the growing storm, the deeps arise,
Foam o'er the rocks, and thunder to the skies.
So to the fight the thick battalions throng,
Shields urged on shields, and men drove men along
Sedate and silent move the numerous bands;
No sound, no whisper, but the chief's commands,
Those only heard; with awe the rest obey,
As if some god had snatch'd their voice away.
Not so the Trojans; from their host ascends
A general shout that all the region rends.
As when the fleecy flocks unnumber'd stand
In wealthy folds, and wait the milker's hand,
The hollow vales incessant bleating fills,
The lambs reply from all the neighbouring hills:
Such clamours rose from various nations round,
Mix'd was the murmur, and confused the sound.
Each host now joins, and each a god inspires,
These Mars incites, and those Minerva fires,
Pale flight around, and dreadful terror reign;
And discord raging bathes the purple plain;
Discord! dire sister of the slaughtering power,
Small at her birth, but rising every hour,
While scarce the skies her horrid head can bound,
She stalks on earth, and shakes the world around;
The nations bleed, where'er her steps she turns,
The groan still deepens, and the combat burns.
Now shield with shield, with helmet helmet closed,
To armour armour, lance to lance opposed,
Host against host with shadowy squadrons drew,
The sounding darts in iron tempests flew,
Victors and vanquish'd join'd promiscuous cries,
And shrilling shouts and dying groans arise;
With streaming blood the slippery fields are dyed,
And slaughter'd heroes swell the dreadful tide.

As torrents roll, increased by numerous rills,
With rage impetuous, down their echoing hills
Rush to the vales, and pour'd along the plain,
Roar through a thousand channels to the main:
The distant shepherd trembling hears the sound;
So mix both hosts, and so their cries rebound.
The bold Antilochus the slaughter led,
The first who struck a valiant Trojan dead:
At great Echepolus the lance arrives,
Razed his high crest, and through his helmet drives;
Warm'd in the brain the brazen weapon lies,
And shades eternal settle o'er his eyes.
So sinks a tower, that long assaults had stood
Of force and fire, its walls besmear'd with blood.
Him, the bold leader of the Abantian throng,
Seized to despoil, and dragg'd the corpse along:
But while he strove to tug the inserted dart,
Agenor's javelin reach'd the hero's heart.
His flank, unguarded by his ample shield,
Admits the lance: he falls, and spurns the field;
The nerves, unbraced, support his limbs no more;
The soul comes floating in a tide of gore.
Trojans and Greeks now gather round the slain;
The war renews, the warriors bleed again:
As o'er their prey rapacious wolves engage,
Man dies on man, and all is blood and rage.
In blooming youth fair Simoisius fell,
Sent by great Ajax to the shades of hell;
Fair Simoisius, whom his mother bore
Amid the flocks on silver Simois' shore:
The nymph descending from the hills of Ide,
To seek her parents on his flowery side,
Brought forth the babe, their common care and joy,
And thence from Simois named the lovely boy.
Short was his date! by dreadful Ajax slain,
He falls, and renders all their cares in vain!
So falls a poplar, that in watery ground
Raised high the head, with stately branches crown'd,
(Fell'd by some artist with his shining steel,
To shape the circle of the bending wheel,)
Cut down it lies, tall, smooth, and largely spread,
With all its beauteous honours on its head
There, left a subject to the wind and rain,
And scorch'd by suns, it withers on the plain
Thus pierced by Ajax, Simoisius lies
Stretch'd on the shore, and thus neglected dies.

At Ajax, Antiphus his javelin threw;
The pointed lance with erring fury flew,
And Leucus, loved by wise Ulysses, slew.
He drops the corpse of Simoisius slain,
And sinks a breathless carcase on the plain.
This saw Ulysses, and with grief enraged,
Strode where the foremost of the foes engaged;
Arm'd with his spear, he meditates the wound,
In act to throw; but cautious look'd around,
Struck at his sight the Trojans backward drew,
And trembling heard the javelin as it flew.
A chief stood nigh, who from Abydos came,
Old Priam's son, Democoon was his name.
The weapon entered close above his ear,
Cold through his temples glides the whizzing spear;
With piercing shrieks the youth resigns his breath,
His eye-balls darken with the shades of death;
Ponderous he falls; his clanging arms resound,
And his broad buckler rings against the ground.
Seized with affright the boldest foes appear;
E'en godlike Hector seems himself to fear;
Slow he gave way, the rest tumultuous fled;
The Greeks with shouts press on, and spoil the dead:
But Phœbus now from Ilion's towering height
Shines forth reveal'd, and animates the fight.
"Trojans, be bold, and force with force oppose;
Your foaming steeds urge headlong on the foes!
Nor are their bodies rocks, nor ribb'd with steel;
Your weapons enter, and your strokes they feel.
Have ye forgot what seem'd your dread before?
The great, the fierce Achilles fights no more."
Apollo thus from Ilion's lofty towers,
Array'd in terrors, roused the Trojan powers:
While war's fierce goddess fires the Grecian foe,
And shouts and thunders in the fields below.
Then great Diores fell, by doom divine,
In vain his valour and illustrious line.
A broken rock the force of Pyrus threw,
(Who from cold Ænus led the Thracian crew,)
Full on his ankle dropp'd the ponderous stone,
Burst the strong nerves, and crash'd the solid bone.
Supine he tumbles on the crimson sands,
Before his helpless friends, and native bands,
And spreads for aid his unavailing hands.
The foe rush'd furious as he pants for breath,
And through his navel drove the pointed death:

His gushing entrails smoked upon the ground,
And the warm life came issuing from the wound.
His lance bold Thoas at the conqueror sent,
Deep in his breast above the pap it went,
Amid the lungs was fix'd the winged wood,
And quivering in his heaving bosom stood:
Till from the dying chief, approaching near,
The Ætolian warrior tugg'd his weighty spear:
Then sudden waved his flaming falchion round,
And gash'd his belly with a ghastly wound;
The corpse now breathless on the bloody plain,
To spoil his arms the victor strove in vain;
The Thracian bands against the victor press'd,
A grove of lances glitter'd at his breast.
Stern Thoas, glaring with revengeful eyes,
In sullen fury slowly quits the prize.
Thus fell two heroes; one the pride of Thrace,
And one the leader of the Epeian race;
Death's sable shade at once o'ercast their eyes,
In dust the vanquish'd and the victor lies.
With copious slaughter all the fields are red,
And heap'd with growing mountains of the dead.
Had some brave chief this martial scene beheld,
By Pallas guarded through the dreadful field;
Might darts be bid to turn their points away,
And swords around him innocently play;
The war's whole art with wonder had he seen,
And counted heroes where he counted men.
So fought each host, with thirst of glory fired,
And crowds on crowds triumphantly expired.

BOOK V.

THE ACTS OF DIOMED.

But Pallas now Tydides' soul inspires,
Fills with her force, and warms with all her fires,
Above the Greeks his deathless fame to raise,
And crown her hero with distinguish'd praise.
High on his helm celestial lightnings play,

His beamy shield emits a living ray;
The unwearied blaze incessant streams supplies,
Like the red star that fires the autumnal skies,
When fresh he rears his radiant orb to sight,
And, bathed in ocean, shoots a keener light.
Such glories Pallas on the chief bestow'd,
Such, from his arms, the fierce effulgence flow'd:
Onward she drives him, furious to engage,
Where the fight burns, and where the thickest rage.
The sons of Dares first the combat sought,
A wealthy priest, but rich without a fault;
In Vulcan's fane the father's days were led,
The sons to toils of glorious battle bred;
These singled from their troops the fight maintain,
These, from their steeds, Tydides on the plain.
Fierce for renown the brother-chiefs draw near,
And first bold Phegeus cast his sounding spear,
Which o'er the warrior's shoulder took its course,
And spent in empty air its erring force.
Not so, Tydides, flew thy lance in vain,
But pierced his breast, and stretch'd him on the plain.
Seized with unusual fear, Idæus fled,
Left the rich chariot, and his brother dead.
And had not Vulcan lent celestial aid,
He too had sunk to death's eternal shade;
But in a smoky cloud the god of fire
Preserved the son, in pity to the sire.
The steeds and chariot, to the navy led,
Increased the spoils of gallant Diomed.
Struck with amaze and shame, the Trojan crew,
Or slain, or fled, the sons of Dares view;
When by the blood-stain'd hand Minerva press'd
The god of battles, and this speech address'd:
"Stern power of war! by whom the mighty fall,
Who bathe in blood, and shake the lofty wall!
Let the brave chiefs their glorious toils divide;
And whose the conquest, mighty Jove decide:
While we from interdicted fields retire,
Nor tempt the wrath of heaven's avenging sire."
Her words allay the impetuous warrior's heat,
The god of arms and martial maid retreat;
Removed from fight, on Xanthus' flowery bounds
They sat, and listen'd to the dying sounds.
Meantime, the Greeks the Trojan race pursue,
And some bold chieftain every leader slew:
First Odius falls, and bites the bloody sand,

His death ennobled by Atrides' hand:
As he to flight his wheeling car address'd,
The speedy javelin drove from back to breast.
In dust the mighty Halizonian lay,
His arms resound, the spirit wings its way.
Thy fate was next, O Phæstus! doom'd to feel
The great Idomeneus' protended steel;
Whom Borus sent (his son and only joy)
From fruitful Tarne to the fields of Troy.
The Cretan javelin reach'd him from afar,
And pierced his shoulder as he mounts his car;
Back from the car he tumbles to the ground,
And everlasting shades his eyes surround.
Then died Scamandrius, expert in the chase,
In woods and wilds to wound the savage race;
Diana taught him all her sylvan arts,
To bend the bow, and aim unerring darts:
But vainly here Diana's arts he tries,
The fatal lance arrests him as he flies;
From Menelaus' arm the weapon sent,
Through his broad back and heaving bosom went:
Down sinks the warrior with a thundering sound,
His brazen armour rings against the ground.
Next artful Phereclus untimely fell;
Bold Merion sent him to the realms of hell.
Thy father's skill, O Phereclus! was thine,
The graceful fabric and the fair design;
For loved by Pallas, Pallas did impart
To him the shipwright's and the builder's art.
Beneath his hand the fleet of Paris rose,
The fatal cause of all his country's woes;
But he, the mystic will of heaven unknown,
Nor saw his country's peril, nor his own.
The hapless artist, while confused he fled,
The spear of Merion mingled with the dead.
Through his right hip, with forceful fury cast,
Between the bladder and the bone it pass'd;
Prone on his knees he falls with fruitless cries,
And death in lasting slumber seals his eyes.
From Meges' force the swift Pedaeus fled,
Antenor's offspring from a foreign bed,
Whose generous spouse, Theanor, heavenly fair,
Nursed the young stranger with a mother's care.
How vain those cares! when Meges in the rear
Full in his nape infix'd the fatal spear;
Swift through his crackling jaws the weapon glides,

And the cold tongue and grinning teeth divides.
Then died Hypsenor, generous and divine,
Sprung from the brave Dolopion's mighty line,
Who near adored Scamander made abode,
Priest of the stream, and honoured as a god.
On him, amidst the flying numbers found,
Eurypylus inflicts a deadly wound;
On his broad shoulders fell the forceful brand,
Thence glancing downwards, lopp'd his holy hand,
Which stain'd with sacred blood the blushing sand.
Down sunk the priest: the purple hand of death
Closed his dim eye, and fate suppress'd his breath.
Thus toil'd the chiefs, in different parts engaged.
In every quarter fierce Tydides raged;
Amid the Greek, amid the Trojan train,
Rapt through the ranks he thunders o'er the plain;
Now here, now there, he darts from place to place,
Pours on the rear, or lightens in their face.
Thus from high hills the torrents swift and strong
Deluge whole fields, and sweep the trees along,
Through ruin'd moles the rushing wave resounds,
O'erwhelm's the bridge, and bursts the lofty bounds;
The yellow harvests of the ripen'd year,
And flatted vineyards, one sad waste appear!
While Jove descends in sluicy sheets of rain,
And all the labours of mankind are vain.
So raged Tydides, boundless in his ire,
Drove armies back, and made all Troy retire.
With grief the leader of the Lycian band
Saw the wide waste of his destructive hand:
His bended bow against the chief he drew;
Swift to the mark the thirsty arrow flew,
Whose forky point the hollow breastplate tore,
Deep in his shoulder pierced, and drank the gore:
The rushing stream his brazen armour dyed,
While the proud archer thus exulting cried:
"Hither, ye Trojans, hither drive your steeds!
Lo! by our hand the bravest Grecian bleeds,
Not long the deathful dart he can sustain;
Or Phœbus urged me to these fields in vain."
So spoke he, boastful: but the winged dart
Stopp'd short of life, and mock'd the shooter's art.
The wounded chief, behind his car retired,
The helping hand of Sthenelus required;
Swift from his seat he leap'd upon the ground,
And tugg'd the weapon from the gushing wound;

When thus the king his guardian power address'd,
The purple current wandering o'er his vest:
"O progeny of Jove! unconquer'd maid!
If e'er my godlike sire deserved thy aid,
If e'er I felt thee in the fighting field;
Now, goddess, now, thy sacred succour yield.
O give my lance to reach the Trojan knight,
Whose arrow wounds the chief thou guard'st in fight;
And lay the boaster grovelling on the shore,
That vaunts these eyes shall view the light no more."
Thus pray'd Tydides, and Minerva heard,
His nerves confirm'd, his languid spirits cheer'd;
He feels each limb with wonted vigour light;
His beating bosom claim'd the promised fight.
"Be bold, (she cried), in every combat shine,
War be thy province, thy protection mine;
Rush to the fight, and every foe control;
Wake each paternal virtue in thy soul:
Strength swells thy boiling breast, infused by me,
And all thy godlike father breathes in thee;
Yet more, from mortal mists I purge thy eyes,
And set to view the warring deities.
These see thou shun, through all the embattled plain;
Nor rashly strive where human force is vain.
If Venus mingle in the martial band,
Her shalt thou wound: so Pallas gives command."
With that, the blue-eyed virgin wing'd her flight;
The hero rush'd impetuous to the fight;
With tenfold ardour now invades the plain,
Wild with delay, and more enraged by pain.
As on the fleecy flocks when hunger calls,
Amidst the field a brindled lion falls;
If chance some shepherd with a distant dart
The savage wound, he rouses at the smart,
He foams, he roars; the shepherd dares not stay,
But trembling leaves the scattering flocks a prey;
Heaps fall on heaps; he bathes with blood the ground,
Then leaps victorious o'er the lofty mound.
Not with less fury stern Tydides flew;
And two brave leaders at an instant slew;
Astynous breathless fell, and by his side,
His people's pastor, good Hypenor, died;
Astynous' breast the deadly lance receives,
Hypenor's shoulder his broad falchion cleaves.
Those slain he left, and sprung with noble rage
Abas and Polyidus to engage;

Sons of Eurydamus, who, wise and old,
Could fate foresee, and mystic dreams unfold;
The youths return'd not from the doubtful plain,
And the sad father tried his arts in vain;
No mystic dream could make their fates appear,
Though now determined by Tydides' spear.
Young Xanthus next, and Thoon felt his rage;
The joy and hope of Phaenops' feeble age:
Vast was his wealth, and these the only heirs
Of all his labours and a life of cares.
Cold death o'ertakes them in their blooming years,
And leaves the father unavailing tears:
To strangers now descends his heapy store,
The race forgotten, and the name no more.
Two sons of Priam in one chariot ride,
Glittering in arms, and combat side by side.
As when the lordly lion seeks his food
Where grazing heifers range the lonely wood,
He leaps amidst them with a furious bound,
Bends their strong necks, and tears them to the ground:
So from their seats the brother chiefs are torn,
Their steeds and chariot to the navy borne.
With deep concern divine Æneas view'd
The foe prevailing, and his friends pursued;
Through the thick storm of singing spears he flies,
Exploring Pandarus with careful eyes.
At length he found Lycaon's mighty son;
To whom the chief of Venus' race begun:
"Where, Pandarus, are all thy honours now,
Thy winged arrows and unerring bow,
Thy matchless skill, thy yet unrivall'd fame,
And boasted glory of the Lycian name?
O pierce that mortal! if we mortal call
That wondrous force by which whole armies fall;
Or god incensed, who quits the distant skies
To punish Troy for slighted sacrifice;
(Which, oh avert from our unhappy state!
For what so dreadful as celestial hate)?
Whoe'er he be, propitiate Jove with prayer;
If man, destroy; if god, entreat to spare."
To him the Lycian: "Whom your eyes behold,
If right I judge, is Diomed the bold:
Such coursers whirl him o'er the dusty field,
So towers his helmet, and so flames his shield.
If 'tis a god, he wears that chief's disguise:
Or if that chief, some guardian of the skies,

Involved in clouds, protects him in the fray,
And turns unseen the frustrate dart away.
I wing'd an arrow, which not idly fell,
The stroke had fix'd him to the gates of hell;
And, but some god, some angry god withstands,
His fate was due to these unerring hands.
Skill'd in the bow, on foot I sought the war,
Nor join'd swift horses to the rapid car.
Ten polish'd chariots I possess'd at home,
And still they grace Lycaon's princely dome:
There veil'd in spacious coverlets they stand;
And twice ten coursers wait their lord's command.
The good old warrior bade me trust to these,
When first for Troy I sail'd the sacred seas;
In fields, aloft, the whirling car to guide,
And through the ranks of death triumphant ride.
But vain with youth, and yet to thrift inclined,
I heard his counsels with unheedful mind,
And thought the steeds (your large supplies unknown)
Might fail of forage in the straiten'd town;
So took my bow and pointed darts in hand
And left the chariots in my native land.
"Too late, O friend! my rashness I deplore;
These shafts, once fatal, carry death no more.
Tydeus' and Atreus' sons their points have found,
And undissembled gore pursued the wound.
In vain they bleed: this unavailing bow
Serves, not to slaughter, but provoke the foe.
In evil hour these bended horns I strung,
And seized the quiver where it idly hung.
Cursed be the fate that sent me to the field
Without a warrior's arms, the spear and shield!
If e'er with life I quit the Trojan plain,
If e'er I see my spouse and sire again,
This bow, unfaithful to my glorious aims,
Broke by my hand, shall feed the blazing flames."
To whom the leader of the Dardan race:
"Be calm, nor Phœbus' honour'd gift disgrace.
The distant dart be praised, though here we need
The rushing chariot and the bounding steed.
Against yon hero let us bend our course,
And, hand to hand, encounter force with force.
Now mount my seat, and from the chariot's height
Observe my father's steeds, renown'd in fight;
Practised alike to turn, to stop, to chase,
To dare the shock, or urge the rapid race;

Secure with these, through fighting fields we go;
Or safe to Troy, if Jove assist the foe.
Haste, seize the whip, and snatch the guiding rein;
The warrior's fury let this arm sustain;
Or, if to combat thy bold heart incline,
Take thou the spear, the chariot's care be mine."
"O prince! (Lycaon's valiant son replied)
As thine the steeds, be thine the task to guide.
The horses, practised to their lord's command,
Shall bear the rein, and answer to thy hand;
But, if, unhappy, we desert the fight,
Thy voice alone can animate their flight;
Else shall our fates be number'd with the dead,
And these, the victor's prize, in triumph led.
Thine be the guidance, then: with spear and shield
Myself will charge this terror of the field."
And now both heroes mount the glittering car;
The bounding coursers rush amidst the war;
Their fierce approach bold Sthenelus espied,
Who thus, alarm'd, to great Tydides cried:
"O friend! two chiefs of force immense I see,
Dreadful they come, and bend their rage on thee:
Lo the brave heir of old Lycaon's line,
And great Æneas, sprung from race divine!
Enough is given to fame. Ascend thy car!
And save a life, the bulwark of our war."
At this the hero cast a gloomy look,
Fix'd on the chief with scorn; and thus he spoke:
"Me dost thou bid to shun the coming fight?
Me wouldst thou move to base, inglorious flight?
Know, 'tis not honest in my soul to fear,
Nor was Tydides born to tremble here.
I hate the cumbrous chariot's slow advance,
And the long distance of the flying lance;
But while my nerves are strong, my force entire,
Thus front the foe, and emulate my sire.
Nor shall yon steeds, that fierce to fight convey
Those threatening heroes, bear them both away;
One chief at least beneath this arm shall die;
So Pallas tells me, and forbids to fly.
But if she dooms, and if no god withstand,
That both shall fall by one victorious hand,
Then heed my words: my horses here detain,
Fix'd to the chariot by the straiten'd rein;
Swift to Æneas' empty seat proceed,
And seize the coursers of ethereal breed;

The race of those, which once the thundering god
For ravish'd Ganymede on Tros bestow'd,
The best that e'er on earth's broad surface run,
Beneath the rising or the setting sun.
Hence great Anchises stole a breed unknown,
By mortal mares, from fierce Laomedon:
Four of this race his ample stalls contain,
And two transport Æneas o'er the plain.
These, were the rich immortal prize our own,
Through the wide world should make our glory known."
Thus while they spoke, the foe came furious on,
And stern Lycaon's warlike race begun:
"Prince, thou art met. Though late in vain assail'd,
The spear may enter where the arrow fail'd."
He said, then shook the ponderous lance, and flung;
On his broad shield the sounding weapon rung,
Pierced the tough orb, and in his cuirass hung,
"He bleeds! the pride of Greece! (the boaster cries,)
Our triumph now, the mighty warrior lies!"
"Mistaken vaunter! (Diomed replied;)
Thy dart has erred, and now my spear be tried;
Ye 'scape not both; one, headlong from his car,
With hostile blood shall glut the god of war."
He spoke, and rising hurl'd his forceful dart,
Which, driven by Pallas, pierced a vital part;
Full in his face it enter'd, and betwixt
The nose and eye-ball the proud Lycian fix'd;
Crash'd all his jaws, and cleft the tongue within,
Till the bright point look'd out beneath the chin.
Headlong he falls, his helmet knocks the ground:
Earth groans beneath him, and his arms resound;
The starting coursers tremble with affright;
The soul indignant seeks the realms of night.
To guard his slaughter'd friend, Æneas flies,
His spear extending where the carcase lies;
Watchful he wheels, protects it every way,
As the grim lion stalks around his prey.
O'er the fall'n trunk his ample shield display'd,
He hides the hero with his mighty shade,
And threats aloud! the Greeks with longing eyes
Behold at distance, but forbear the prize.
Then fierce Tydides stoops; and from the fields
Heaved with vast force, a rocky fragment wields.
Not two strong men the enormous weight could raise,
Such men as live in these degenerate days:
He swung it round; and, gathering strength to throw,

Discharged the ponderous ruin at the foe.
Where to the hip the inserted thigh unites,
Full on the bone the pointed marble lights;
Through both the tendons broke the rugged stone,
And stripp'd the skin, and crack'd the solid bone.
Sunk on his knees, and staggering with his pains,
His falling bulk his bended arm sustains;
Lost in a dizzy mist the warrior lies;
A sudden cloud comes swimming o'er his eyes.
There the brave chief, who mighty numbers sway'd,
Oppress'd had sunk to death's eternal shade,
But heavenly Venus, mindful of the love
She bore Anchises in the Idaean grove,
His danger views with anguish and despair,
And guards her offspring with a mother's care.
About her much-loved son her arms she throws,
Her arms whose whiteness match the falling snows.
Screen'd from the foe behind her shining veil,
The swords wave harmless, and the javelins fail;
Safe through the rushing horse, and feather'd flight
Of sounding shafts, she bears him from the fight.
Nor Sthenelus, with unassisting hands,
Remain'd unheedful of his lord's commands:
His panting steeds, removed from out the war,
He fix'd with straiten'd traces to the car,
Next, rushing to the Dardan spoil, detains
The heavenly coursers with the flowing manes:
These in proud triumph to the fleet convey'd,
No longer now a Trojan lord obey'd.
That charge to bold Deipylus he gave,
(Whom most he loved, as brave men love the brave,)
Then mounting on his car, resumed the rein,
And follow'd where Tydides swept the plain.
Meanwhile (his conquest ravished from his eyes)
The raging chief in chase of Venus flies:
No goddess she, commission'd to the field,
Like Pallas dreadful with her sable shield,
Or fierce Bellona thundering at the wall,
While flames ascend, and mighty ruins fall;
He knew soft combats suit the tender dame,
New to the field, and still a foe to fame.
Through breaking ranks his furious course he bends,
And at the goddess his broad lance extends;
Through her bright veil the daring weapon drove,
The ambrosial veil which all the Graces wove;
Her snowy hand the razing steel profaned,

And the transparent skin with crimson stain'd,
From the clear vein a stream immortal flow'd,
Such stream as issues from a wounded god;
Pure emanation! uncorrupted flood!
Unlike our gross, diseased, terrestrial blood:
(For not the bread of man their life sustains,
Nor wine's inflaming juice supplies their veins:)
With tender shrieks the goddess fill'd the place,
And dropp'd her offspring from her weak embrace.
Him Phœbus took: he casts a cloud around
The fainting chief, and wards the mortal wound.
Then with a voice that shook the vaulted skies,
The king insults the goddess as she flies:
"Ill with Jove's daughter bloody fights agree,
The field of combat is no scene for thee:
Go, let thy own soft sex employ thy care,
Go, lull the coward, or delude the fair.
Taught by this stroke renounce the war's alarms,
And learn to tremble at the name of arms."
Tydides thus. The goddess, seized with dread,
Confused, distracted, from the conflict fled.
To aid her, swift the winged Iris flew,
Wrapt in a mist above the warring crew.
The queen of love with faded charms she found.
Pale was her cheek, and livid look'd the wound.
To Mars, who sat remote, they bent their way:
Far, on the left, with clouds involved he lay;
Beside him stood his lance, distain'd with gore,
And, rein'd with gold, his foaming steeds before.
Low at his knee, she begg'd with streaming eyes
Her brother's car, to mount the distant skies,
And show'd the wound by fierce Tydides given,
A mortal man, who dares encounter heaven.
Stern Mars attentive hears the queen complain,
And to her hand commits the golden rein;
She mounts the seat, oppress'd with silent woe,
Driven by the goddess of the painted bow.
The lash resounds, the rapid chariot flies,
And in a moment scales the lofty skies:
They stopp'd the car, and there the coursers stood,
Fed by fair Iris with ambrosial food;
Before her mother, love's bright queen appears,
O'erwhelmed with anguish, and dissolved in tears:
She raised her in her arms, beheld her bleed,
And ask'd what god had wrought this guilty deed?

Then she: "This insult from no god I found,
An impious mortal gave the daring wound!
Behold the deed of haughty Diomed!
'Twas in the son's defence the mother bled.
The war with Troy no more the Grecians wage;
But with the gods (the immortal gods) engage."
Dione then: "Thy wrongs with patience bear,
And share those griefs inferior powers must share:
Unnumber'd woes mankind from us sustain,
And men with woes afflict the gods again.
The mighty Mars in mortal fetters bound,
And lodged in brazen dungeons underground,
Full thirteen moons imprison'd roar'd in vain;
Otus and Ephialtes held the chain:
Perhaps had perish'd had not Hermes' care
Restored the groaning god to upper air.
Great Juno's self has borne her weight of pain,
The imperial partner of the heavenly reign;
Amphitryon's son infix'd the deadly dart,
And fill'd with anguish her immortal heart.
E'en hell's grim king Alcides' power confess'd,
The shaft found entrance in his iron breast;
To Jove's high palace for a cure he fled,
Pierced in his own dominions of the dead;
Where Paeon, sprinkling heavenly balm around,
Assuaged the glowing pangs, and closed the wound.
Rash, impious man! to stain the bless'd abodes,
And drench his arrows in the blood of gods!

"But thou (though Pallas urged thy frantic deed),
Whose spear ill-fated makes a goddess bleed,
Know thou, whoe'er with heavenly power contends,
Short is his date, and soon his glory ends;
From fields of death when late he shall retire,
No infant on his knees shall call him sire.
Strong as thou art, some god may yet be found,
To stretch thee pale and gasping on the ground;
Thy distant wife, Ægialé the fair,
Starting from sleep with a distracted air,
Shall rouse thy slaves, and her lost lord deplore,
The brave, the great, the glorious now no more!"
This said, she wiped from Venus' wounded palm
The sacred ichor, and infused the balm.
Juno and Pallas with a smile survey'd,
And thus to Jove began the blue-eyed maid:
"Permit thy daughter, gracious Jove! to tell

How this mischance the Cyprian queen befell,
As late she tried with passion to inflame
The tender bosom of a Grecian dame;
Allured the fair, with moving thoughts of joy,
To quit her country for some youth of Troy;
The clasping zone, with golden buckles bound,
Razed her soft hand with this lamented wound."
The sire of gods and men superior smiled,
And, calling Venus, thus address'd his child:
"Not these, O daughter are thy proper cares,
Thee milder arts befit, and softer wars;
Sweet smiles are thine, and kind endearing charms;
To Mars and Pallas leave the deeds of arms."
Thus they in heaven: while on the plain below
The fierce Tydides charged his Dardan foe,
Flush'd with celestial blood pursued his way,
And fearless dared the threatening god of day;
Already in his hopes he saw him kill'd,
Though screen'd behind Apollo's mighty shield.
Thrice rushing furious, at the chief he strook;
His blazing buckler thrice Apollo shook:
He tried the fourth: when, breaking from the cloud,
A more than mortal voice was heard aloud.
"O son of Tydeus, cease! be wise and see
How vast the difference of the gods and thee;
Distance immense! between the powers that shine
Above, eternal, deathless, and divine,
And mortal man! a wretch of humble birth,
A short-lived reptile in the dust of earth."
So spoke the god who darts celestial fires:
He dreads his fury, and some steps retires.
Then Phœbus bore the chief of Venus' race
To Troy's high fane, and to his holy place;
Latona there and Phoebe heal'd the wound,
With vigour arm'd him, and with glory crown'd.
This done, the patron of the silver bow
A phantom raised, the same in shape and show
With great Æneas; such the form he bore,
And such in fight the radiant arms he wore.
Around the spectre bloody wars are waged,
And Greece and Troy with clashing shields engaged.
Meantime on Ilion's tower Apollo stood,
And calling Mars, thus urged the raging god:
"Stern power of arms, by whom the mighty fall;
Who bathest in blood, and shakest the embattled wall,
Rise in thy wrath! to hell's abhorr'd abodes

Despatch yon Greek, and vindicate the gods.
First rosy Venus felt his brutal rage;
Me next he charged, and dares all heaven engage:
The wretch would brave high heaven's immortal sire,
His triple thunder, and his bolts of fire."
The god of battle issues on the plain,
Stirs all the ranks, and fires the Trojan train;
In form like Acamas, the Thracian guide,
Enraged to Troy's retiring chiefs he cried:
"How long, ye sons of Priam! will ye fly,
And unrevenged see Priam's people die?
Still unresisted shall the foe destroy,
And stretch the slaughter to the gates of Troy?
Lo, brave Æneas sinks beneath his wound,
Not godlike Hector more in arms renown'd:
Haste all, and take the generous warrior's part.
He said;—new courage swell'd each hero's heart.
Sarpedon first his ardent soul express'd,
And, turn'd to Hector, these bold words address'd:
"Say, chief, is all thy ancient valour lost?
Where are thy threats, and where thy glorious boast,
That propp'd alone by Priam's race should stand
Troy's sacred walls, nor need a foreign hand?
Now, now thy country calls her wonted friends,
And the proud vaunt in just derision ends.
Remote they stand while alien troops engage,
Like trembling hounds before the lion's rage.
Far distant hence I held my wide command,
Where foaming Xanthus laves the Lycian land;
With ample wealth (the wish of mortals) bless'd,
A beauteous wife, and infant at her breast;
With those I left whatever dear could be:
Greece, if she conquers, nothing wins from me;
Yet first in fight my Lycian bands I cheer,
And long to meet this mighty man ye fear;
While Hector idle stands, nor bids the brave
Their wives, their infants, and their altars save.
Haste, warrior, haste! preserve thy threaten'd state,
Or one vast burst of all-involving fate
Full o'er your towers shall fall, and sweep away
Sons, sires, and wives, an undistinguish'd prey.
Rouse all thy Trojans, urge thy aids to fight;
These claim thy thoughts by day, thy watch by night;
With force incessant the brave Greeks oppose;
Such cares thy friends deserve, and such thy foes."
Stung to the heart the generous Hector hears,

But just reproof with decent silence bears.
From his proud car the prince impetuous springs,
On earth he leaps, his brazen armour rings.
Two shining spears are brandish'd in his hands;
Thus arm'd, he animates his drooping bands,
Revives their ardour, turns their steps from flight,
And wakes anew the dying flames of fight.
They turn, they stand; the Greeks their fury dare,
Condense their powers, and wait the growing war.
As when, on Ceres' sacred floor, the swain
Spreads the wide fan to clear the golden grain,
And the light chaff, before the breezes borne,
Ascends in clouds from off the heapy corn;
The grey dust, rising with collected winds,
Drives o'er the barn, and whitens all the hinds:
So white with dust the Grecian host appears,
From trampling steeds, and thundering charioteers.
The dusky clouds from labour'd earth arise,
And roll in smoking volumes to the skies.
Mars hovers o'er them with his sable shield,
And adds new horrors to the darken'd field:
Pleased with his charge, and ardent to fulfil,
In Troy's defence, Apollo's heavenly will:
Soon as from fight the blue-eyed maid retires,
Each Trojan bosom with new warmth he fires.
And now the god, from forth his sacred fane,
Produced Æneas to the shouting train;
Alive, unharm'd, with all his peers around,
Erect he stood, and vigorous from his wound:
Inquiries none they made; the dreadful day
No pause of words admits, no dull delay;
Fierce Discord storms, Apollo loud exclaims,
Fame calls, Mars thunders, and the field's in flames.
Stern Diomed with either Ajax stood,
And great Ulysses, bathed in hostile blood.
Embodied close, the labouring Grecian train
The fiercest shock of charging hosts sustain.
Unmoved and silent, the whole war they wait
Serenely dreadful, and as fix'd as fate.
So when the embattled clouds in dark array,
Along the skies their gloomy lines display;
When now the North his boisterous rage has spent,
And peaceful sleeps the liquid element:
The low-hung vapours, motionless and still,
Rest on the summits of the shaded hill;
Till the mass scatters as the winds arise,

Dispersed and broken through the ruffled skies.
Nor was the general wanting to his train;
From troop to troop he toils through all the plain,
"Ye Greeks, be men! the charge of battle bear;
Your brave associates and yourselves revere!
Let glorious acts more glorious acts inspire,
And catch from breast to breast the noble fire!
On valour's side the odds of combat lie,
The brave live glorious, or lamented die;
The wretch who trembles in the field of fame,
Meets death, and worse than death, eternal shame!"
These words he seconds with his flying lance,
To meet whose point was strong Deicoon's chance:
Æneas' friend, and in his native place
Honour'd and loved like Priam's royal race:
Long had he fought the foremost in the field,
But now the monarch's lance transpierced his shield:
His shield too weak the furious dart to stay,
Through his broad belt the weapon forced its way:
The grisly wound dismiss'd his soul to hell,
His arms around him rattled as he fell.
Then fierce Æneas, brandishing his blade,
In dust Orsilochus and Crethon laid,
Whose sire Diocleus, wealthy, brave and great,
In well-built Pheræ held his lofty seat:
Sprung from Alpheus' plenteous stream, that yields
Increase of harvests to the Pylian fields.
He got Orsilochus, Diocleus he,
And these descended in the third degree.
Too early expert in the martial toil,
In sable ships they left their native soil,
To avenge Atrides: now, untimely slain,
They fell with glory on the Phrygian plain.
So two young mountain lions, nursed with blood
In deep recesses of the gloomy wood,
Rush fearless to the plains, and uncontroll'd
Depopulate the stalls and waste the fold:
Till pierced at distance from their native den,
O'erpowered they fall beneath the force of men.
Prostrate on earth their beauteous bodies lay,
Like mountain firs, as tall and straight as they.
Great Menelaus views with pitying eyes,
Lifts his bright lance, and at the victor flies;
Mars urged him on; yet, ruthless in his hate,
The god but urged him to provoke his fate.
He thus advancing, Nestor's valiant son

Shakes for his danger, and neglects his own;
Struck with the thought, should Helen's lord be slain,
And all his country's glorious labours vain.
Already met, the threatening heroes stand;
The spears already tremble in their hand:
In rush'd Antilochus, his aid to bring,
And fall or conquer by the Spartan king.
These seen, the Dardan backward turn'd his course,
Brave as he was, and shunn'd unequal force.
The breathless bodies to the Greeks they drew,
Then mix in combat, and their toils renew.
First, Pylæmenes, great in battle, bled,
Who sheathed in brass the Paphlagonians led.
Atrides mark'd him where sublime he stood;
Fix'd in his throat the javelin drank his blood.
The faithful Mydon, as he turn'd from fight
His flying coursers, sunk to endless night;
A broken rock by Nestor's son was thrown:
His bended arm received the falling stone;
From his numb'd hand the ivory-studded reins,
Dropp'd in the dust, are trail'd along the plains:
Meanwhile his temples feel a deadly wound;
He groans in death, and ponderous sinks to ground:
Deep drove his helmet in the sands, and there
The head stood fix'd, the quivering legs in air,
Till trampled flat beneath the coursers' feet:
The youthful victor mounts his empty seat,
And bears the prize in triumph to the fleet.
Great Hector saw, and, raging at the view,
Pours on the Greeks: the Trojan troops pursue:
He fires his host with animating cries,
And brings along the furies of the skies,
Mars, stern destroyer! and Bellona dread,
Flame in the front, and thunder at their head:
This swells the tumult and the rage of fight;
That shakes a spear that casts a dreadful light.
Where Hector march'd, the god of battles shined,
Now storm'd before him, and now raged behind.
Tydides paused amidst his full career;
Then first the hero's manly breast knew fear.
As when some simple swain his cot forsakes,
And wide through fens an unknown journey takes:
If chance a swelling brook his passage stay,
And foam impervious 'cross the wanderer's way,
Confused he stops, a length of country pass'd,
Eyes the rough waves, and tired, returns at last.

Amazed no less the great Tydides stands:
He stay'd, and turning thus address'd his bands:
"No wonder, Greeks! that all to Hector yield;
Secure of favouring gods, he takes the field;
His strokes they second, and avert our spears.
Behold where Mars in mortal arms appears!
Retire then, warriors, but sedate and slow;
Retire, but with your faces to the foe.
Trust not too much your unavailing might;
'Tis not with Troy, but with the gods ye fight."
Now near the Greeks the black battalions drew;
And first two leaders valiant Hector slew:
His force Anchialus and Mnesthes found,
In every art of glorious war renown'd;
In the same car the chiefs to combat ride,
And fought united, and united died.
Struck at the sight, the mighty Ajax glows
With thirst of vengeance, and assaults the foes.
His massy spear with matchless fury sent,
Through Amphius' belt and heaving belly went;
Amphius Apæsus' happy soil possess'd,
With herds abounding, and with treasure bless'd;
But fate resistless from his country led
The chief, to perish at his people's head.
Shook with his fall his brazen armour rung,
And fierce, to seize it, conquering Ajax sprung;
Around his head an iron tempest rain'd;
A wood of spears his ample shield sustain'd:
Beneath one foot the yet warm corpse he press'd,
And drew his javelin from the bleeding breast:
He could no more; the showering darts denied
To spoil his glittering arms, and plumy pride.
Now foes on foes came pouring on the fields,
With bristling lances, and compacted shields;
Till in the steely circle straiten'd round,
Forced he gives way, and sternly quits the ground.
While thus they strive, Tlepolemus the great,
Urged by the force of unresisted fate,
Burns with desire Sarpedon's strength to prove;
Alcides' offspring meets the son of Jove.
Sheathed in bright arms each adverse chief came on.
Jove's great descendant, and his greater son.
Prepared for combat, ere the lance he toss'd,
The daring Rhodian vents his haughty boast:
"What brings this Lycian counsellor so far,
To tremble at our arms, not mix in war!

Know thy vain self, nor let their flattery move,
Who style thee son of cloud-compelling Jove.
How far unlike those chiefs of race divine,
How vast the difference of their deeds and thine!
Jove got such heroes as my sire, whose soul
No fear could daunt, nor earth nor hell control.
Troy felt his arm, and yon proud ramparts stand
Raised on the ruins of his vengeful hand:
With six small ships, and but a slender train,
He left the town a wide-deserted plain.
But what art thou, who deedless look'st around,
While unrevenged thy Lycians bite the ground!
Small aid to Troy thy feeble force can be;
But wert thou greater, thou must yield to me.
Pierced by my spear, to endless darkness go!
I make this present to the shades below."
The son of Hercules, the Rhodian guide,
Thus haughty spoke. The Lycian king replied:
"Thy sire, O prince! o'erturn'd the Trojan state,
Whose perjured monarch well deserved his fate;
Those heavenly steeds the hero sought so far,
False he detain'd, the just reward of war.
Nor so content, the generous chief defied,
With base reproaches and unmanly pride.
But you, unworthy the high race you boast,
Shall raise my glory when thy own is lost:
Now meet thy fate, and by Sarpedon slain,
Add one more ghost to Pluto's gloomy reign."
He said: both javelins at an instant flew;
Both struck, both wounded, but Sarpedon's slew:
Full in the boaster's neck the weapon stood,
Transfix'd his throat, and drank the vital blood;
The soul disdainful seeks the caves of night,
And his seal'd eyes for ever lose the light.
Yet not in vain, Tlepolemus, was thrown
Thy angry lance; which piercing to the bone
Sarpedon's thigh, had robb'd the chief of breath;
But Jove was present, and forbade the death.
Borne from the conflict by his Lycian throng,
The wounded hero dragg'd the lance along.
(His friends, each busied in his several part,
Through haste, or danger, had not drawn the dart.)
The Greeks with slain Tlepolemus retired;
Whose fall Ulysses view'd, with fury fired;
Doubtful if Jove's great son he should pursue,
Or pour his vengeance on the Lycian crew.

But heaven and fate the first design withstand,
Nor this great death must grace Ulysses' hand.
Minerva drives him on the Lycian train;
Alastor, Cronius, Halius, strew'd the plain,
Alcander, Prytanis, Noëmon fell:
And numbers more his sword had sent to hell,
But Hector saw; and, furious at the sight,
Rush'd terrible amidst the ranks of fight.
With joy Sarpedon view'd the wish'd relief,
And, faint, lamenting, thus implored the chief:
"O suffer not the foe to bear away
My helpless corpse, an unassisted prey;
If I, unbless'd, must see my son no more,
My much-loved consort, and my native shore,
Yet let me die in Ilion's sacred wall;
Troy, in whose cause I fell, shall mourn my fall."
He said, nor Hector to the chief replies,
But shakes his plume, and fierce to combat flies;
Swift as a whirlwind, drives the scattering foes;
And dyes the ground with purple as he goes.
Beneath a beech, Jove's consecrated shade,
His mournful friends divine Sarpedon laid:
Brave Pelagon, his favourite chief, was nigh,
Who wrench'd the javelin from his sinewy thigh.
The fainting soul stood ready wing'd for flight,
And o'er his eye-balls swam the shades of night;
But Boreas rising fresh, with gentle breath,
Recall'd his spirit from the gates of death.
The generous Greeks recede with tardy pace,
Though Mars and Hector thunder in their face;
None turn their backs to mean ignoble flight,
Slow they retreat, and even retreating fight.
Who first, who last, by Mars' and Hector's hand,
Stretch'd in their blood, lay gasping on the sand?
Tenthras the great, Orestes the renown'd
For managed steeds, and Trechus press'd the ground;
Next Œnomaus and Œnops' offspring died;
Oresbius last fell groaning at their side:
Oresbius, in his painted mitre gay,
In fat Bœotia held his wealthy sway,
Where lakes surround low Hylè's watery plain;
A prince and people studious of their gain.
The carnage Juno from the skies survey'd,
And touch'd with grief bespoke the blue-eyed maid:
"Oh, sight accursed! Shall faithless Troy prevail,
And shall our promise to our people fail?

How vain the word to Menelaus given
By Jove's great daughter and the queen of heaven,
Beneath his arms that Priam's towers should fall,
If warring gods for ever guard the wall!
Mars, red with slaughter, aids our hated foes:
Haste, let us arm, and force with force oppose!"
She spoke; Minerva burns to meet the war:
And now heaven's empress calls her blazing car.
At her command rush forth the steeds divine;
Rich with immortal gold their trappings shine.
Bright Hebe waits; by Hebe, ever young,
The whirling wheels are to the chariot hung.
On the bright axle turns the bidden wheel
Of sounding brass; the polished axle steel.
Eight brazen spokes in radiant order flame;
The circles gold, of uncorrupted frame,
Such as the heavens produce: and round the gold
Two brazen rings of work divine were roll'd.
The bossy naves of sold silver shone;
Braces of gold suspend the moving throne:
The car, behind, an arching figure bore;
The bending concave form'd an arch before.
Silver the beam, the extended yoke was gold,
And golden reins the immortal coursers hold.
Herself, impatient, to the ready car,
The coursers joins, and breathes revenge and war.
Pallas disrobes; her radiant veil untied,
With flowers adorn'd, with art diversified,
(The laboured veil her heavenly fingers wove,)
Flows on the pavement of the court of Jove.
Now heaven's dread arms her mighty limbs invest,
Jove's cuirass blazes on her ample breast;
Deck'd in sad triumph for the mournful field,
O'er her broad shoulders hangs his horrid shield,
Dire, black, tremendous! Round the margin roll'd,
A fringe of serpents hissing guards the gold:
Here all the terrors of grim War appear,
Here rages Force, here tremble Flight and Fear,
Here storm'd Contention, and here Fury frown'd,
And the dire orb portentous Gorgon crown'd.
The massy golden helm she next assumes,
That dreadful nods with four o'ershading plumes;
So vast, the broad circumference contains
A hundred armies on a hundred plains.
The goddess thus the imperial car ascends;
Shook by her arm the mighty javelin bends,

Ponderous and huge; that when her fury burns,
Proud tyrants humbles, and whole hosts o'erturns.
Swift at the scourge the ethereal coursers fly,
While the smooth chariot cuts the liquid sky.
Heaven's gates spontaneous open to the powers,
Heaven's golden gates, kept by the winged Hours;
Commission'd in alternate watch they stand,
The sun's bright portals and the skies command,
Involve in clouds the eternal gates of day,
Or the dark barrier roll with ease away.
The sounding hinges ring, on either side
The gloomy volumes, pierced with light, divide.
The chariot mounts, where deep in ambient skies,
Confused, Olympus' hundred heads arise;
Where far apart the Thunderer fills his throne,
O'er all the gods superior and alone.
There with her snowy hand the queen restrains
The fiery steeds, and thus to Jove complains:
"O sire! can no resentment touch thy soul?
Can Mars rebel, and does no thunder roll?
What lawless rage on yon forbidden plain,
What rash destruction! and what heroes slain!
Venus, and Phœbus with the dreadful bow,
Smile on the slaughter, and enjoy my woe.
Mad, furious power! whose unrelenting mind
No god can govern, and no justice bind.
Say, mighty father! shall we scourge this pride,
And drive from fight the impetuous homicide?"
To whom assenting, thus the Thunderer said:
"Go! and the great Minerva be thy aid.
To tame the monster-god Minerva knows,
And oft afflicts his brutal breast with woes."
He said; Saturnia, ardent to obey,
Lash'd her white steeds along the aerial way.
Swift down the steep of heaven the chariot rolls,
Between the expanded earth and starry poles.
Far as a shepherd, from some point on high,
O'er the wide main extends his boundless eye,
Through such a space of air, with thundering sound,
At every leap the immortal coursers bound
Troy now they reach'd and touch'd those banks divine,
Where silver Simois and Scamander join.
There Juno stopp'd, and (her fair steeds unloosed)
Of air condensed a vapour circumfused:
For these, impregnate with celestial dew,
On Simois' brink ambrosial herbage grew.

Thence to relieve the fainting Argive throng,
Smooth as the sailing doves they glide along.
The best and bravest of the Grecian band
(A warlike circle) round Tydides stand.
Such was their look as lions bathed in blood,
Or foaming boars, the terror of the wood.
Heaven's empress mingles with the mortal crowd,
And shouts, in Stentor's sounding voice, aloud;
Stentor the strong, endued with brazen lungs,
Whose throats surpass'd the force of fifty tongues.
"Inglorious Argives! to your race a shame,
And only men in figure and in name!
Once from the walls your timorous foes engaged,
While fierce in war divine Achilles raged;
Now issuing fearless they possess the plain,
Now win the shores, and scarce the seas remain."
Her speech new fury to their hearts convey'd;
While near Tydides stood the Athenian maid;
The king beside his panting steeds she found,
O'erspent with toil reposing on the ground;
To cool his glowing wound he sat apart,
(The wound inflicted by the Lycian dart.)
Large drops of sweat from all his limbs descend,
Beneath his ponderous shield his sinews bend,
Whose ample belt, that o'er his shoulder lay,
He eased; and wash'd the clotted gore away.
The goddess leaning o'er the bending yoke,
Beside his coursers, thus her silence broke:
"Degenerate prince! and not of Tydeus' kind,
Whose little body lodged a mighty mind;
Foremost he press'd in glorious toils to share,
And scarce refrain'd when I forbade the war.
Alone, unguarded, once he dared to go,
And feast, incircled by the Theban foe;
There braved, and vanquish'd, many a hardy knight;
Such nerves I gave him, and such force in fight.
Thou too no less hast been my constant care;
Thy hands I arm'd, and sent thee forth to war:
But thee or fear deters, or sloth detains;
No drop of all thy father warms thy veins."
The chief thus answered mild: "Immortal maid!
I own thy presence, and confess thy aid.
Not fear, thou know'st, withholds me from the plains,
Nor sloth hath seized me, but thy word restrains:
From warring gods thou bad'st me turn my spear,
And Venus only found resistance here.

Hence, goddess! heedful of thy high commands,
Loth I gave way, and warn'd our Argive bands:
For Mars, the homicide, these eyes beheld,
With slaughter red, and raging round the field."
Then thus Minerva:—"Brave Tydides, hear!
Not Mars himself, nor aught immortal, fear.
Full on the god impel thy foaming horse:
Pallas commands, and Pallas lends thee force.
Rash, furious, blind, from these to those he flies,
And every side of wavering combat tries;
Large promise makes, and breaks the promise made:
Now gives the Grecians, now the Trojans aid."
She said, and to the steeds approaching near,
Drew from his seat the martial charioteer.
The vigorous power the trembling car ascends,
Fierce for revenge; and Diomed attends:
The groaning axle bent beneath the load;
So great a hero, and so great a god.
She snatch'd the reins, she lash'd with all her force,
And full on Mars impelled the foaming horse:
But first, to hide her heavenly visage, spread
Black Orcus' helmet o'er her radiant head.

Just then gigantic Periphas lay slain,
The strongest warrior of the Ætolian train;
The god, who slew him, leaves his prostrate prize
Stretch'd where he fell, and at Tydides flies.
Now rushing fierce, in equal arms appear
The daring Greek, the dreadful god of war!
Full at the chief, above his courser's head,
From Mars's arm the enormous weapon fled:
Pallas opposed her hand, and caused to glance
Far from the car the strong immortal lance.
Then threw the force of Tydeus' warlike son;
The javelin hiss'd; the goddess urged it on:
Where the broad cincture girt his armour round,
It pierced the god: his groin received the wound.
From the rent skin the warrior tugs again
The smoking steel. Mars bellows with the pain:
Loud as the roar encountering armies yield,
When shouting millions shake the thundering field.
Both armies start, and trembling gaze around;
And earth and heaven re-bellow to the sound.
As vapours blown by Auster's sultry breath,
Pregnant with plagues, and shedding seeds of death,
Beneath the rage of burning Sirius rise,

Choke the parch'd earth, and blacken all the skies;
In such a cloud the god from combat driven,
High o'er the dusky whirlwind scales the heaven.
Wild with his pain, he sought the bright abodes,
There sullen sat beneath the sire of gods,
Show'd the celestial blood, and with a groan
Thus pour'd his plaints before the immortal throne:
"Can Jove, supine, flagitious facts survey,
And brook the furies of this daring day?
For mortal men celestial powers engage,
And gods on gods exert eternal rage:
From thee, O father! all these ills we bear,
And thy fell daughter with the shield and spear;
Thou gavest that fury to the realms of light,
Pernicious, wild, regardless of the right.
All heaven beside reveres thy sovereign sway,
Thy voice we hear, and thy behests obey:
'Tis hers to offend, and even offending share
Thy breast, thy counsels, thy distinguish'd care:
So boundless she, and thou so partial grown,
Well may we deem the wondrous birth thy own.
Now frantic Diomed, at her command,
Against the immortals lifts his raging hand:
The heavenly Venus first his fury found,
Me next encountering, me he dared to wound;
Vanquish'd I fled; even I, the god of fight,
From mortal madness scarce was saved by flight.
Else hadst thou seen me sink on yonder plain,
Heap'd round, and heaving under loads of slain!
Or pierced with Grecian darts, for ages lie,
Condemn'd to pain, though fated not to die."
Him thus upbraiding, with a wrathful look
The lord of thunders view'd, and stern bespoke:
"To me, perfidious! this lamenting strain?
Of lawless force shall lawless Mars complain?
Of all the gods who tread the spangled skies,
Thou most unjust, most odious in our eyes!
Inhuman discord is thy dire delight,
The waste of slaughter, and the rage of fight.
No bounds, no law, thy fiery temper quells,
And all thy mother in thy soul rebels.
In vain our threats, in vain our power we use;
She gives the example, and her son pursues.
Yet long the inflicted pangs thou shall not mourn,
Sprung since thou art from Jove, and heavenly-born.
Else, singed with lightning, hadst thou hence been thrown,

Where chain'd on burning rocks the Titans groan."
Thus he who shakes Olympus with his nod;
Then gave to Pæon's care the bleeding god.
With gentle hand the balm he pour'd around,
And heal'd the immortal flesh, and closed the wound.
As when the fig's press'd juice, infused in cream,
To curds coagulates the liquid stream,
Sudden the fluids fix the parts combined;
Such, and so soon, the ethereal texture join'd.
Cleansed from the dust and gore, fair Hebe dress'd
His mighty limbs in an immortal vest.
Glorious he sat, in majesty restored,
Fast by the throne of heaven's superior lord.
Juno and Pallas mount the bless'd abodes,
Their task perform'd, and mix among the gods.

BOOK VI.

THE EPISODES OF GLAUCUS AND DIOMED, AND OF HEC-
TOR AND ANDROMACHE.

Now heaven forsakes the fight: the immortals yield
To human force and human skill the field:
Dark showers of javelins fly from foes to foes;
Now here, now there, the tide of combat flows;
While Troy's famed streams, that bound the deathful plain
On either side, run purple to the main.
Great Ajax first to conquest led the way,
Broke the thick ranks, and turn'd the doubtful day.
The Thracian Acamas his falchion found,
And hew'd the enormous giant to the ground;
His thundering arm a deadly stroke impress'd
Where the black horse-hair nodded o'er his crest;
Fix'd in his front the brazen weapon lies,
And seals in endless shades his swimming eyes.
Next Teuthras' son distain'd the sands with blood,
Axylus, hospitable, rich, and good:
In fair Arisbe's walls (his native place)
He held his seat! a friend to human race.
Fast by the road, his ever-open door

Obliged the wealthy, and relieved the poor.
To stern Tydides now he falls a prey,
No friend to guard him in the dreadful day!
Breathless the good man fell, and by his side
His faithful servant, old Calesius died.
By great Euryalus was Dresus slain,
And next he laid Opheltius on the plain.
Two twins were near, bold, beautiful, and young,
From a fair naiad and Bucolion sprung:
(Laomedon's white flocks Bucolion fed,
That monarch's first-born by a foreign bed;
In secret woods he won the naiad's grace,
And two fair infants crown'd his strong embrace:)
Here dead they lay in all their youthful charms;
The ruthless victor stripp'd their shining arms.
Astyalus by Polypœtes fell;
Ulysses' spear Pidytes sent to hell;
By Teucer's shaft brave Aretaon bled,
And Nestor's son laid stern Ablerus dead;
Great Agamemnon, leader of the brave,
The mortal wound of rich Elatus gave,
Who held in Pedasus his proud abode,
And till'd the banks where silver Satnio flow'd.
Melanthius by Eurypylus was slain;
And Phylacus from Leitus flies in vain.
Unbless'd Adrastus next at mercy lies
Beneath the Spartan spear, a living prize.
Scared with the din and tumult of the fight,
His headlong steeds, precipitate in flight,
Rush'd on a tamarisk's strong trunk, and broke
The shatter'd chariot from the crooked yoke;
Wide o'er the field, resistless as the wind,
For Troy they fly, and leave their lord behind.
Prone on his face he sinks beside the wheel:
Atrides o'er him shakes his vengeful steel;
The fallen chief in suppliant posture press'd
The victor's knees, and thus his prayer address'd:
"O spare my youth, and for the life I owe
Large gifts of price my father shall bestow.
When fame shall tell, that, not in battle slain,
Thy hollow ships his captive son detain:
Rich heaps of brass shall in thy tent be told,
And steel well-temper'd, and persuasive gold."
He said: compassion touch'd the hero's heart
He stood, suspended with the lifted dart:
As pity pleaded for his vanquish'd prize,

Stern Agamemnon swift to vengeance flies,
And, furious, thus: "Oh impotent of mind!
Shall these, shall these Atrides' mercy find?
Well hast thou known proud Troy's perfidious land,
And well her natives merit at thy hand!
Not one of all the race, nor sex, nor age,
Shall save a Trojan from our boundless rage:
Ilion shall perish whole, and bury all;
Her babes, her infants at the breast, shall fall;
A dreadful lesson of exampled fate,
To warn the nations, and to curb the great!"
The monarch spoke; the words, with warmth address'd,
To rigid justice steel'd his brother's breast.
Fierce from his knees the hapless chief he thrust;
The monarch's javelin stretch'd him in the dust,
Then pressing with his foot his panting heart,
Forth from the slain he tugg'd the reeking dart.
Old Nestor saw, and roused the warrior's rage;
"Thus, heroes! thus the vigorous combat wage;
No son of Mars descend, for servile gains,
To touch the booty, while a foe remains.
Behold yon glittering host, your future spoil!
First gain the conquest, then reward the toil."
And now had Greece eternal fame acquired,
And frighted Troy within her walls, retired,
Had not sage Helenus her state redress'd,
Taught by the gods that moved his sacred breast.
Where Hector stood, with great Æneas join'd,
The seer reveal'd the counsels of his mind:
"Ye generous chiefs! on whom the immortals lay
The cares and glories of this doubtful day;
On whom your aids, your country's hopes depend;
Wise to consult, and active to defend!
Here, at our gates, your brave efforts unite,
Turn back the routed, and forbid the flight,
Ere yet their wives' soft arms the cowards gain,
The sport and insult of the hostile train.
When your commands have hearten'd every band,
Ourselves, here fix'd, will make the dangerous stand;
Press'd as we are, and sore of former fight,
These straits demand our last remains of might.
Meanwhile thou, Hector, to the town retire,
And teach our mother what the gods require:
Direct the queen to lead the assembled train
Of Troy's chief matrons to Minerva's fane;
Unbar the sacred gates, and seek the power,

With offer'd vows, in Ilion's topmost tower.
The largest mantle her rich wardrobes hold,
Most prized for art, and labour'd o'er with gold,
Before the goddess' honour'd knees be spread,
And twelve young heifers to her altars led:
If so the power, atoned by fervent prayer,
Our wives, our infants, and our city spare,
And far avert Tydides' wasteful ire,
That mows whole troops, and makes all Troy retire;
Not thus Achilles taught our hosts to dread,
Sprung though he was from more than mortal bed;
Not thus resistless ruled the stream of fight,
In rage unbounded, and unmatch'd in might."
Hector obedient heard: and, with a bound,
Leap'd from his trembling chariot to the ground;
Through all his host inspiring force he flies,
And bids the thunder of the battle rise.
With rage recruited the bold Trojans glow,
And turn the tide of conflict on the foe:
Fierce in the front he shakes two dazzling spears;
All Greece recedes, and 'midst her triumphs fears;
Some god, they thought, who ruled the fate of wars,
Shot down avenging from the vault of stars.
Then thus aloud: "Ye dauntless Dardans, hear!
And you whom distant nations send to war!
Be mindful of the strength your fathers bore;
Be still yourselves, and Hector asks no more.
One hour demands me in the Trojan wall,
To bid our altars flame, and victims fall:
Nor shall, I trust, the matrons' holy train,
And reverend elders, seek the gods in vain."
This said, with ample strides the hero pass'd;
The shield's large orb behind his shoulder cast,
His neck o'ershading, to his ankle hung;
And as he march'd the brazen buckler rung.
Now paused the battle (godlike Hector gone),
Where daring Glaucus and great Tydeus' son
Between both armies met: the chiefs from far
Observed each other, and had mark'd for war.
Near as they drew, Tydides thus began:
"What art thou, boldest of the race of man?
Our eyes till now that aspect ne'er beheld,
Where fame is reap'd amid the embattled field;
Yet far before the troops thou dar'st appear,
And meet a lance the fiercest heroes fear.
Unhappy they, and born of luckless sires,

Who tempt our fury when Minerva fires!
But if from heaven, celestial, thou descend,
Know with immortals we no more contend.
Not long Lycurgus view'd the golden light,
That daring man who mix'd with gods in fight.
Bacchus, and Bacchus' votaries, he drove,
With brandish'd steel, from Nyssa's sacred grove:
Their consecrated spears lay scatter'd round,
With curling vines and twisted ivy bound;
While Bacchus headlong sought the briny flood,
And Thetis' arms received the trembling god.
Nor fail'd the crime the immortals' wrath to move;
(The immortals bless'd with endless ease above;)
Deprived of sight by their avenging doom,
Cheerless he breathed, and wander'd in the gloom,
Then sunk unpitied to the dire abodes,
A wretch accursed, and hated by the gods!
I brave not heaven: but if the fruits of earth
Sustain thy life, and human be thy birth,
Bold as thou art, too prodigal of breath,
Approach, and enter the dark gates of death."
"What, or from whence I am, or who my sire,
(Replied the chief,) can Tydeus' son inquire?
Like leaves on trees the race of man is found,
Now green in youth, now withering on the ground;
Another race the following spring supplies;
They fall successive, and successive rise:
So generations in their course decay;
So flourish these, when those are pass'd away.
But if thou still persist to search my birth,
Then hear a tale that fills the spacious earth.
"A city stands on Argos' utmost bound,
(Argos the fair, for warlike steeds renown'd,)
Æolian Sisyphus, with wisdom bless'd,
In ancient time the happy wall possess'd,
Then call'd Ephyre: Glaucus was his son;
Great Glaucus, father of Bellerophon,
Who o'er the sons of men in beauty shined,
Loved for that valour which preserves mankind.
Then mighty Praetus Argos' sceptre sway'd,
Whose hard commands Bellerophon obey'd.
With direful jealousy the monarch raged,
And the brave prince in numerous toils engaged.
For him Antaea burn'd with lawless flame,
And strove to tempt him from the paths of fame:
In vain she tempted the relentless youth,

Endued with wisdom, sacred fear, and truth.
Fired at his scorn the queen to Praetus fled,
And begg'd revenge for her insulted bed:
Incensed he heard, resolving on his fate;
But hospitable laws restrain'd his hate:
To Lycia the devoted youth he sent,
With tablets seal'd, that told his dire intent.
Now bless'd by every power who guards the good,
The chief arrived at Xanthus' silver flood:
There Lycia's monarch paid him honours due,
Nine days he feasted, and nine bulls he slew.
But when the tenth bright morning orient glow'd,
The faithful youth his monarch's mandate show'd:
The fatal tablets, till that instant seal'd,
The deathful secret to the king reveal'd.
First, dire Chimaera's conquest was enjoin'd;
A mingled monster of no mortal kind!
Behind, a dragon's fiery tail was spread;
A goat's rough body bore a lion's head;
Her pitchy nostrils flaky flames expire;
Her gaping throat emits infernal fire.
"This pest he slaughter'd, (for he read the skies,
And trusted heaven's informing prodigies,)
Then met in arms the Solymæan crew,
(Fiercest of men,) and those the warrior slew;
Next the bold Amazons' whole force defied;
And conquer'd still, for heaven was on his side.
"Nor ended here his toils: his Lycian foes,
At his return, a treacherous ambush rose,
With levell'd spears along the winding shore:
There fell they breathless, and return'd no more.
"At length the monarch, with repentant grief,
Confess'd the gods, and god-descended chief;
His daughter gave, the stranger to detain,
With half the honours of his ample reign:
The Lycians grant a chosen space of ground,
With woods, with vineyards, and with harvests crown'd.
There long the chief his happy lot possess'd,
With two brave sons and one fair daughter bless'd;
(Fair e'en in heavenly eyes: her fruitful love
Crown'd with Sarpedon's birth the embrace of Jove;)
But when at last, distracted in his mind,
Forsook by heaven, forsaking humankind,
Wide o'er the Aleian field he chose to stray,
A long, forlorn, uncomfortable way!
Woes heap'd on woes consumed his wasted heart:

His beauteous daughter fell by Phoebe's dart;
His eldest born by raging Mars was slain,
In combat on the Solymaean plain.
Hippolochus survived: from him I came,
The honour'd author of my birth and name;
By his decree I sought the Trojan town;
By his instructions learn to win renown,
To stand the first in worth as in command,
To add new honours to my native land,
Before my eyes my mighty sires to place,
And emulate the glories of our race."
He spoke, and transport fill'd Tydides' heart;
In earth the generous warrior fix'd his dart,
Then friendly, thus the Lycian prince address'd:
"Welcome, my brave hereditary guest!
Thus ever let us meet, with kind embrace,
Nor stain the sacred friendship of our race.
Know, chief, our grandsires have been guests of old;
Œneus the strong, Bellerophon the bold:
Our ancient seat his honour'd presence graced,
Where twenty days in genial rites he pass'd.
The parting heroes mutual presents left;
A golden goblet was thy grandsire's gift;
Œneus a belt of matchless work bestowed,
That rich with Tyrian dye refulgent glow'd.
(This from his pledge I learn'd, which, safely stored
Among my treasures, still adorns my board:
For Tydeus left me young, when Thebe's wall
Beheld the sons of Greece untimely fall.)
Mindful of this, in friendship let us join;
If heaven our steps to foreign lands incline,
My guest in Argos thou, and I in Lycia thine.
Enough of Trojans to this lance shall yield,
In the full harvest of yon ample field;
Enough of Greeks shall dye thy spear with gore;
But thou and Diomed be foes no more.
Now change we arms, and prove to either host
We guard the friendship of the line we boast."
Thus having said, the gallant chiefs alight,
Their hands they join, their mutual faith they plight;
Brave Glaucus then each narrow thought resign'd,
(Jove warm'd his bosom, and enlarged his mind,)
For Diomed's brass arms, of mean device,
For which nine oxen paid, (a vulgar price,)
He gave his own, of gold divinely wrought,
A hundred beeves the shining purchase bought.

Meantime the guardian of the Trojan state,
Great Hector, enter'd at the Scæan gate.
Beneath the beech-tree's consecrated shades,
The Trojan matrons and the Trojan maids
Around him flock'd, all press'd with pious care
For husbands, brothers, sons, engaged in war.
He bids the train in long procession go,
And seek the gods, to avert the impending woe.
And now to Priam's stately courts he came,
Rais'd on arch'd columns of stupendous frame;
O'er these a range of marble structure runs,
The rich pavilions of his fifty sons,
In fifty chambers lodged: and rooms of state,
Opposed to those, where Priam's daughters sate.
Twelve domes for them and their loved spouses shone,
Of equal beauty, and of polish'd stone.
Hither great Hector pass'd, nor pass'd unseen
Of royal Hecuba, his mother-queen.
(With her Laodice, whose beauteous face
Surpass'd the nymphs of Troy's illustrious race.)
Long in a strict embrace she held her son,
And press'd his hand, and tender thus begun:
"O Hector! say, what great occasion calls
My son from fight, when Greece surrounds our walls;
Com'st thou to supplicate the almighty power
With lifted hands, from Ilion's lofty tower?
Stay, till I bring the cup with Bacchus crown'd,
In Jove's high name, to sprinkle on the ground,
And pay due vows to all the gods around.
Then with a plenteous draught refresh thy soul,
And draw new spirits from the generous bowl;
Spent as thou art with long laborious fight,
The brave defender of thy country's right."
"Far hence be Bacchus' gifts; (the chief rejoin'd;)
Inflaming wine, pernicious to mankind,
Unnerves the limbs, and dulls the noble mind.
Let chiefs abstain, and spare the sacred juice
To sprinkle to the gods, its better use.
By me that holy office were profaned;
Ill fits it me, with human gore distain'd,
To the pure skies these horrid hands to raise,
Or offer heaven's great Sire polluted praise.
You, with your matrons, go! a spotless train,
And burn rich odours in Minerva's fane.
The largest mantle your full wardrobes hold,
Most prized for art, and labour'd o'er with gold,

Before the goddess' honour'd knees be spread,
And twelve young heifers to her altar led.
So may the power, atoned by fervent prayer,
Our wives, our infants, and our city spare;
And far avert Tydides' wasteful ire,
Who mows whole troops, and makes all Troy retire.
Be this, O mother, your religious care:
I go to rouse soft Paris to the war;
If yet not lost to all the sense of shame,
The recreant warrior hear the voice of fame.
Oh, would kind earth the hateful wretch embrace,
That pest of Troy, that ruin of our race!
Deep to the dark abyss might he descend,
Troy yet should flourish, and my sorrows end."
This heard, she gave command: and summon'd came
Each noble matron and illustrious dame.
The Phrygian queen to her rich wardrobe went,
Where treasured odours breathed a costly scent.
There lay the vestures of no vulgar art,
Sidonian maids embroider'd every part,
Whom from soft Sidon youthful Paris bore,
With Helen touching on the Tyrian shore.
Here, as the queen revolved with careful eyes
The various textures and the various dyes,
She chose a veil that shone superior far,
And glow'd refulgent as the morning star.
Herself with this the long procession leads;
The train majestically slow proceeds.
Soon as to Ilion's topmost tower they come,
And awful reach the high Palladian dome,
Antenor's consort, fair Theano, waits
As Pallas' priestess, and unbars the gates.
With hands uplifted and imploring eyes,
They fill the dome with supplicating cries.
The priestess then the shining veil displays,
Placed on Minerva's knees, and thus she prays:
"Oh awful goddess! ever-dreadful maid,
Troy's strong defence, unconquer'd Pallas, aid!
Break thou Tydides' spear, and let him fall
Prone on the dust before the Trojan wall!
So twelve young heifers, guiltless of the yoke,
Shall fill thy temple with a grateful smoke.
But thou, atoned by penitence and prayer,
Ourselves, our infants, and our city spare!"
So pray'd the priestess in her holy fane;
So vow'd the matrons, but they vow'd in vain.

While these appear before the power with prayers,
Hector to Paris' lofty dome repairs.
Himself the mansion raised, from every part
Assembling architects of matchless art.
Near Priam's court and Hector's palace stands
The pompous structure, and the town commands.
A spear the hero bore of wondrous strength,
Of full ten cubits was the lance's length,
The steely point with golden ringlets join'd,
Before him brandish'd, at each motion shined
Thus entering, in the glittering rooms he found
His brother-chief, whose useless arms lay round,
His eyes delighting with their splendid show,
Brightening the shield, and polishing the bow.
Beside him Helen with her virgins stands,
Guides their rich labours, and instructs their hands.
Him thus inactive, with an ardent look
The prince beheld, and high-resenting spoke.
"Thy hate to Troy, is this the time to show?
(O wretch ill-fated, and thy country's foe!)
Paris and Greece against us both conspire,
Thy close resentment, and their vengeful ire.
For thee great Ilion's guardian heroes fall,
Till heaps of dead alone defend her wall,
For thee the soldier bleeds, the matron mourns,
And wasteful war in all its fury burns.
Ungrateful man! deserves not this thy care,
Our troops to hearten, and our toils to share?
Rise, or behold the conquering flames ascend,
And all the Phrygian glories at an end."
"Brother, 'tis just, (replied the beauteous youth,)
Thy free remonstrance proves thy worth and truth:
Yet charge my absence less, O generous chief!
On hate to Troy, than conscious shame and grief:
Here, hid from human eyes, thy brother sate,
And mourn'd, in secret, his and Ilion's fate.
'Tis now enough; now glory spreads her charms,
And beauteous Helen calls her chief to arms.
Conquest to-day my happier sword may bless,
'Tis man's to fight, but heaven's to give success.
But while I arm, contain thy ardent mind;
Or go, and Paris shall not lag behind."

He said, nor answer'd Priam's warlike son;
When Helen thus with lowly grace begun:
"Oh, generous brother! (if the guilty dame

That caused these woes deserve a sister's name!)
Would heaven, ere all these dreadful deeds were done,
The day that show'd me to the golden sun
Had seen my death! why did not whirlwinds bear
The fatal infant to the fowls of air?
Why sunk I not beneath the whelming tide,
And midst the roarings of the waters died?
Heaven fill'd up all my ills, and I accursed
Bore all, and Paris of those ills the worst.
Helen at least a braver spouse might claim,
Warm'd with some virtue, some regard of fame!
Now tired with toils, thy fainting limbs recline,
With toils, sustain'd for Paris' sake and mine
The gods have link'd our miserable doom,
Our present woe, and infamy to come:
Wide shall it spread, and last through ages long,
Example sad! and theme of future song."
The chief replied: "This time forbids to rest;
The Trojan bands, by hostile fury press'd,
Demand their Hector, and his arm require;
The combat urges, and my soul's on fire.
Urge thou thy knight to march where glory calls,
And timely join me, ere I leave the walls.
Ere yet I mingle in the direful fray,
My wife, my infant, claim a moment's stay;
This day (perhaps the last that sees me here)
Demands a parting word, a tender tear:
This day, some god who hates our Trojan land
May vanquish Hector by a Grecian hand."
He said, and pass'd with sad presaging heart
To seek his spouse, his soul's far dearer part;
At home he sought her, but he sought in vain;
She, with one maid of all her menial train,
Had hence retired; and with her second joy,
The young Astyanax, the hope of Troy,
Pensive she stood on Ilion's towery height,
Beheld the war, and sicken'd at the sight;
There her sad eyes in vain her lord explore,
Or weep the wounds her bleeding country bore.
But he who found not whom his soul desired,
Whose virtue charm'd him as her beauty fired,
Stood in the gates, and ask'd "what way she bent
Her parting step? If to the fane she went,
Where late the mourning matrons made resort;
Or sought her sisters in the Trojan court?"
"Not to the court, (replied the attendant train,)

Nor mix'd with matrons to Minerva's fane:
To Ilion's steepy tower she bent her way,
To mark the fortunes of the doubtful day.
Troy fled, she heard, before the Grecian sword;
She heard, and trembled for her absent lord:
Distracted with surprise, she seem'd to fly,
Fear on her cheek, and sorrow in her eye.
The nurse attended with her infant boy,
The young Astyanax, the hope of Troy."
Hector this heard, return'd without delay;
Swift through the town he trod his former way,
Through streets of palaces, and walks of state;
And met the mourner at the Scæan gate.
With haste to meet him sprung the joyful fair.
His blameless wife, Aëtion's wealthy heir
(Cilician Thebe great Aëtion sway'd,
And Hippoplacus' wide extended shade):
The nurse stood near, in whose embraces press'd,
His only hope hung smiling at her breast,
Whom each soft charm and early grace adorn,
Fair as the new-born star that gilds the morn.
To this loved infant Hector gave the name
Scamandrius, from Scamander's honour'd stream;
Astyanax the Trojans call'd the boy,
From his great father, the defence of Troy.
Silent the warrior smiled, and pleased resign'd
To tender passions all his mighty mind;
His beauteous princess cast a mournful look,
Hung on his hand, and then dejected spoke;
Her bosom laboured with a boding sigh,
And the big tear stood trembling in her eye.

"Too daring prince! ah, whither dost thou run?
Ah, too forgetful of thy wife and son!
And think'st thou not how wretched we shall be,
A widow I, a helpless orphan he?
For sure such courage length of life denies,
And thou must fall, thy virtue's sacrifice.
Greece in her single heroes strove in vain;
Now hosts oppose thee, and thou must be slain.
O grant me, gods, ere Hector meets his doom,
All I can ask of heaven, an early tomb!
So shall my days in one sad tenor run,
And end with sorrows as they first begun.
No parent now remains my griefs to share,
No father's aid, no mother's tender care.

The fierce Achilles wrapt our walls in fire,
Laid Thebe waste, and slew my warlike sire!
His fate compassion in the victor bred;
Stern as he was, he yet revered the dead,
His radiant arms preserved from hostile spoil,
And laid him decent on the funeral pile;
Then raised a mountain where his bones were burn'd,
The mountain-nymphs the rural tomb adorn'd,
Jove's sylvan daughters bade their elms bestow
A barren shade, and in his honour grow.
"By the same arm my seven brave brothers fell;
In one sad day beheld the gates of hell;
While the fat herds and snowy flocks they fed,
Amid their fields the hapless heroes bled!
My mother lived to wear the victor's bands,
The queen of Hippoplacia's sylvan lands:
Redeem'd too late, she scarce beheld again
Her pleasing empire and her native plain,
When ah! oppress'd by life-consuming woe,
She fell a victim to Diana's bow.
"Yet while my Hector still survives, I see
My father, mother, brethren, all, in thee:
Alas! my parents, brothers, kindred, all
Once more will perish, if my Hector fall,
Thy wife, thy infant, in thy danger share:
Oh, prove a husband's and a father's care!
That quarter most the skilful Greeks annoy,
Where yon wild fig-trees join the wall of Troy;
Thou, from this tower defend the important post;
There Agamemnon points his dreadful host,
That pass Tydides, Ajax, strive to gain,
And there the vengeful Spartan fires his train.
Thrice our bold foes the fierce attack have given,
Or led by hopes, or dictated from heaven.
Let others in the field their arms employ,
But stay my Hector here, and guard his Troy."
The chief replied: "That post shall be my care,
Not that alone, but all the works of war.
How would the sons of Troy, in arms renown'd,
And Troy's proud dames, whose garments sweep the ground
Attaint the lustre of my former name,
Should Hector basely quit the field of fame?
My early youth was bred to martial pains,
My soul impels me to the embattled plains!
Let me be foremost to defend the throne,
And guard my father's glories, and my own.

"Yet come it will, the day decreed by fates!
(How my heart trembles while my tongue relates!)
The day when thou, imperial Troy! must bend,
And see thy warriors fall, thy glories end.
And yet no dire presage so wounds my mind,
My mother's death, the ruin of my kind,
Not Priam's hoary hairs defiled with gore,
Not all my brothers gasping on the shore;
As thine, Andromache! Thy griefs I dread:
I see thee trembling, weeping, captive led!
In Argive looms our battles to design,
And woes, of which so large a part was thine!
To bear the victor's hard commands, or bring
The weight of waters from Hyperia's spring.
There while you groan beneath the load of life,
They cry, 'Behold the mighty Hector's wife!'
Some haughty Greek, who lives thy tears to see,
Imbitters all thy woes, by naming me.
The thoughts of glory past, and present shame,
A thousand griefs shall waken at the name!
May I lie cold before that dreadful day,
Press'd with a load of monumental clay!
Thy Hector, wrapt in everlasting sleep,
Shall neither hear thee sigh, nor see thee weep."
Thus having spoke, the illustrious chief of Troy
Stretch'd his fond arms to clasp the lovely boy.
The babe clung crying to his nurse's breast,
Scared at the dazzling helm, and nodding crest.
With secret pleasure each fond parent smiled,
And Hector hasted to relieve his child,
The glittering terrors from his brows unbound,
And placed the beaming helmet on the ground;
Then kiss'd the child, and, lifting high in air,
Thus to the gods preferr'd a father's prayer:
"O thou! whose glory fills the ethereal throne,
And all ye deathless powers! protect my son!
Grant him, like me, to purchase just renown,
To guard the Trojans, to defend the crown,
Against his country's foes the war to wage,
And rise the Hector of the future age!
So when triumphant from successful toils
Of heroes slain he bears the reeking spoils,
Whole hosts may hail him with deserved acclaim,
And say, 'This chief transcends his father's fame:'
While pleased amidst the general shouts of Troy,
His mother's conscious heart o'erflows with joy."

He spoke, and fondly gazing on her charms,
Restored the pleasing burden to her arms;
Soft on her fragrant breast the babe she laid,
Hush'd to repose, and with a smile survey'd.
The troubled pleasure soon chastised by fear,
She mingled with a smile a tender tear.
The soften'd chief with kind compassion view'd,
And dried the falling drops, and thus pursued:
"Andromache! my soul's far better part,
Why with untimely sorrows heaves thy heart?
No hostile hand can antedate my doom,
Till fate condemns me to the silent tomb.
Fix'd is the term to all the race of earth;
And such the hard condition of our birth:
No force can then resist, no flight can save,
All sink alike, the fearful and the brave.
No more—but hasten to thy tasks at home,
There guide the spindle, and direct the loom:
Me glory summons to the martial scene,
The field of combat is the sphere for men.
Where heroes war, the foremost place I claim,
The first in danger as the first in fame."
Thus having said, the glorious chief resumes
His towery helmet, black with shading plumes.
His princess parts with a prophetic sigh,
Unwilling parts, and oft reverts her eye
That stream'd at every look; then, moving slow,
Sought her own palace, and indulged her woe.
There, while her tears deplored the godlike man,
Through all her train the soft infection ran;
The pious maids their mingled sorrows shed,
And mourn the living Hector, as the dead.
But now, no longer deaf to honour's call,
Forth issues Paris from the palace wall.
In brazen arms that cast a gleamy ray,
Swift through the town the warrior bends his way.
The wanton courser thus with reins unbound
Breaks from his stall, and beats the trembling ground;
Pamper'd and proud, he seeks the wonted tides,
And laves, in height of blood his shining sides;
His head now freed, he tosses to the skies;
His mane dishevell'd o'er his shoulders flies;
He snuffs the females in the distant plain,
And springs, exulting, to his fields again.
With equal triumph, sprightly, bold, and gay,
In arms refulgent as the god of day,

The son of Priam, glorying in his might,
Rush'd forth with Hector to the fields of fight.
And now, the warriors passing on the way,
The graceful Paris first excused his stay.
To whom the noble Hector thus replied:
"O chief! in blood, and now in arms, allied!
Thy power in war with justice none contest;
Known is thy courage, and thy strength confess'd.
What pity sloth should seize a soul so brave,
Or godlike Paris live a woman's slave!
My heart weeps blood at what the Trojans say,
And hopes thy deeds shall wipe the stain away.
Haste then, in all their glorious labours share,
For much they suffer, for thy sake, in war.
These ills shall cease, whene'er by Jove's decree
We crown the bowl to heaven and liberty:
While the proud foe his frustrate triumphs mourns,
And Greece indignant through her seas returns."

BOOK VII.

THE SINGLE COMBAT OF HECTOR AND AJAX.

So spoke the guardian of the Trojan state,
Then rush'd impetuous through the Scæan gate.
Him Paris follow'd to the dire alarms;
Both breathing slaughter, both resolved in arms.
As when to sailors labouring through the main,
That long have heaved the weary oar in vain,
Jove bids at length the expected gales arise;
The gales blow grateful, and the vessel flies.
So welcome these to Troy's desiring train,
The bands are cheer'd, the war awakes again.
Bold Paris first the work of death begun
On great Menestheus, Areithous' son,
Sprung from the fair Philomeda's embrace,
The pleasing Arnè was his native place.
Then sunk Eioneus to the shades below,
Beneath his steely casque he felt the blow

Full on his neck, from Hector's weighty hand;
And roll'd, with limbs relax'd, along the land.
By Glaucus' spear the bold Iphinous bleeds,
Fix'd in the shoulder as he mounts his steeds;
Headlong he tumbles: his slack nerves unbound,
Drop the cold useless members on the ground.
When now Minerva saw her Argives slain,
From vast Olympus to the gleaming plain
Fierce she descends: Apollo marked her flight,
Nor shot less swift from Ilion's towery height.
Radiant they met, beneath the beechen shade;
When thus Apollo to the blue-eyed maid:
"What cause, O daughter of Almighty Jove!
Thus wings thy progress from the realms above?
Once more impetuous dost thou bend thy way,
To give to Greece the long divided day?
Too much has Troy already felt thy hate,
Now breathe thy rage, and hush the stern debate;
This day, the business of the field suspend;
War soon shall kindle, and great Ilion bend;
Since vengeful goddesses confederate join
To raze her walls, though built by hands divine."
To whom the progeny of Jove replies:
"I left, for this, the council of the skies:
But who shall bid conflicting hosts forbear,
What art shall calm the furious sons of war?"
To her the god: "Great Hector's soul incite
To dare the boldest Greek to single fight,
Till Greece, provoked, from all her numbers show
A warrior worthy to be Hector's foe."
At this agreed, the heavenly powers withdrew;
Sage Helenus their secret counsels knew;
Hector, inspired, he sought: to him address'd,
Thus told the dictates of his sacred breast:
"O son of Priam! let thy faithful ear
Receive my words: thy friend and brother hear!
Go forth persuasive, and a while engage
The warring nations to suspend their rage;
Then dare the boldest of the hostile train
To mortal combat on the listed plain.
For not this day shall end thy glorious date;
The gods have spoke it, and their voice is fate."
He said: the warrior heard the word with joy;
Then with his spear restrain'd the youth of Troy,
Held by the midst athwart. On either hand
The squadrons part; the expecting Trojans stand;

Great Agamemnon bids the Greeks forbear:
They breathe, and hush the tumult of the war.
The Athenian maid, and glorious god of day,
With silent joy the settling hosts survey:
In form of vultures, on the beech's height
They sit conceal'd, and wait the future fight.
The thronging troops obscure the dusky fields,
Horrid with bristling spears, and gleaming shields.
As when a general darkness veils the main,
(Soft Zephyr curling the wide wat'ry plain,)
The waves scarce heave, the face of ocean sleeps,
And a still horror saddens all the deeps;
Thus in thick orders settling wide around,
At length composed they sit, and shade the ground.
Great Hector first amidst both armies broke
The solemn silence, and their powers bespoke:
"Hear, all ye Trojan, all ye Grecian bands,
What my soul prompts, and what some god commands.
Great Jove, averse our warfare to compose,
O'erwhelms the nations with new toils and woes;
War with a fiercer tide once more returns,
Till Ilion falls, or till yon navy burns.
You then, O princes of the Greeks! appear;
'Tis Hector speaks, and calls the gods to hear:
From all your troops select the boldest knight,
And him, the boldest, Hector dares to fight.
Here if I fall, by chance of battle slain,
Be his my spoil, and his these arms remain;
But let my body, to my friends return'd,
By Trojan hands and Trojan flames be burn'd.
And if Apollo, in whose aid I trust,
Shall stretch your daring champion in the dust;
If mine the glory to despoil the foe;
On Phœbus' temple I'll his arms bestow:
The breathless carcase to your navy sent,
Greece on the shore shall raise a monument;
Which when some future mariner surveys,
Wash'd by broad Hellespont's resounding seas,
Thus shall he say, 'A valiant Greek lies there,
By Hector slain, the mighty man of war,'
The stone shall tell your vanquish'd hero's name
And distant ages learn the victor's fame."
This fierce defiance Greece astonish'd heard,
Blush'd to refuse, and to accept it fear'd.
Stern Menelaus first the silence broke,
And, inly groaning, thus opprobrious spoke:

"Women of Greece! O scandal of your race,
Whose coward souls your manly form disgrace,
How great the shame, when every age shall know
That not a Grecian met this noble foe!
Go then! resolve to earth, from whence ye grew,
A heartless, spiritless, inglorious crew!
Be what ye seem, unanimated clay,
Myself will dare the danger of the day;
'Tis man's bold task the generous strife to try,
But in the hands of God is victory."
These words scarce spoke, with generous ardour press'd,
His manly limbs in azure arms he dress'd.
That day, Atrides! a superior hand
Had stretch'd thee breathless on the hostile strand;
But all at once, thy fury to compose,
The kings of Greece, an awful band, arose;
Even he their chief, great Agamemnon, press'd
Thy daring hand, and this advice address'd:
"Whither, O Menelaus! wouldst thou run,
And tempt a fate which prudence bids thee shun?
Grieved though thou art, forbear the rash design;
Great Hector's arm is mightier far than thine:
Even fierce Achilles learn'd its force to fear,
And trembling met this dreadful son of war.
Sit thou secure, amidst thy social band;
Greece in our cause shall arm some powerful hand.
The mightiest warrior of the Achaian name,
Though bold and burning with desire of fame,
Content the doubtful honour might forego,
So great the danger, and so brave the foe."
He said, and turn'd his brother's vengeful mind;
He stoop'd to reason, and his rage resign'd,
No longer bent to rush on certain harms;
His joyful friends unbrace his azure arms.
He from whose lips divine persuasion flows,
Grave Nestor, then, in graceful act arose;
Thus to the kings he spoke: "What grief, what shame
Attend on Greece, and all the Grecian name!
How shall, alas! her hoary heroes mourn
Their sons degenerate, and their race a scorn!
What tears shall down thy silvery beard be roll'd,
O Peleus, old in arms, in wisdom old!
Once with what joy the generous prince would hear
Of every chief who fought this glorious war,
Participate their fame, and pleased inquire
Each name, each action, and each hero's sire!

Gods! should he see our warriors trembling stand,
And trembling all before one hostile hand;
How would he lift his aged arms on high,
Lament inglorious Greece, and beg to die!
Oh! would to all the immortal powers above,
Minerva, Phœbus, and almighty Jove!
Years might again roll back, my youth renew,
And give this arm the spring which once it knew
When fierce in war, where Jardan's waters fall,
I led my troops to Phea's trembling wall,
And with the Arcadian spears my prowess tried,
Where Celadon rolls down his rapid tide.
There Ereuthalion braved us in the field,
Proud Areithous' dreadful arms to wield;
Great Areithous, known from shore to shore
By the huge, knotted, iron mace he bore;
No lance he shook, nor bent the twanging bow,
But broke, with this, the battle of the foe.
Him not by manly force Lycurgus slew,
Whose guileful javelin from the thicket flew,
Deep in a winding way his breast assailed,
Nor aught the warrior's thundering mace avail'd.
Supine he fell: those arms which Mars before
Had given the vanquish'd, now the victor bore:
But when old age had dimm'd Lycurgus' eyes,
To Ereuthalion he consign'd the prize.
Furious with this he crush'd our levell'd bands,
And dared the trial of the strongest hands;
Nor could the strongest hands his fury stay:
All saw, and fear'd, his huge tempestuous sway
Till I, the youngest of the host, appear'd,
And, youngest, met whom all our army fear'd.
I fought the chief: my arms Minerva crown'd:
Prone fell the giant o'er a length of ground.
What then I was, O were your Nestor now!
Not Hector's self should want an equal foe.
But, warriors, you that youthful vigour boast,
The flower of Greece, the examples of our host,
Sprung from such fathers, who such numbers sway,
Can you stand trembling, and desert the day?"
His warm reproofs the listening kings inflame;
And nine, the noblest of the Grecian name,
Up-started fierce: but far before the rest
The king of men advanced his dauntless breast:
Then bold Tydides, great in arms, appear'd;
And next his bulk gigantic Ajax rear'd;

Oïleus follow'd; Idomen was there,
And Merion, dreadful as the god of war:
With these Eurypylus and Thoas stand,
And wise Ulysses closed the daring band.
All these, alike inspired with noble rage,
Demand the fight. To whom the Pylian sage:
"Lest thirst of glory your brave souls divide,
What chief shall combat, let the gods decide.
Whom heaven shall choose, be his the chance to raise
His country's fame, his own immortal praise."
The lots produced, each hero signs his own:
Then in the general's helm the fates are thrown,
The people pray, with lifted eyes and hands,
And vows like these ascend from all the bands:
"Grant, thou Almighty! in whose hand is fate,
A worthy champion for the Grecian state:
This task let Ajax or Tydides prove,
Or he, the king of kings, beloved by Jove."
Old Nestor shook the casque. By heaven inspired,
Leap'd forth the lot, of every Greek desired.
This from the right to left the herald bears,
Held out in order to the Grecian peers;
Each to his rival yields the mark unknown,
Till godlike Ajax finds the lot his own;
Surveys the inscription with rejoicing eyes,
Then casts before him, and with transport cries:
"Warriors! I claim the lot, and arm with joy;
Be mine the conquest of this chief of Troy.
Now while my brightest arms my limbs invest,
To Saturn's son be all your vows address'd:
But pray in secret, lest the foes should hear,
And deem your prayers the mean effect of fear.
Said I in secret? No, your vows declare
In such a voice as fills the earth and air,
Lives there a chief whom Ajax ought to dread?
Ajax, in all the toils of battle bred!
From warlike Salamis I drew my birth,
And, born to combats, fear no force on earth."
He said. The troops with elevated eyes,
Implore the god whose thunder rends the skies:
"O father of mankind, superior lord!
On lofty Ida's holy hill adored:
Who in the highest heaven hast fix'd thy throne,
Supreme of gods! unbounded and alone:
Grant thou, that Telamon may bear away
The praise and conquest of this doubtful day;

Or, if illustrious Hector be thy care,
That both may claim it, and that both may share."
Now Ajax braced his dazzling armour on;
Sheathed in bright steel the giant-warrior shone:
He moves to combat with majestic pace;
So stalks in arms the grisly god of Thrace,
When Jove to punish faithless men prepares,
And gives whole nations to the waste of wars,
Thus march'd the chief, tremendous as a god;
Grimly he smiled; earth trembled as he strode:
His massy javelin quivering in his hand,
He stood, the bulwark of the Grecian band.
Through every Argive heart new transport ran;
All Troy stood trembling at the mighty man:
Even Hector paused; and with new doubt oppress'd,
Felt his great heart suspended in his breast:
'Twas vain to seek retreat, and vain to fear;
Himself had challenged, and the foe drew near.
Stern Telamon behind his ample shield,
As from a brazen tower, o'erlook'd the field.
Huge was its orb, with seven thick folds o'ercast,
Of tough bull-hides; of solid brass the last,
(The work of Tychius, who in Hylè dwell'd
And in all arts of armoury excell'd,)
This Ajax bore before his manly breast,
And, threatening, thus his adverse chief address'd:
"Hector! approach my arm, and singly know
What strength thou hast, and what the Grecian foe.
Achilles shuns the fight; yet some there are,
Not void of soul, and not unskill'd in war:
Let him, unactive on the sea-beat shore,
Indulge his wrath, and aid our arms no more;
Whole troops of heroes Greece has yet to boast,
And sends thee one, a sample of her host,
Such as I am, I come to prove thy might;
No more—be sudden, and begin the fight."
"O son of Telamon, thy country's pride!
(To Ajax thus the Trojan prince replied)
Me, as a boy, or woman, wouldst thou fright,
New to the field, and trembling at the fight?
Thou meet'st a chief deserving of thy arms,
To combat born, and bred amidst alarms:
I know to shift my ground, remount the car,
Turn, charge, and answer every call of war;
To right, to left, the dexterous lance I wield,
And bear thick battle on my sounding shield/

But open be our fight, and bold each blow;
I steal no conquest from a noble foe."
He said, and rising, high above the field
Whirl'd the long lance against the sevenfold shield.
Full on the brass descending from above
Through six bull-hides the furious weapon drove,
Till in the seventh it fix'd. Then Ajax threw;
Through Hector's shield the forceful javelin flew,
His corslet enters, and his garment rends,
And glancing downwards, near his flank descends.
The wary Trojan shrinks, and bending low
Beneath his buckler, disappoints the blow.
From their bored shields the chiefs their javelins drew,
Then close impetuous, and the charge renew;
Fierce as the mountain-lions bathed in blood,
Or foaming boars, the terror of the wood.
At Ajax, Hector his long lance extends;
The blunted point against the buckler bends;
But Ajax, watchful as his foe drew near,
Drove through the Trojan targe the knotty spear;
It reach'd his neck, with matchless strength impell'd!
Spouts the black gore, and dims his shining shield.
Yet ceased not Hector thus; but stooping down,
In his strong hand up-heaved a flinty stone,
Black, craggy, vast: to this his force he bends;
Full on the brazen boss the stone descends;
The hollow brass resounded with the shock:
Then Ajax seized the fragment of a rock,
Applied each nerve, and swinging round on high,
With force tempestuous, let the ruin fly;
The huge stone thundering through his buckler broke:
His slacken'd knees received the numbing stroke;
Great Hector falls extended on the field,
His bulk supporting on the shatter'd shield:
Nor wanted heavenly aid: Apollo's might
Confirm'd his sinews, and restored to fight.
And now both heroes their broad falchions drew
In flaming circles round their heads they flew;
But then by heralds' voice the word was given.
The sacred ministers of earth and heaven:
Divine Talthybius, whom the Greeks employ,
And sage Idæus on the part of Troy,
Between the swords their peaceful sceptres rear'd;
And first Idæus' awful voice was heard:

"Forbear, my sons! your further force to prove,

Both dear to men, and both beloved of Jove.
To either host your matchless worth is known,
Each sounds your praise, and war is all your own.
But now the Night extends her awful shade;
The goddess parts you; be the night obey'd."
To whom great Ajax his high soul express'd:
"O sage! to Hector be these words address'd.
Let him, who first provoked our chiefs to fight,
Let him demand the sanction of the night;
If first he ask'd it, I content obey,
And cease the strife when Hector shows the way."
"O first of Greeks! (his noble foe rejoin'd)
Whom heaven adorns, superior to thy kind,
With strength of body, and with worth of mind!
Now martial law commands us to forbear;
Hereafter we shall meet in glorious war,
Some future day shall lengthen out the strife,
And let the gods decide of death or life!
Since, then, the night extends her gloomy shade,
And heaven enjoins it, be the night obey'd.
Return, brave Ajax, to thy Grecian friends,
And joy the nations whom thy arm defends;
As I shall glad each chief, and Trojan wife,
Who wearies heaven with vows for Hector's life.
But let us, on this memorable day,
Exchange some gift: that Greece and Troy may say,
'Not hate, but glory, made these chiefs contend;
And each brave foe was in his soul a friend.'"
With that, a sword with stars of silver graced,
The baldric studded, and the sheath enchased,
He gave the Greek. The generous Greek bestow'd
A radiant belt that rich with purple glow'd.
Then with majestic grace they quit the plain;
This seeks the Grecian, that the Phrygian train.
The Trojan bands returning Hector wait,
And hail with joy the Champion of their state;
Escaped great Ajax, they survey him round,
Alive, unarm'd, and vigorous from his wound;
To Troy's high gates the godlike man they bear
Their present triumph, as their late despair.
But Ajax, glorying in his hardy deed,
The well-arm'd Greeks to Agamemnon lead.
A steer for sacrifice the king design'd,
Of full five years, and of the nobler kind.
The victim falls; they strip the smoking hide,
The beast they quarter, and the joints divide;

Then spread the tables, the repast prepare,
Each takes his seat, and each receives his share.
The king himself (an honorary sign)
Before great Ajax placed the mighty chine.
When now the rage of hunger was removed,
Nestor, in each persuasive art approved,
The sage whose counsels long had sway'd the rest,
In words like these his prudent thought express'd:
"How dear, O kings! this fatal day has cost,
What Greeks are perish'd! what a people lost!
What tides of blood have drench'd Scamander's shore!
What crowds of heroes sunk to rise no more!
Then hear me, chief! nor let the morrow's light
Awake thy squadrons to new toils of fight:
Some space at least permit the war to breathe,
While we to flames our slaughter'd friends bequeath,
From the red field their scatter'd bodies bear,
And nigh the fleet a funeral structure rear;
So decent urns their snowy bones may keep,
And pious children o'er their ashes weep.
Here, where on one promiscuous pile they blazed,
High o'er them all a general tomb be raised;
Next, to secure our camp and naval powers,
Raise an embattled wall, with lofty towers;
From space to space be ample gates around,
For passing chariots; and a trench profound.
So Greece to combat shall in safety go,
Nor fear the fierce incursions of the foe."
'Twas thus the sage his wholesome counsel moved;
The sceptred kings of Greece his words approved.
Meanwhile, convened at Priam's palace-gate,
The Trojan peers in nightly council sate;
A senate void of order, as of choice:
Their hearts were fearful, and confused their voice.
Antenor, rising, thus demands their ear:
"Ye Trojans, Dardans, and auxiliars, hear!
'Tis heaven the counsel of my breast inspires,
And I but move what every god requires:
Let Sparta's treasures be this hour restored,
And Argive Helen own her ancient lord.
The ties of faith, the sworn alliance, broke,
Our impious battles the just gods provoke.
As this advice ye practise, or reject,
So hope success, or dread the dire effect."
The senior spoke and sate. To whom replied
The graceful husband of the Spartan bride:

"Cold counsels, Trojan, may become thy years
But sound ungrateful in a warrior's ears:
Old man, if void of fallacy or art,
Thy words express the purpose of thy heart,
Thou, in thy time, more sound advice hast given;
But wisdom has its date, assign'd by heaven.
Then hear me, princes of the Trojan name!
Their treasures I'll restore, but not the dame;
My treasures too, for peace, I will resign;
But be this bright possession ever mine."
'Twas then, the growing discord to compose,
Slow from his seat the reverend Priam rose:
His godlike aspect deep attention drew:
He paused, and these pacific words ensue:
"Ye Trojans, Dardans, and auxiliar bands!
Now take refreshment as the hour demands;
Guard well the walls, relieve the watch of night.
Till the new sun restores the cheerful light.
Then shall our herald, to the Atrides sent,
Before their ships proclaim my son's intent.
Next let a truce be ask'd, that Troy may burn
Her slaughter'd heroes, and their bones inurn;
That done, once more the fate of war be tried,
And whose the conquest, mighty Jove decide!"
The monarch spoke: the warriors snatch'd with haste
(Each at his post in arms) a short repast.
Soon as the rosy morn had waked the day,
To the black ships Idæus bent his way;
There, to the sons of Mars, in council found,
He raised his voice: the host stood listening round.
"Ye sons of Atreus, and ye Greeks, give ear!
The words of Troy, and Troy's great monarch, hear.
Pleased may ye hear (so heaven succeed my prayers)
What Paris, author of the war, declares.
The spoils and treasures he to Ilion bore
(Oh had he perish'd ere they touch'd our shore!)
He proffers injured Greece: with large increase
Of added Trojan wealth to buy the peace.
But to restore the beauteous bride again,
This Greece demands, and Troy requests in vain.
Next, O ye chiefs! we ask a truce to burn
Our slaughter'd heroes, and their bones inurn.
That done, once more the fate of war be tried,
And whose the conquest, mighty Jove decide!"
The Greeks gave ear, but none the silence broke;
At length Tydides rose, and rising spoke:

"Oh, take not, friends! defrauded of your fame,
Their proffer'd wealth, nor even the Spartan dame.
Let conquest make them ours: fate shakes their wall,
And Troy already totters to her fall."
The admiring chiefs, and all the Grecian name,
With general shouts return'd him loud acclaim.
Then thus the king of kings rejects the peace:
"Herald! in him thou hear'st the voice of Greece
For what remains; let funeral flames be fed
With heroes' corps: I war not with the dead:
Go search your slaughtered chiefs on yonder plain,
And gratify the manes of the slain.
Be witness, Jove, whose thunder rolls on high!"
He said, and rear'd his sceptre to the sky.
To sacred Troy, where all her princes lay
To wait the event, the herald bent his way.
He came, and standing in the midst, explain'd
The peace rejected, but the truce obtain'd.
Straight to their several cares the Trojans move,
Some search the plains, some fell the sounding grove:
Nor less the Greeks, descending on the shore,
Hew'd the green forests, and the bodies bore.
And now from forth the chambers of the main,
To shed his sacred light on earth again,
Arose the golden chariot of the day,
And tipp'd the mountains with a purple ray.
In mingled throngs the Greek and Trojan train
Through heaps of carnage search'd the mournful plain.
Scarce could the friend his slaughter'd friend explore,
With dust dishonour'd, and deformed with gore.
The wounds they wash'd, their pious tears they shed,
And, laid along their cars, deplored the dead.
Sage Priam check'd their grief: with silent haste
The bodies decent on the piles were placed:
With melting hearts the cold remains they burn'd,
And, sadly slow, to sacred Troy return'd.
Nor less the Greeks their pious sorrows shed,
And decent on the pile dispose the dead;
The cold remains consume with equal care;
And slowly, sadly, to their fleet repair.
Now, ere the morn had streak'd with reddening light
The doubtful confines of the day and night,
About the dying flames the Greeks appear'd,
And round the pile a general tomb they rear'd.
Then, to secure the camp and naval powers,
They raised embattled walls with lofty towers:

From space to space were ample gates around,
For passing chariots, and a trench profound
Of large extent; and deep in earth below,
Strong piles infix'd stood adverse to the foe.
So toil'd the Greeks: meanwhile the gods above,
In shining circle round their father Jove,
Amazed beheld the wondrous works of man:
Then he, whose trident shakes the earth, began:
"What mortals henceforth shall our power adore,
Our fanes frequent, our oracles implore,
If the proud Grecians thus successful boast
Their rising bulwarks on the sea-beat coast?
See the long walls extending to the main,
No god consulted, and no victim slain!
Their fame shall fill the world's remotest ends,
Wide as the morn her golden beam extends;
While old Laomedon's divine abodes,
Those radiant structures raised by labouring gods,
Shall, razed and lost, in long oblivion sleep."
Thus spoke the hoary monarch of the deep.
The almighty Thunderer with a frown replies,
That clouds the world, and blackens half the skies:
"Strong god of ocean! thou, whose rage can make
The solid earth's eternal basis shake!
What cause of fear from mortal works could move
The meanest subject of our realms above?
Where'er the sun's refulgent rays are cast,
Thy power is honour'd, and thy fame shall last.
But yon proud work no future age shall view,
No trace remain where once the glory grew.
The sapp'd foundations by thy force shall fall,
And, whelm'd beneath the waves, drop the huge wall:
Vast drifts of sand shall change the former shore:
The ruin vanish'd, and the name no more."
Thus they in heaven: while, o'er the Grecian train,
The rolling sun descending to the main
Beheld the finish'd work. Their bulls they slew;
Back from the tents the savoury vapour flew.
And now the fleet, arrived from Lemnos' strands,
With Bacchus' blessings cheered the generous bands.
Of fragrant wines the rich Eunaeus sent
A thousand measures to the royal tent.
(Eunaeus, whom Hypsipyle of yore
To Jason, shepherd of his people, bore,)
The rest they purchased at their proper cost,
And well the plenteous freight supplied the host:

Each, in exchange, proportion'd treasures gave;
Some, brass or iron; some, an ox, or slave.
All night they feast, the Greek and Trojan powers:
Those on the fields, and these within their towers.
But Jove averse the signs of wrath display'd,
And shot red lightnings through the gloomy shade:
Humbled they stood; pale horror seized on all,
While the deep thunder shook the aerial hall.
Each pour'd to Jove before the bowl was crown'd;
And large libations drench'd the thirsty ground:
Then late, refresh'd with sleep from toils of fight,
Enjoy'd the balmy blessings of the night.

BOOK VIII.

THE SECOND BATTLE, AND THE DISTRESS OF THE
GREEKS.

Aurora now, fair daughter of the dawn,
Sprinkled with rosy light the dewy lawn;
When Jove convened the senate of the skies,
Where high Olympus' cloudy tops arise,
The sire of gods his awful silence broke;
The heavens attentive trembled as he spoke:
"Celestial states! immortal gods! give ear,
Hear our decree, and reverence what ye hear;
The fix'd decree which not all heaven can move;
Thou, fate! fulfil it! and, ye powers, approve!
What god but enters yon forbidden field,
Who yields assistance, or but wills to yield,
Back to the skies with shame he shall be driven,
Gash'd with dishonest wounds, the scorn of heaven;
Or far, oh far, from steep Olympus thrown,
Low in the dark Tartarean gulf shall groan,
With burning chains fix'd to the brazen floors,
And lock'd by hell's inexorable doors;
As deep beneath the infernal centre hurl'd,
As from that centre to the ethereal world.

Let him who tempts me, dread those dire abodes:
And know, the Almighty is the god of gods.
League all your forces, then, ye powers above,
Join all, and try the omnipotence of Jove.
Let down our golden everlasting chain
Whose strong embrace holds heaven, and earth, and main
Strive all, of mortal and immortal birth,
To drag, by this, the Thunderer down to earth:
Ye strive in vain! if I but stretch this hand,
I heave the gods, the ocean, and the land;
I fix the chain to great Olympus' height,
And the vast world hangs trembling in my sight!
For such I reign, unbounded and above;
And such are men, and gods, compared to Jove."
The all-mighty spoke, nor durst the powers reply:
A reverend horror silenced all the sky;
Trembling they stood before their sovereign's look;
At length his best-beloved, the power of wisdom, spoke:
"O first and greatest! God, by gods adored
We own thy might, our father and our lord!
But, ah! permit to pity human state:
If not to help, at least lament their fate.
From fields forbidden we submiss refrain,
With arms unaiding mourn our Argives slain;
Yet grant my counsels still their breasts may move,
Or all must perish in the wrath of Jove."
The cloud-compelling god her suit approved,
And smiled superior on his best beloved;
Then call'd his coursers, and his chariot took;
The stedfast firmament beneath them shook:
Rapt by the ethereal steeds the chariot roll'd;
Brass were their hoofs, their curling manes of gold:
Of heaven's undrossy gold the gods array,
Refulgent, flash'd intolerable day.
High on the throne he shines: his coursers fly
Between the extended earth and starry sky.
But when to Ida's topmost height he came,
(Fair nurse of fountains, and of savage game,)
Where o'er her pointed summits proudly raised,
His fane breathed odours, and his altar blazed:
There, from his radiant car, the sacred sire
Of gods and men released the steeds of fire:
Blue ambient mists the immortal steeds embraced;
High on the cloudy point his seat he placed;
Thence his broad eye the subject world surveys,
The town, and tents, and navigable seas.

Now had the Grecians snatch'd a short repast,
And buckled on their shining arms with haste.
Troy roused as soon; for on this dreadful day
The fate of fathers, wives, and infants lay.
The gates unfolding pour forth all their train;
Squadrons on squadrons cloud the dusky plain:
Men, steeds, and chariots shake the trembling ground,
The tumult thickens, and the skies resound;
And now with shouts the shocking armies closed,
To lances lances, shields to shields opposed,
Host against host with shadowy legends drew,
The sounding darts in iron tempests flew;
Victors and vanquish'd join promiscuous cries,
Triumphant shouts and dying groans arise;
With streaming blood the slippery fields are dyed,
And slaughter'd heroes swell the dreadful tide.
Long as the morning beams, increasing bright,
O'er heaven's clear azure spread the sacred light,
Commutual death the fate of war confounds,
Each adverse battle gored with equal wounds.
But when the sun the height of heaven ascends,
The sire of gods his golden scales suspends,
With equal hand: in these explored the fate
Of Greece and Troy, and poised the mighty weight:
Press'd with its load, the Grecian balance lies
Low sunk on earth, the Trojan strikes the skies.
Then Jove from Ida's top his horrors spreads;
The clouds burst dreadful o'er the Grecian heads;
Thick lightnings flash; the muttering thunder rolls;
Their strength he withers, and unmans their souls.
Before his wrath the trembling hosts retire;
The gods in terrors, and the skies on fire.
Nor great Idomeneus that sight could bear,
Nor each stern Ajax, thunderbolts of war:
Nor he, the king of war, the alarm sustain'd
Nestor alone, amidst the storm remain'd.
Unwilling he remain'd, for Paris' dart
Had pierced his courser in a mortal part;
Fix'd in the forehead, where the springing mane
Curl'd o'er the brow, it stung him to the brain;
Mad with his anguish, he begins to rear,
Paw with his hoofs aloft, and lash the air.
Scarce had his falchion cut the reins, and freed
The encumber'd chariot from the dying steed,
When dreadful Hector, thundering through the war,
Pour'd to the tumult on his whirling car.

That day had stretch'd beneath his matchless hand
The hoary monarch of the Pylian band,
But Diomed beheld; from forth the crowd
He rush'd, and on Ulysses call'd aloud:
"Whither, oh whither does Ulysses run?
Oh, flight unworthy great Laertes' son!
Mix'd with the vulgar shall thy fate be found,
Pierced in the back, a vile, dishonest wound?
Oh turn and save from Hector's direful rage
The glory of the Greeks, the Pylian sage."
His fruitless words are lost unheard in air,
Ulysses seeks the ships, and shelters there.
But bold Tydides to the rescue goes,
A single warrior midst a host of foes;
Before the coursers with a sudden spring
He leap'd, and anxious thus bespoke the king:
"Great perils, father! wait the unequal fight;
These younger champions will oppress thy might.
Thy veins no more with ancient vigour glow,
Weak is thy servant, and thy coursers slow.
Then haste, ascend my seat, and from the car
Observe the steeds of Tros, renown'd in war.
Practised alike to turn, to stop, to chase,
To dare the fight, or urge the rapid race:
These late obey'd Æneas' guiding rein;
Leave thou thy chariot to our faithful train;
With these against yon Trojans will we go,
Nor shall great Hector want an equal foe;
Fierce as he is, even he may learn to fear
The thirsty fury of my flying spear."
Thus said the chief; and Nestor, skill'd in war,
Approves his counsel, and ascends the car:
The steeds he left, their trusty servants hold;
Eurymedon, and Sthenelus the bold:
The reverend charioteer directs the course,
And strains his aged arm to lash the horse.
Hector they face; unknowing how to fear,
Fierce he drove on; Tydides whirl'd his spear.
The spear with erring haste mistook its way,
But plunged in Eniopeus' bosom lay.
His opening hand in death forsakes the rein;
The steeds fly back: he falls, and spurns the plain.
Great Hector sorrows for his servant kill'd,
Yet unrevenged permits to press the field;
Till, to supply his place and rule the car,
Rose Archeptolemus, the fierce in war.

And now had death and horror cover'd all;
Like timorous flocks the Trojans in their wall
Inclosed had bled: but Jove with awful sound
Roll'd the big thunder o'er the vast profound:
Full in Tydides' face the lightning flew;
The ground before him flamed with sulphur blue;
The quivering steeds fell prostrate at the sight;
And Nestor's trembling hand confess'd his fright:
He dropp'd the reins: and, shook with sacred dread,
Thus, turning, warn'd the intrepid Diomed:
"O chief! too daring in thy friend's defence
Retire advised, and urge the chariot hence.
This day, averse, the sovereign of the skies
Assists great Hector, and our palm denies.
Some other sun may see the happier hour,
When Greece shall conquer by his heavenly power.
'Tis not in man his fix'd decree to move:
The great will glory to submit to Jove."
"O reverend prince! (Tydides thus replies)
Thy years are awful, and thy words are wise.
But ah, what grief! should haughty Hector boast
I fled inglorious to the guarded coast.
Before that dire disgrace shall blast my fame,
O'erwhelm me, earth; and hide a warrior's shame!"
To whom Gerenian Nestor thus replied:
"Gods! can thy courage fear the Phrygian's pride?
Hector may vaunt, but who shall heed the boast?
Not those who felt thy arm, the Dardan host,
Nor Troy, yet bleeding in her heroes lost;
Not even a Phrygian dame, who dreads the sword
That laid in dust her loved, lamented lord."
He said, and, hasty, o'er the gasping throng
Drives the swift steeds: the chariot smokes along;
The shouts of Trojans thicken in the wind;
The storm of hissing javelins pours behind.
Then with a voice that shakes the solid skies,
Pleased, Hector braves the warrior as he flies.
"Go, mighty hero! graced above the rest
In seats of council and the sumptuous feast:
Now hope no more those honours from thy train;
Go less than woman, in the form of man!
To scale our walls, to wrap our towers in flames,
To lead in exile the fair Phrygian dames,
Thy once proud hopes, presumptuous prince! are fled;
This arm shall reach thy heart, and stretch thee dead."
Now fears dissuade him, and now hopes invite.

To stop his coursers, and to stand the fight;
Thrice turn'd the chief, and thrice imperial Jove
On Ida's summits thunder'd from above.
Great Hector heard; he saw the flashing light,
(The sign of conquest,) and thus urged the fight:
"Hear, every Trojan, Lycian, Dardan band,
All famed in war, and dreadful hand to hand.
Be mindful of the wreaths your arms have won,
Your great forefathers' glories, and your own.
Heard ye the voice of Jove? Success and fame
Await on Troy, on Greece eternal shame.
In vain they skulk behind their boasted wall,
Weak bulwarks; destined by this arm to fall.
High o'er their slighted trench our steeds shall bound,
And pass victorious o'er the levell'd mound.
Soon as before yon hollow ships we stand,
Fight each with flames, and toss the blazing brand;
Till, their proud navy wrapt in smoke and fires,
All Greece, encompass'd, in one blaze expires."
Furious he said; then bending o'er the yoke,
Encouraged his proud steeds, while thus he spoke:
"Now, Xanthus, Æthon, Lampus, urge the chase,
And thou, Podargus! prove thy generous race;
Be fleet, be fearless, this important day,
And all your master's well-spent care repay.
For this, high-fed, in plenteous stalls ye stand,
Served with pure wheat, and by a princess' hand;
For this my spouse, of great Aëtion's line,
So oft has steep'd the strengthening grain in wine.
Now swift pursue, now thunder uncontroll'd:
Give me to seize rich Nestor's shield of gold;
From Tydeus' shoulders strip the costly load,
Vulcanian arms, the labour of a god:
These if we gain, then victory, ye powers!
This night, this glorious night, the fleet is ours!"
That heard, deep anguish stung Saturnia's soul;
She shook her throne, that shook the starry pole:
And thus to Neptune: "Thou, whose force can make
The stedfast earth from her foundations shake,
Seest thou the Greeks by fates unjust oppress'd,
Nor swells thy heart in that immortal breast?
Yet Ægae, Helicè, thy power obey,
And gifts unceasing on thine altars lay.
Would all the deities of Greece combine,
In vain the gloomy Thunderer might repine:
Sole should he sit, with scarce a god to friend,

And see his Trojans to the shades descend:
Such be the scene from his Idaean bower;
Ungrateful prospect to the sullen power!"
Neptune with wrath rejects the rash design:
"What rage, what madness, furious queen! is thine?
I war not with the highest. All above
Submit and tremble at the hand of Jove."
Now godlike Hector, to whose matchless might
Jove gave the glory of the destined fight,
Squadrons on squadrons drives, and fills the fields
With close-ranged chariots, and with thicken'd shields.
Where the deep trench in length extended lay,
Compacted troops stand wedged in firm array,
A dreadful front! they shake the brands, and threat
With long-destroying flames the hostile fleet.
The king of men, by Juno's self inspired,
Toil'd through the tents, and all his army fired.
Swift as he moved, he lifted in his hand
His purple robe, bright ensign of command.
High on the midmost bark the king appear'd:
There, from Ulysses' deck, his voice was heard:
To Ajax and Achilles reach'd the sound,
Whose distant ships the guarded navy bound.
"O Argives! shame of human race! (he cried:
The hollow vessels to his voice replied,)
Where now are all your glorious boasts of yore,
Your hasty triumphs on the Lemnian shore?
Each fearless hero dares a hundred foes,
While the feast lasts, and while the goblet flows;
But who to meet one martial man is found,
When the fight rages, and the flames surround?
O mighty Jove! O sire of the distress'd!
Was ever king like me, like me oppress'd?
With power immense, with justice arm'd in vain;
My glory ravish'd, and my people slain!
To thee my vows were breathed from every shore;
What altar smoked not with our victims' gore?
With fat of bulls I fed the constant flame,
And ask'd destruction to the Trojan name.
Now, gracious god! far humbler our demand;
Give these at least to 'scape from Hector's hand,
And save the relics of the Grecian land!"
Thus pray'd the king, and heaven's great father heard
His vows, in bitterness of soul preferr'd:
The wrath appeased, by happy signs declares,
And gives the people to their monarch's prayers.

His eagle, sacred bird of heaven! he sent,
A fawn his talons truss'd, (divine portent!)
High o'er the wondering hosts he soar'd above,
Who paid their vows to Panomphaean Jove;
Then let the prey before his altar fall;
The Greeks beheld, and transport seized on all:
Encouraged by the sign, the troops revive,
And fierce on Troy with doubled fury drive.
Tydides first, of all the Grecian force,
O'er the broad ditch impell'd his foaming horse,
Pierced the deep ranks, their strongest battle tore,
And dyed his javelin red with Trojan gore.
Young Agelaus (Phradmon was his sire)
With flying coursers shunn'd his dreadful ire;
Struck through the back, the Phrygian fell oppress'd;
The dart drove on, and issued at his breast:
Headlong he quits the car: his arms resound;
His ponderous buckler thunders on the ground.
Forth rush a tide of Greeks, the passage freed;
The Atridae first, the Ajaces next succeed:
Meriones, like Mars in arms renown'd,
And godlike Idomen, now passed the mound;
Evaemon's son next issues to the foe,
And last young Teucer with his bended bow.
Secure behind the Telamonian shield
The skilful archer wide survey'd the field,
With every shaft some hostile victim slew,
Then close beneath the sevenfold orb withdrew:
The conscious infant so, when fear alarms,
Retires for safety to the mother's arms.
Thus Ajax guards his brother in the field,
Moves as he moves, and turns the shining shield.
Who first by Teucer's mortal arrows bled?
Orsilochus; then fell Ormenus dead:
The godlike Lycophon next press'd the plain,
With Chromius, Daetor, Ophelestes slain:
Bold Hamopaon breathless sunk to ground;
The bloody pile great Melanippus crown'd.
Heaps fell on heaps, sad trophies of his art,
A Trojan ghost attending every dart.
Great Agamemnon views with joyful eye
The ranks grow thinner as his arrows fly:
"O youth forever dear! (the monarch cried)
Thus, always thus, thy early worth be tried;
Thy brave example shall retrieve our host,
Thy country's saviour, and thy father's boast!

Sprung from an alien's bed thy sire to grace,
The vigorous offspring of a stolen embrace:
Proud of his boy, he own'd the generous flame,
And the brave son repays his cares with fame.
Now hear a monarch's vow: If heaven's high powers
Give me to raze Troy's long-defended towers;
Whatever treasures Greece for me design,
The next rich honorary gift be thine:
Some golden tripod, or distinguished car,
With coursers dreadful in the ranks of war:
Or some fair captive, whom thy eyes approve,
Shall recompense the warrior's toils with love."
To this the chief: "With praise the rest inspire,
Nor urge a soul already fill'd with fire.
What strength I have, be now in battle tried,
Till every shaft in Phrygian blood be dyed.
Since rallying from our wall we forced the foe,
Still aim'd at Hector have I bent my bow:
Eight forky arrows from this hand have fled,
And eight bold heroes by their points lie dead:
But sure some god denies me to destroy
This fury of the field, this dog of Troy."
He said, and twang'd the string. The weapon flies
At Hector's breast, and sings along the skies:
He miss'd the mark; but pierced Gorgythio's heart,
And drench'd in royal blood the thirsty dart.
(Fair Castianira, nymph of form divine,
This offspring added to king Priam's line.)
As full-blown poppies, overcharged with rain,
Decline the head, and drooping kiss the plain;
So sinks the youth: his beauteous head, depress'd
Beneath his helmet, drops upon his breast.
Another shaft the raging archer drew,
That other shaft with erring fury flew,
(From Hector, Phœbus turn'd the flying wound,)
Yet fell not dry or guiltless to the ground:
Thy breast, brave Archeptolemus! it tore,
And dipp'd its feathers in no vulgar gore.
Headlong he falls: his sudden fall alarms
The steeds, that startle at his sounding arms.
Hector with grief his charioteer beheld
All pale and breathless on the sanguine field:
Then bids Cebriones direct the rein,
Quits his bright car, and issues on the plain.
Dreadful he shouts: from earth a stone he took,
And rush'd on Teucer with the lifted rock.

The youth already strain'd the forceful yew;
The shaft already to his shoulder drew;
The feather in his hand, just wing'd for flight,
Touch'd where the neck and hollow chest unite;
There, where the juncture knits the channel bone,
The furious chief discharged the craggy stone:
The bow-string burst beneath the ponderous blow,
And his numb'd hand dismiss'd his useless bow.
He fell: but Ajax his broad shield display'd,
And screen'd his brother with the mighty shade;
Till great Alaster, and Mecistheus, bore
The batter'd archer groaning to the shore.
Troy yet found grace before the Olympian sire,
He arm'd their hands, and fill'd their breasts with fire.
The Greeks repulsed, retreat behind their wall,
Or in the trench on heaps confusedly fall.
First of the foe, great Hector march'd along,
With terror clothed, and more than mortal strong.
As the bold hound, that gives the lion chase,
With beating bosom, and with eager pace,
Hangs on his haunch, or fastens on his heels,
Guards as he turns, and circles as he wheels;
Thus oft the Grecians turn'd, but still they flew;
Thus following, Hector still the hindmost slew.
When flying they had pass'd the trench profound,
And many a chief lay gasping on the ground;
Before the ships a desperate stand they made,
And fired the troops, and called the gods to aid.
Fierce on his rattling chariot Hector came:
His eyes like Gorgon shot a sanguine flame
That wither'd all their host: like Mars he stood:
Dire as the monster, dreadful as the god!
Their strong distress the wife of Jove survey'd;
Then pensive thus, to war's triumphant maid:
"O daughter of that god, whose arm can wield
The avenging bolt, and shake the sable shield!
Now, in this moment of her last despair,
Shall wretched Greece no more confess our care,
Condemn'd to suffer the full force of fate,
And drain the dregs of heaven's relentless hate?
Gods! shall one raging hand thus level all?
What numbers fell! what numbers yet shall fall!
What power divine shall Hector's wrath assuage?
Still swells the slaughter, and still grows the rage!"
So spake the imperial regent of the skies;
To whom the goddess with the azure eyes:

"Long since had Hector stain'd these fields with gore,
Stretch'd by some Argive on his native shore:
But he above, the sire of heaven, withstands,
Mocks our attempts, and slights our just demands;
The stubborn god, inflexible and hard,
Forgets my service and deserved reward:
Saved I, for this, his favourite son distress'd,
By stern Eurystheus with long labours press'd?
He begg'd, with tears he begg'd, in deep dismay;
I shot from heaven, and gave his arm the day.
Oh had my wisdom known this dire event,
When to grim Pluto's gloomy gates he went;
The triple dog had never felt his chain,
Nor Styx been cross'd, nor hell explored in vain.
Averse to me of all his heaven of gods,
At Thetis' suit the partial Thunderer nods;
To grace her gloomy, fierce, resenting son,
My hopes are frustrate, and my Greeks undone.
Some future day, perhaps, he may be moved
To call his blue-eyed maid his best beloved.
Haste, launch thy chariot, through yon ranks to ride;
Myself will arm, and thunder at thy side.
Then, goddess! say, shall Hector glory then?
(That terror of the Greeks, that man of men)
When Juno's self, and Pallas shall appear,
All dreadful in the crimson walks of war!
What mighty Trojan then, on yonder shore,
Expiring, pale, and terrible no more,
Shall feast the fowls, and glut the dogs with gore?"
She ceased, and Juno rein'd the steeds with care:
(Heaven's awful empress, Saturn's other heir:)
Pallas, meanwhile, her various veil unbound,
With flowers adorn'd, with art immortal crown'd;
The radiant robe her sacred fingers wove
Floats in rich waves, and spreads the court of Jove.
Her father's arms her mighty limbs invest,
His cuirass blazes on her ample breast.
The vigorous power the trembling car ascends:
Shook by her arm, the massy javelin bends:
Huge, ponderous, strong! that when her fury burns
Proud tyrants humbles, and whole hosts o'erturns.
Saturnia lends the lash; the coursers fly;
Smooth glides the chariot through the liquid sky.
Heaven's gates spontaneous open to the powers,
Heaven's golden gates, kept by the winged Hours.
Commission'd in alternate watch they stand,

The sun's bright portals and the skies command;
Close, or unfold, the eternal gates of day
Bar heaven with clouds, or roll those clouds away.
The sounding hinges ring, the clouds divide.
Prone down the steep of heaven their course they guide.
But Jove, incensed, from Ida's top survey'd,
And thus enjoin'd the many-colour'd maid.

"Thaumantia! mount the winds, and stop their car;
Against the highest who shall wage the war?
If furious yet they dare the vain debate,
Thus have I spoke, and what I speak is fate:
Their coursers crush'd beneath the wheels shall lie,
Their car in fragments, scatter'd o'er the sky:
My lightning these rebellious shall confound,
And hurl them flaming, headlong, to the ground,
Condemn'd for ten revolving years to weep
The wounds impress'd by burning thunder deep.
So shall Minerva learn to fear our ire,
Nor dare to combat hers and nature's sire.
For Juno, headstrong and imperious still,
She claims some title to transgress our will."
Swift as the wind, the various-colour'd maid
From Ida's top her golden wings display'd;
To great Olympus' shining gate she flies,
There meets the chariot rushing down the skies,
Restrains their progress from the bright abodes,
And speaks the mandate of the sire of gods.
"What frenzy goddesses! what rage can move
Celestial minds to tempt the wrath of Jove?
Desist, obedient to his high command:
This is his word; and know his word shall stand:
His lightning your rebellion shall confound,
And hurl ye headlong, flaming, to the ground;
Your horses crush'd beneath the wheels shall lie,
Your car in fragments scatter'd o'er the sky;
Yourselves condemn'd ten rolling years to weep
The wounds impress'd by burning thunder deep.
So shall Minerva learn to fear his ire,
Nor dare to combat hers and nature's sire.
For Juno, headstrong and imperious still,
She claims some title to transgress his will:
But thee, what desperate insolence has driven
To lift thy lance against the king of heaven?"
Then, mounting on the pinions of the wind,
She flew; and Juno thus her rage resign'd:

"O daughter of that god, whose arm can wield
The avenging bolt, and shake the saber shield!
No more let beings of superior birth
Contend with Jove for this low race of earth;
Triumphant now, now miserably slain,
They breathe or perish as the fates ordain:
But Jove's high counsels full effect shall find;
And, ever constant, ever rule mankind."
She spoke, and backward turn'd her steeds of light,
Adorn'd with manes of gold, and heavenly bright.
The Hours unloosed them, panting as they stood,
And heap'd their mangers with ambrosial food.
There tied, they rest in high celestial stalls;
The chariot propp'd against the crystal walls,
The pensive goddesses, abash'd, controll'd,
Mix with the gods, and fill their seats of gold.

And now the Thunderer meditates his flight
From Ida's summits to the Olympian height.
Swifter than thought, the wheels instinctive fly,
Flame through the vast of air, and reach the sky.
'Twas Neptune's charge his coursers to unbrace,
And fix the car on its immortal base;
There stood the chariot, beaming forth its rays,
Till with a snowy veil he screen'd the blaze.
He, whose all-conscious eyes the world behold,
The eternal Thunderer sat, enthroned in gold.
High heaven the footstool of his feet he makes,
And wide beneath him all Olympus shakes.
Trembling afar the offending powers appear'd,
Confused and silent, for his frown they fear'd.
He saw their soul, and thus his word imparts:
"Pallas and Juno! say, why heave your hearts?
Soon was your battle o'er: proud Troy retired
Before your face, and in your wrath expired.
But know, whoe'er almighty power withstand!
Unmatch'd our force, unconquer'd is our hand:
Who shall the sovereign of the skies control?
Not all the gods that crown the starry pole.
Your hearts shall tremble, if our arms we take,
And each immortal nerve with horror shake.
For thus I speak, and what I speak shall stand;
What power soe'er provokes our lifted hand,
On this our hill no more shall hold his place;
Cut off, and exiled from the ethereal race."
Juno and Pallas grieving hear the doom,

But feast their souls on Ilion's woes to come.
Though secret anger swell'd Minerva's breast,
The prudent goddess yet her wrath repress'd;
But Juno, impotent of rage, replies:
"What hast thou said, O tyrant of the skies!
Strength and omnipotence invest thy throne;
'Tis thine to punish; ours to grieve alone.
For Greece we grieve, abandon'd by her fate
To drink the dregs of thy unmeasured hate.
From fields forbidden we submiss refrain,
With arms unaiding see our Argives slain;
Yet grant our counsels still their breasts may move,
Lest all should perish in the rage of Jove."
The goddess thus; and thus the god replies,
Who swells the clouds, and blackens all the skies:
"The morning sun, awaked by loud alarms,
Shall see the almighty Thunderer in arms.
What heaps of Argives then shall load the plain,
Those radiant eyes shall view, and view in vain.
Nor shall great Hector cease the rage of fight,
The navy flaming, and thy Greeks in flight,
Even till the day when certain fates ordain
That stern Achilles (his Patroclus slain)
Shall rise in vengeance, and lay waste the plain.
For such is fate, nor canst thou turn its course
With all thy rage, with all thy rebel force.
Fly, if thy wilt, to earth's remotest bound,
Where on her utmost verge the seas resound;
Where cursed Iapetus and Saturn dwell,
Fast by the brink, within the streams of hell;
No sun e'er gilds the gloomy horrors there;
No cheerful gales refresh the lazy air:
There arm once more the bold Titanian band;
And arm in vain; for what I will, shall stand."
Now deep in ocean sunk the lamp of light,
And drew behind the cloudy veil of night:
The conquering Trojans mourn his beams decay'd;
The Greeks rejoicing bless the friendly shade.
The victors keep the field; and Hector calls
A martial council near the navy walls;
These to Scamander's bank apart he led,
Where thinly scatter'd lay the heaps of dead.
The assembled chiefs, descending on the ground,
Attend his order, and their prince surround.
A massy spear he bore of mighty strength,
Of full ten cubits was the lance's length;

The point was brass, refulgent to behold,
Fix'd to the wood with circling rings of gold:
The noble Hector on his lance reclined,
And, bending forward, thus reveal'd his mind:
"Ye valiant Trojans, with attention hear!
Ye Dardan bands, and generous aids, give ear!
This day, we hoped, would wrap in conquering flame
Greece with her ships, and crown our toils with fame.
But darkness now, to save the cowards, falls,
And guards them trembling in their wooden walls.
Obey the night, and use her peaceful hours
Our steeds to forage, and refresh our powers.
Straight from the town be sheep and oxen sought,
And strengthening bread and generous wine be brought.
Wide o'er the field, high blazing to the sky,
Let numerous fires the absent sun supply,
The flaming piles with plenteous fuel raise,
Till the bright morn her purple beam displays;
Lest, in the silence and the shades of night,
Greece on her sable ships attempt her flight.
Not unmolested let the wretches gain
Their lofty decks, or safely cleave the main;
Some hostile wound let every dart bestow,
Some lasting token of the Phrygian foe,
Wounds, that long hence may ask their spouses' care.
And warn their children from a Trojan war.
Now through the circuit of our Ilion wall,
Let sacred heralds sound the solemn call;
To bid the sires with hoary honours crown'd,
And beardless youths, our battlements surround.
Firm be the guard, while distant lie our powers,
And let the matrons hang with lights the towers;
Lest, under covert of the midnight shade,
The insidious foe the naked town invade.
Suffice, to-night, these orders to obey;
A nobler charge shall rouse the dawning day.
The gods, I trust, shall give to Hector's hand
From these detested foes to free the land,
Who plough'd, with fates averse, the watery way:
For Trojan vultures a predestined prey.
Our common safety must be now the care;
But soon as morning paints the fields of air,
Sheathed in bright arms let every troop engage,
And the fired fleet behold the battle rage.
Then, then shall Hector and Tydides prove
Whose fates are heaviest in the scales of Jove.

To-morrow's light (O haste the glorious morn!)
Shall see his bloody spoils in triumph borne,
With this keen javelin shall his breast be gored,
And prostrate heroes bleed around their lord.
Certain as this, oh! might my days endure,
From age inglorious, and black death secure;
So might my life and glory know no bound,
Like Pallas worshipp'd, like the sun renown'd!
As the next dawn, the last they shall enjoy,
Shall crush the Greeks, and end the woes of Troy."
The leader spoke. From all his host around
Shouts of applause along the shores resound.
Each from the yoke the smoking steeds untied,
And fix'd their headstalls to his chariot-side.
Fat sheep and oxen from the town are led,
With generous wine, and all-sustaining bread,
Full hecatombs lay burning on the shore:
The winds to heaven the curling vapours bore.
Ungrateful offering to the immortal powers!
Whose wrath hung heavy o'er the Trojan towers:
Nor Priam nor his sons obtain'd their grace;
Proud Troy they hated, and her guilty race.
The troops exulting sat in order round,
And beaming fires illumined all the ground.
As when the moon, refulgent lamp of night,
O'er heaven's pure azure spreads her sacred light,
When not a breath disturbs the deep serene,
And not a cloud o'ercasts the solemn scene,
Around her throne the vivid planets roll,
And stars unnumber'd gild the glowing pole,
O'er the dark trees a yellower verdure shed,
And tip with silver every mountain's head:
Then shine the vales, the rocks in prospect rise,
A flood of glory bursts from all the skies:
The conscious swains, rejoicing in the sight,
Eye the blue vault, and bless the useful light.
So many flames before proud Ilion blaze,
And lighten glimmering Xanthus with their rays.
The long reflections of the distant fires
Gleam on the walls, and tremble on the spires.
A thousand piles the dusky horrors gild,
And shoot a shady lustre o'er the field.
Full fifty guards each flaming pile attend,
Whose umber'd arms, by fits, thick flashes send,
Loud neigh the coursers o'er their heaps of corn,
And ardent warriors wait the rising morn.

BOOK IX.

THE EMBASSY TO ACHILLES.

Thus joyful Troy maintain'd the watch of night;
While fear, pale comrade of inglorious flight,
And heaven-bred horror, on the Grecian part,
Sat on each face, and sadden'd every heart.
As from its cloudy dungeon issuing forth,
A double tempest of the west and north
Swells o'er the sea, from Thracia's frozen shore,
Heaps waves on waves, and bids the Ægean roar:
This way and that the boiling deeps are toss'd:
Such various passions urged the troubled host,
Great Agamemnon grieved above the rest;
Superior sorrows swell'd his royal breast;
Himself his orders to the heralds bears,
To bid to council all the Grecian peers,
But bid in whispers: these surround their chief,
In solemn sadness and majestic grief.
The king amidst the mournful circle rose:
Down his wan cheek a briny torrent flows.
So silent fountains, from a rock's tall head,
In sable streams soft-trickling waters shed.
With more than vulgar grief he stood oppress'd;
Words, mix'd with sighs, thus bursting from his breast:
"Ye sons of Greece! partake your leader's care;
Fellows in arms and princes of the war!
Of partial Jove too justly we complain,
And heavenly oracles believed in vain.
A safe return was promised to our toils,
With conquest honour'd and enrich'd with spoils:
Now shameful flight alone can save the host;
Our wealth, our people, and our glory lost.
So Jove decrees, almighty lord of all!
Jove, at whose nod whole empires rise or fall,
Who shakes the feeble props of human trust,
And towers and armies humbles to the dust.
Haste then, for ever quit these fatal fields,

Haste to the joys our native country yields;
Spread all your canvas, all your oars employ,
Nor hope the fall of heaven-defended Troy."
He said: deep silence held the Grecian band;
Silent, unmov'd in dire dismay they stand;
A pensive scene! till Tydeus' warlike son
Roll'd on the king his eyes, and thus begun:
"When kings advise us to renounce our fame,
First let him speak who first has suffer'd shame.
If I oppose thee, prince! thy wrath withhold,
The laws of council bid my tongue be bold.
Thou first, and thou alone, in fields of fight,
Durst brand my courage, and defame my might:
Nor from a friend the unkind reproach appear'd,
The Greeks stood witness, all our army heard.
The gods, O chief! from whom our honours spring,
The gods have made thee but by halves a king:
They gave thee sceptres, and a wide command;
They gave dominion o'er the seas and land;
The noblest power that might the world control
They gave thee not—a brave and virtuous soul.
Is this a general's voice, that would suggest
Fears like his own to every Grecian breast?
Confiding in our want of worth, he stands;
And if we fly, 'tis what our king commands.
Go thou, inglorious! from the embattled plain;
Ships thou hast store, and nearest to the main;
A noble care the Grecians shall employ,
To combat, conquer, and extirpate Troy.
Here Greece shall stay; or, if all Greece retire,
Myself shall stay, till Troy or I expire;
Myself, and Sthenelus, will fight for fame;
God bade us fight, and 'twas with God we came."
He ceased; the Greeks loud acclamations raise,
And voice to voice resounds Tydides' praise.
Wise Nestor then his reverend figure rear'd;
He spoke: the host in still attention heard:
"O truly great! in whom the gods have join'd
Such strength of body with such force of mind:
In conduct, as in courage, you excel,
Still first to act what you advise so well.
These wholesome counsels which thy wisdom moves,
Applauding Greece with common voice approves.
Kings thou canst blame; a bold but prudent youth:
And blame even kings with praise, because with truth.
And yet those years that since thy birth have run

Would hardly style thee Nestor's youngest son.
Then let me add what yet remains behind,
A thought unfinish'd in that generous mind;
Age bids me speak! nor shall the advice I bring
Distaste the people, or offend the king:
"Cursed is the man, and void of law and right,
Unworthy property, unworthy light,
Unfit for public rule, or private care,
That wretch, that monster, who delights in war;
Whose lust is murder, and whose horrid joy,
To tear his country, and his kind destroy!
This night, refresh and fortify thy train;
Between the trench and wall let guards remain:
Be that the duty of the young and bold;
But thou, O king, to council call the old;
Great is thy sway, and weighty are thy cares;
Thy high commands must spirit all our wars.
With Thracian wines recruit thy honour'd guests,
For happy counsels flow from sober feasts.
Wise, weighty counsels aid a state distress'd,
And such a monarch as can choose the best.
See what a blaze from hostile tents aspires,
How near our fleet approach the Trojan fires!
Who can, unmoved, behold the dreadful light?
What eye beholds them, and can close to-night?
This dreadful interval determines all;
To-morrow, Troy must flame, or Greece must fall."
Thus spoke the hoary sage: the rest obey;
Swift through the gates the guards direct their way.
His son was first to pass the lofty mound,
The generous Thrasymed, in arms renown'd:
Next him, Ascalaphus, Iälmen, stood,
The double offspring of the warrior-god:
Deipyrus, Aphareus, Merion join,
And Lycomed of Creon's noble line.
Seven were the leaders of the nightly bands,
And each bold chief a hundred spears commands.
The fires they light, to short repasts they fall,
Some line the trench, and others man the wall.
The king of men, on public counsels bent,
Convened the princes in his ample tent,
Each seized a portion of the kingly feast,
But stay'd his hand when thirst and hunger ceased.
Then Nestor spoke, for wisdom long approved,
And slowly rising, thus the council moved.
"Monarch of nations! whose superior sway

Assembled states, and lords of earth obey,
The laws and sceptres to thy hand are given,
And millions own the care of thee and Heaven.
O king! the counsels of my age attend;
With thee my cares begin, with thee must end.
Thee, prince! it fits alike to speak and hear,
Pronounce with judgment, with regard give ear,
To see no wholesome motion be withstood,
And ratify the best for public good.
Nor, though a meaner give advice, repine,
But follow it, and make the wisdom thine.
Hear then a thought, not now conceived in haste,
At once my present judgment and my past.
When from Pelides' tent you forced the maid,
I first opposed, and faithful, durst dissuade;
But bold of soul, when headlong fury fired,
You wronged the man, by men and gods admired:
Now seek some means his fatal wrath to end,
With prayers to move him, or with gifts to bend."
To whom the king. "With justice hast thou shown
A prince's faults, and I with reason own.
That happy man, whom Jove still honours most,
Is more than armies, and himself a host.
Bless'd in his love, this wondrous hero stands;
Heaven fights his war, and humbles all our bands.
Fain would my heart, which err'd through frantic rage,
The wrathful chief and angry gods assuage.
If gifts immense his mighty soul can bow,
Hear, all ye Greeks, and witness what I vow.
Ten weighty talents of the purest gold,
And twice ten vases of refulgent mould:
Seven sacred tripods, whose unsullied frame
Yet knows no office, nor has felt the flame;
Twelve steeds unmatch'd in fleetness and in force,
And still victorious in the dusty course;
(Rich were the man whose ample stores exceed
The prizes purchased by their winged speed;)
Seven lovely captives of the Lesbian line,
Skill'd in each art, unmatch'd in form divine,
The same I chose for more than vulgar charms,
When Lesbos sank beneath the hero's arms:
All these, to buy his friendship, shall be paid,
And join'd with these the long-contested maid;
With all her charms, Briseïs I resign,
And solemn swear those charms were never mine;
Untouch'd she stay'd, uninjured she removes,

Pure from my arms, and guiltless of my loves,
These instant shall be his; and if the powers
Give to our arms proud Ilion's hostile towers,
Then shall he store (when Greece the spoil divides)
With gold and brass his loaded navy's sides:
Besides, full twenty nymphs of Trojan race
With copious love shall crown his warm embrace,
Such as himself will choose; who yield to none,
Or yield to Helen's heavenly charms alone.
Yet hear me further: when our wars are o'er,
If safe we land on Argos' fruitful shore,
There shall he live my son, our honours share,
And with Orestes' self divide my care.
Yet more—three daughters in my court are bred,
And each well worthy of a royal bed;
Laodice and Iphigenia fair,
And bright Chrysothemis with golden hair;
Her let him choose whom most his eyes approve,
I ask no presents, no reward for love:
Myself will give the dower; so vast a store
As never father gave a child before.
Seven ample cities shall confess his sway,
Him Enope, and Pheræ him obey,
Cardamyle with ample turrets crown'd,
And sacred Pedasus for vines renown'd;
Æpea fair, the pastures Hira yields,
And rich Antheia with her flowery fields:
The whole extent to Pylos' sandy plain,
Along the verdant margin of the main.
There heifers graze, and labouring oxen toil;
Bold are the men, and generous is the soil;
There shall he reign, with power and justice crown'd,
And rule the tributary realms around.
All this I give, his vengeance to control,
And sure all this may move his mighty soul.
Pluto, the grisly god, who never spares,
Who feels no mercy, and who hears no prayers,
Lives dark and dreadful in deep hell's abodes,
And mortals hate him, as the worst of gods.
Great though he be, it fits him to obey,
Since more than his my years, and more my sway."

The monarch thus. The reverend Nestor then:
"Great Agamemnon! glorious king of men!
Such are thy offers as a prince may take,
And such as fits a generous king to make.

Let chosen delegates this hour be sent
(Myself will name them) to Pelides' tent.
Let Phœnix lead, revered for hoary age,
Great Ajax next, and Ithacus the sage.
Yet more to sanctify the word you send,
Let Hodius and Eurybates attend.
Now pray to Jove to grant what Greece demands;
Pray in deep silence, and with purest hands."

He said; and all approved. The heralds bring
The cleansing water from the living spring.
The youth with wine the sacred goblets crown'd,
And large libations drench'd the sands around.
The rite perform'd, the chiefs their thirst allay,
Then from the royal tent they take their way;
Wise Nestor turns on each his careful eye,
Forbids to offend, instructs them to apply;
Much he advised them all, Ulysses most,
To deprecate the chief, and save the host.
Through the still night they march, and hear the roar
Of murmuring billows on the sounding shore.
To Neptune, ruler of the seas profound,
Whose liquid arms the mighty globe surround,
They pour forth vows, their embassy to bless,
And calm the rage of stern Æacides.
And now, arrived, where on the sandy bay
The Myrmidonian tents and vessels lay;
Amused at ease, the godlike man they found,
Pleased with the solemn harp's harmonious sound.
(The well wrought harp from conquered Thebae came;
Of polish'd silver was its costly frame.)
With this he soothes his angry soul, and sings
The immortal deeds of heroes and of kings.
Patroclus only of the royal train,
Placed in his tent, attends the lofty strain:
Full opposite he sat, and listen'd long,
In silence waiting till he ceased the song.
Unseen the Grecian embassy proceeds
To his high tent; the great Ulysses leads.
Achilles starting, as the chiefs he spied,
Leap'd from his seat, and laid the harp aside.
With like surprise arose Menoetius' son:
Pelides grasp'd their hands, and thus begun:
"Princes, all hail! whatever brought you here,
Or strong necessity, or urgent fear;
Welcome, though Greeks! for not as foes ye came;

To me more dear than all that bear the name."
With that, the chiefs beneath his roof he led,
And placed in seats with purple carpets spread.
Then thus—"Patroclus, crown a larger bowl,
Mix purer wine, and open every soul.
Of all the warriors yonder host can send,
Thy friend most honours these, and these thy friend."
He said: Patroclus o'er the blazing fire
Heaps in a brazen vase three chines entire:
The brazen vase Automedon sustains,
Which flesh of porker, sheep, and goat contains.
Achilles at the genial feast presides,
The parts transfixes, and with skill divides.
Meanwhile Patroclus sweats, the fire to raise;
The tent is brighten'd with the rising blaze:
Then, when the languid flames at length subside,
He strows a bed of glowing embers wide,
Above the coals the smoking fragments turns
And sprinkles sacred salt from lifted urns;
With bread the glittering canisters they load,
Which round the board Menoetius' son bestow'd;
Himself, opposed to Ulysses full in sight,
Each portion parts, and orders every rite.
The first fat offering to the immortals due,
Amidst the greedy flames Patroclus threw;
Then each, indulging in the social feast,
His thirst and hunger soberly repress'd.
That done, to Phœnix Ajax gave the sign:
Not unperceived; Ulysses crown'd with wine
The foaming bowl, and instant thus began,
His speech addressing to the godlike man.
"Health to Achilles! happy are thy guests!
Not those more honour'd whom Atrides feasts:
Though generous plenty crown thy loaded boards,
That, Agamemnon's regal tent affords;
But greater cares sit heavy on our souls,
Nor eased by banquets or by flowing bowls.
What scenes of slaughter in yon fields appear!
The dead we mourn, and for the living fear;
Greece on the brink of fate all doubtful stands,
And owns no help but from thy saving hands:
Troy and her aids for ready vengeance call;
Their threatening tents already shade our wall:
Hear how with shouts their conquest they proclaim,
And point at every ship their vengeful flame!
For them the father of the gods declares,

Theirs are his omens, and his thunder theirs.
See, full of Jove, avenging Hector rise!
See! heaven and earth the raging chief defies;
What fury in his breast, what lightning in his eyes!
He waits but for the morn, to sink in flame
The ships, the Greeks, and all the Grecian name.
Heavens! how my country's woes distract my mind,
Lest Fate accomplish all his rage design'd!
And must we, gods! our heads inglorious lay
In Trojan dust, and this the fatal day?
Return, Achilles: oh return, though late,
To save thy Greeks, and stop the course of Fate;
If in that heart or grief or courage lies,
Rise to redeem; ah, yet to conquer, rise!
The day may come, when, all our warriors slain,
That heart shall melt, that courage rise in vain:
Regard in time, O prince divinely brave!
Those wholesome counsels which thy father gave.
When Peleus in his aged arms embraced
His parting son, these accents were his last:
"'My child! with strength, with glory, and success,
Thy arms may Juno and Minerva bless!
Trust that to Heaven: but thou, thy cares engage
To calm thy passions, and subdue thy rage:
From gentler manners let thy glory grow,
And shun contention, the sure source of woe;
That young and old may in thy praise combine,
The virtues of humanity be thine—'
This now-despised advice thy father gave;
Ah! check thy anger; and be truly brave.
If thou wilt yield to great Atrides' prayers,
Gifts worthy thee his royal hand prepares;
If not—but hear me, while I number o'er
The proffer'd presents, an exhaustless store.
Ten weighty talents of the purest gold,
And twice ten vases of refulgent mould;
Seven sacred tripods, whose unsullied frame
Yet knows no office, nor has felt the flame;
Twelve steeds unmatched in fleetness and in force,
And still victorious in the dusty course;
(Rich were the man, whose ample stores exceed
The prizes purchased by their winged speed;)
Seven lovely captives of the Lesbian line,
Skill'd in each art, unmatch'd in form divine,
The same he chose for more than vulgar charms,
When Lesbos sank beneath thy conquering arms.

All these, to buy thy friendship shall be paid,
And, join'd with these, the long-contested maid;
With all her charms, Briseïs he'll resign,
And solemn swear those charms were only thine;
Untouch'd she stay'd, uninjured she removes,
Pure from his arms, and guiltless of his loves.
These instant shall be thine; and if the powers
Give to our arms proud Ilion's hostile towers,
Then shalt thou store (when Greece the spoil divides)
With gold and brass thy loaded navy's sides.
Besides, full twenty nymphs of Trojan race
With copious love shall crown thy warm embrace;
Such as thyself shall chose; who yield to none,
Or yield to Helen's heavenly charms alone.
Yet hear me further: when our wars are o'er,
If safe we land on Argos' fruitful shore,
There shalt thou live his son, his honour share,
And with Orestes' self divide his care.
Yet more—three daughters in his court are bred,
And each well worthy of a royal bed:
Laodice and Iphigenia fair,
And bright Chrysothemis with golden hair:
Her shalt thou wed whom most thy eyes approve;
He asks no presents, no reward for love:
Himself will give the dower; so vast a store
As never father gave a child before.
Seven ample cities shall confess thy sway,
The Enope and Pheræ thee obey,
Cardamyle with ample turrets crown'd,
And sacred Pedasus, for vines renown'd:
Æpea fair, the pastures Hira yields,
And rich Antheia with her flowery fields;
The whole extent to Pylos' sandy plain,
Along the verdant margin of the main.
There heifers graze, and labouring oxen toil;
Bold are the men, and generous is the soil.
There shalt thou reign, with power and justice crown'd,
And rule the tributary realms around.
Such are the proffers which this day we bring,
Such the repentance of a suppliant king.
But if all this, relentless, thou disdain,
If honour and if interest plead in vain,
Yet some redress to suppliant Greece afford,
And be, amongst her guardian gods, adored.
If no regard thy suffering country claim,
Hear thy own glory, and the voice of fame:

For now that chief, whose unresisted ire
Made nations tremble, and whole hosts retire,
Proud Hector, now, the unequal fight demands,
And only triumphs to deserve thy hands."
Then thus the goddess-born: "Ulysses, hear
A faithful speech, that knows nor art nor fear;
What in my secret soul is understood,
My tongue shall utter, and my deeds make good.
Let Greece then know, my purpose I retain:
Nor with new treaties vex my peace in vain.
Who dares think one thing, and another tell,
My heart detests him as the gates of hell.
"Then thus in short my fix'd resolves attend,
Which nor Atrides nor his Greeks can bend;
Long toils, long perils in their cause I bore,
But now the unfruitful glories charm no more.
Fight or not fight, a like reward we claim,
The wretch and hero find their prize the same.
Alike regretted in the dust he lies,
Who yields ignobly, or who bravely dies.
Of all my dangers, all my glorious pains,
A life of labours, lo! what fruit remains?
As the bold bird her helpless young attends,
From danger guards them, and from want defends;
In search of prey she wings the spacious air,
And with the untasted food supplies her care:
For thankless Greece such hardships have I braved,
Her wives, her infants, by my labours saved;
Long sleepless nights in heavy arms I stood,
And sweat laborious days in dust and blood.
I sack'd twelve ample cities on the main,
And twelve lay smoking on the Trojan plain:
Then at Atrides' haughty feet were laid
The wealth I gathered, and the spoils I made.
Your mighty monarch these in peace possess'd;
Some few my soldiers had, himself the rest.
Some present, too, to every prince was paid;
And every prince enjoys the gift he made:
I only must refund, of all his train;
See what pre-eminence our merits gain!
My spoil alone his greedy soul delights:
My spouse alone must bless his lustful nights:
The woman, let him (as he may) enjoy;
But what's the quarrel, then, of Greece to Troy?
What to these shores the assembled nations draws,
What calls for vengeance but a woman's cause?

Are fair endowments and a beauteous face
Beloved by none but those of Atreus' race?
The wife whom choice and passion doth approve,
Sure every wise and worthy man will love.
Nor did my fair one less distinction claim;
Slave as she was, my soul adored the dame.
Wrong'd in my love, all proffers I disdain;
Deceived for once, I trust not kings again.
Ye have my answer—what remains to do,
Your king, Ulysses, may consult with you.
What needs he the defence this arm can make?
Has he not walls no human force can shake?
Has he not fenced his guarded navy round
With piles, with ramparts, and a trench profound?
And will not these (the wonders he has done)
Repel the rage of Priam's single son?
There was a time ('twas when for Greece I fought)
When Hector's prowess no such wonders wrought;
He kept the verge of Troy, nor dared to wait
Achilles' fury at the Scæan gate;
He tried it once, and scarce was saved by fate.
But now those ancient enmities are o'er;
To-morrow we the favouring gods implore;
Then shall you see our parting vessels crown'd,
And hear with oars the Hellespont resound.
The third day hence shall Pythia greet our sails,
If mighty Neptune send propitious gales;
Pythia to her Achilles shall restore
The wealth he left for this detested shore:
Thither the spoils of this long war shall pass,
The ruddy gold, the steel, and shining brass:
My beauteous captives thither I'll convey,
And all that rests of my unravish'd prey.
One only valued gift your tyrant gave,
And that resumed—the fair Lyrnessian slave.
Then tell him: loud, that all the Greeks may hear,
And learn to scorn the wretch they basely fear;
(For arm'd in impudence, mankind he braves,
And meditates new cheats on all his slaves;
Though shameless as he is, to face these eyes
Is what he dares not: if he dares he dies;)
Tell him, all terms, all commerce I decline,
Nor share his council, nor his battle join;
For once deceiv'd, was his; but twice were mine,
No—let the stupid prince, whom Jove deprives
Of sense and justice, run where frenzy drives;

His gifts are hateful: kings of such a kind
Stand but as slaves before a noble mind,
Not though he proffer'd all himself possess'd,
And all his rapine could from others wrest:
Not all the golden tides of wealth that crown
The many-peopled Orchomenian town;
Not all proud Thebes' unrivall'd walls contain,
The world's great empress on the Egyptian plain
(That spreads her conquests o'er a thousand states,
And pours her heroes through a hundred gates,
Two hundred horsemen and two hundred cars
From each wide portal issuing to the wars);
Though bribes were heap'd on bribes, in number more
Than dust in fields, or sands along the shore;
Should all these offers for my friendship call,
'Tis he that offers, and I scorn them all.
Atrides' daughter never shall be led
(An ill-match'd consort) to Achilles' bed;
Like golden Venus though she charm'd the heart,
And vied with Pallas in the works of art;
Some greater Greek let those high nuptials grace,
I hate alliance with a tyrant's race.
If heaven restore me to my realms with life,
The reverend Peleus shall elect my wife;
Thessalian nymphs there are of form divine,
And kings that sue to mix their blood with mine.
Bless'd in kind love, my years shall glide away,
Content with just hereditary sway;
There, deaf for ever to the martial strife,
Enjoy the dear prerogative of life.
Life is not to be bought with heaps of gold.
Not all Apollo's Pythian treasures hold,
Or Troy once held, in peace and pride of sway,
Can bribe the poor possession of a day!
Lost herds and treasures we by arms regain,
And steeds unrivall'd on the dusty plain:
But from our lips the vital spirit fled,
Returns no more to wake the silent dead.
My fates long since by Thetis were disclosed,
And each alternate, life or fame, proposed;
Here, if I stay, before the Trojan town,
Short is my date, but deathless my renown:
If I return, I quit immortal praise
For years on years, and long-extended days.
Convinced, though late, I find my fond mistake,
And warn the Greeks the wiser choice to make;

To quit these shores, their native seats enjoy,
Nor hope the fall of heaven-defended Troy.
Jove's arm display'd asserts her from the skies!
Her hearts are strengthen'd, and her glories rise.
Go then to Greece, report our fix'd design;
Bid all your counsels, all your armies join,
Let all your forces, all your arts conspire,
To save the ships, the troops, the chiefs, from fire.
One stratagem has fail'd, and others will:
Ye find, Achilles is unconquer'd still.
Go then—digest my message as ye may—
But here this night let reverend Phœnix stay:
His tedious toils and hoary hairs demand
A peaceful death in Pythia's friendly land.
But whether he remain or sail with me,
His age be sacred, and his will be free."

The son of Peleus ceased: the chiefs around
In silence wrapt, in consternation drown'd,
Attend the stern reply. Then Phœnix rose;
(Down his white beard a stream of sorrow flows;)
And while the fate of suffering Greece he mourn'd,
With accent weak these tender words return'd.

"Divine Achilles! wilt thou then retire,
And leave our hosts in blood, our fleets on fire?
If wrath so dreadful fill thy ruthless mind,
How shall thy friend, thy Phœnix, stay behind?
The royal Peleus, when from Pythia's coast
He sent thee early to the Achaian host;
Thy youth as then in sage debates unskill'd,
And new to perils of the direful field:
He bade me teach thee all the ways of war,
To shine in councils, and in camps to dare.
Never, ah, never let me leave thy side!
No time shall part us, and no fate divide,
Not though the god, that breathed my life, restore
The bloom I boasted, and the port I bore,
When Greece of old beheld my youthful flames
(Delightful Greece, the land of lovely dames),
My father faithless to my mother's arms,
Old as he was, adored a stranger's charms.
I tried what youth could do (at her desire)
To win the damsel, and prevent my sire.
My sire with curses loads my hated head,
And cries, 'Ye furies! barren be his bed.'

Infernal Jove, the vengeful fiends below,
And ruthless Proserpine, confirm'd his vow.
Despair and grief distract my labouring mind!
Gods! what a crime my impious heart design'd!
I thought (but some kind god that thought suppress'd)
To plunge the poniard in my father's breast;
Then meditate my flight: my friends in vain
With prayers entreat me, and with force detain.
On fat of rams, black bulls, and brawny swine,
They daily feast, with draughts of fragrant wine;
Strong guards they placed, and watch'd nine nights entire;
The roofs and porches flamed with constant fire.
The tenth, I forced the gates, unseen of all:
And, favour'd by the night, o'erleap'd the wall,
My travels thence through spacious Greece extend;
In Phthia's court at last my labours end.
Your sire received me, as his son caress'd,
With gifts enrich'd, and with possessions bless'd.
The strong Dolopians thenceforth own'd my reign,
And all the coast that runs along the main.
By love to thee his bounties I repaid,
And early wisdom to thy soul convey'd:
Great as thou art, my lessons made thee brave:
A child I took thee, but a hero gave.
Thy infant breast a like affection show'd;
Still in my arms (an ever-pleasing load)
Or at my knee, by Phœnix wouldst thou stand;
No food was grateful but from Phœnix' hand.
I pass my watchings o'er thy helpless years,
The tender labours, the compliant cares,
The gods (I thought) reversed their hard decree,
And Phœnix felt a father's joys in thee:
Thy growing virtues justified my cares,
And promised comfort to my silver hairs.
Now be thy rage, thy fatal rage, resign'd;
A cruel heart ill suits a manly mind:
The gods (the only great, and only wise)
Are moved by offerings, vows, and sacrifice;
Offending man their high compassion wins,
And daily prayers atone for daily sins.
Prayers are Jove's daughters, of celestial race,
Lame are their feet, and wrinkled is their face;
With humble mien, and with dejected eyes,
Constant they follow, where injustice flies.
Injustice swift, erect, and unconfined,
Sweeps the wide earth, and tramples o'er mankind,

While Prayers, to heal her wrongs, move slow behind.
Who hears these daughters of almighty Jove,
For him they mediate to the throne above:
When man rejects the humble suit they make,
The sire revenges for the daughters' sake;
From Jove commission'd, fierce injustice then
Descends to punish unrelenting men.
O let not headlong passion bear the sway
These reconciling goddesses obey:
Due honours to the seed of Jove belong,
Due honours calm the fierce, and bend the strong.
Were these not paid thee by the terms we bring,
Were rage still harbour'd in the haughty king;
Nor Greece nor all her fortunes should engage
Thy friend to plead against so just a rage.
But since what honour asks the general sends,
And sends by those whom most thy heart commends;
The best and noblest of the Grecian train;
Permit not these to sue, and sue in vain!
Let me (my son) an ancient fact unfold,
A great example drawn from times of old;
Hear what our fathers were, and what their praise,
Who conquer'd their revenge in former days.
"Where Calydon on rocky mountains stands
Once fought the Ætolian and Curetian bands;
To guard it those; to conquer, these advance;
And mutual deaths were dealt with mutual chance.
The silver Cynthia bade contention rise,
In vengeance of neglected sacrifice;
On Œneus fields she sent a monstrous boar,
That levell'd harvests, and whole forests tore:
This beast (when many a chief his tusks had slain)
Great Meleager stretch'd along the plain,
Then, for his spoils, a new debate arose,
The neighbour nations thence commencing foes.
Strong as they were, the bold Curetes fail'd,
While Meleager's thundering arm prevail'd:
Till rage at length inflamed his lofty breast
(For rage invades the wisest and the best).
"Cursed by Althaea, to his wrath he yields,
And in his wife's embrace forgets the fields.
(She from Marpessa sprung, divinely fair,
And matchless Idas, more than man in war:
The god of day adored the mother's charms;
Against the god the father bent his arms:
The afflicted pair, their sorrows to proclaim,

From Cleopatra changed their daughter's name,
And call'd Alcyone; a name to show
The father's grief, the mourning mother's woe.)
To her the chief retired from stern debate,
But found no peace from fierce Althaea's hate:
Althaea's hate the unhappy warrior drew,
Whose luckless hand his royal uncle slew;
She beat the ground, and call'd the powers beneath
On her own son to wreak her brother's death;
Hell heard her curses from the realms profound,
And the red fiends that walk the nightly round.
In vain Ætolia her deliverer waits,
War shakes her walls, and thunders at her gates.
She sent ambassadors, a chosen band,
Priests of the gods, and elders of the land;
Besought the chief to save the sinking state:
Their prayers were urgent, and their proffers great:
(Full fifty acres of the richest ground,
Half pasture green, and half with vineyards crown'd:)
His suppliant father, aged Œneus, came;
His sisters follow'd; even the vengeful dame,
Althaea, sues; his friends before him fall:
He stands relentless, and rejects them all.
Meanwhile the victor's shouts ascend the skies;
The walls are scaled; the rolling flames arise;
At length his wife (a form divine) appears,
With piercing cries, and supplicating tears;
She paints the horrors of a conquer'd town,
The heroes slain, the palaces o'erthrown,
The matrons ravish'd, the whole race enslaved:
The warrior heard, he vanquish'd, and he saved.
The Ætolians, long disdain'd, now took their turn,
And left the chief their broken faith to mourn.
Learn hence, betimes to curb pernicious ire,
Nor stay till yonder fleets ascend in fire;
Accept the presents; draw thy conquering sword;
And be amongst our guardian gods adored."
Thus he: the stern Achilles thus replied:
"My second father, and my reverend guide:
Thy friend, believe me, no such gifts demands,
And asks no honours from a mortal's hands;
Jove honours me, and favours my designs;
His pleasure guides me, and his will confines;
And here I stay (if such his high behest)
While life's warm spirit beats within my breast.
Yet hear one word, and lodge it in thy heart:

No more molest me on Atrides' part:
Is it for him these tears are taught to flow,
For him these sorrows? for my mortal foe?
A generous friendship no cold medium knows,
Burns with one love, with one resentment glows;
One should our interests and our passions be;
My friend must hate the man that injures me.
Do this, my Phœnix, 'tis a generous part;
And share my realms, my honours, and my heart.
Let these return: our voyage, or our stay,
Rest undetermined till the dawning day."
He ceased; then order'd for the sage's bed
A warmer couch with numerous carpets spread.
With that, stern Ajax his long silence broke,
And thus, impatient, to Ulysses spoke:
"Hence let us go—why waste we time in vain?
See what effect our low submissions gain!
Liked or not liked, his words we must relate,
The Greeks expect them, and our heroes wait.
Proud as he is, that iron heart retains
Its stubborn purpose, and his friends disdains.
Stern and unpitying! if a brother bleed,
On just atonement, we remit the deed;
A sire the slaughter of his son forgives;
The price of blood discharged, the murderer lives:
The haughtiest hearts at length their rage resign,
And gifts can conquer every soul but thine.
The gods that unrelenting breast have steel'd,
And cursed thee with a mind that cannot yield.
One woman-slave was ravish'd from thy arms:
Lo, seven are offer'd, and of equal charms.
Then hear, Achilles! be of better mind;
Revere thy roof, and to thy guests be kind;
And know the men of all the Grecian host,
Who honour worth, and prize thy valour most."
"O soul of battles, and thy people's guide!
(To Ajax thus the first of Greeks replied)
Well hast thou spoke; but at the tyrant's name
My rage rekindles, and my soul's on flame:
'Tis just resentment, and becomes the brave:
Disgraced, dishonour'd, like the vilest slave!
Return, then, heroes! and our answer bear,
The glorious combat is no more my care;
Not till, amidst yon sinking navy slain,
The blood of Greeks shall dye the sable main;
Not till the flames, by Hector's fury thrown,

Consume your vessels, and approach my own;
Just there, the impetuous homicide shall stand,
There cease his battle, and there feel our hand."
This said, each prince a double goblet crown'd,
And cast a large libation on the ground;
Then to their vessels, through the gloomy shades,
The chiefs return; divine Ulysses leads.
Meantime Achilles' slaves prepared a bed,
With fleeces, carpets, and soft linen spread:
There, till the sacred morn restored the day,
In slumber sweet the reverend Phœnix lay.
But in his inner tent, an ampler space,
Achilles slept; and in his warm embrace
Fair Diomede of the Lesbian race.
Last, for Patroclus was the couch prepared,
Whose nightly joys the beauteous Iphis shared;
Achilles to his friend consign'd her charms
When Scyros fell before his conquering arms.
And now the elected chiefs whom Greece had sent,
Pass'd through the hosts, and reach'd the royal tent.
Then rising all, with goblets in their hands,
The peers and leaders of the Achaian bands
Hail'd their return: Atrides first begun:
"Say what success? divine Laertes' son!
Achilles' high resolves declare to all:
Returns the chief, or must our navy fall?"
"Great king of nations! (Ithacus replied)
Fix'd is his wrath, unconquer'd is his pride;
He slights thy friendship, thy proposals scorns,
And, thus implored, with fiercer fury burns.
To save our army, and our fleets to free,
Is not his care; but left to Greece and thee.
Your eyes shall view, when morning paints the sky,
Beneath his oars the whitening billows fly;
Us too he bids our oars and sails employ,
Nor hope the fall of heaven-protected Troy;
For Jove o'ershades her with his arm divine,
Inspires her war, and bids her glory shine.
Such was his word: what further he declared,
These sacred heralds and great Ajax heard.
But Phœnix in his tent the chief retains,
Safe to transport him to his native plains
When morning dawns; if other he decree,
His age is sacred, and his choice is free."
Ulysses ceased: the great Achaian host,
With sorrow seized, in consternation lost,

Attend the stern reply. Tydides broke
The general silence, and undaunted spoke.
"Why should we gifts to proud Achilles send,
Or strive with prayers his haughty soul to bend?
His country's woes he glories to deride,
And prayers will burst that swelling heart with pride.
Be the fierce impulse of his rage obey'd,
Our battles let him or desert or aid;
Then let him arm when Jove or he think fit:
That, to his madness, or to Heaven commit:
What for ourselves we can, is always ours;
This night, let due repast refresh our powers;
(For strength consists in spirits and in blood,
And those are owed to generous wine and food;)
But when the rosy messenger of day
Strikes the blue mountains with her golden ray,
Ranged at the ships, let all our squadrons shine
In flaming arms, a long-extended line:
In the dread front let great Atrides stand,
The first in danger, as in high command."
Shouts of acclaim the listening heroes raise,
Then each to Heaven the due libations pays;
Till sleep, descending o'er the tents, bestows
The grateful blessings of desired repose.

BOOK X.

THE NIGHT-ADVENTURE OF DIOMED AND ULYSSES.

All night the chiefs before their vessels lay,
And lost in sleep the labours of the day:
All but the king: with various thoughts oppress'd,
His country's cares lay rolling in his breast.
As when by lightnings Jove's ethereal power
Foretels the rattling hail, or weighty shower,
Or sends soft snows to whiten all the shore,
Or bids the brazen throat of war to roar;
By fits one flash succeeds as one expires,

And heaven flames thick with momentary fires:
So bursting frequent from Atrides' breast,
Sighs following sighs his inward fears confess'd.
Now o'er the fields, dejected, he surveys
From thousand Trojan fires the mounting blaze;
Hears in the passing wind their music blow,
And marks distinct the voices of the foe.
Now looking backwards to the fleet and coast,
Anxious he sorrows for the endangered host.
He rends his hair, in sacrifice to Jove,
And sues to him that ever lives above:
Inly he groans; while glory and despair
Divide his heart, and wage a double war.
A thousand cares his labouring breast revolves;
To seek sage Nestor now the chief resolves,
With him, in wholesome counsels, to debate
What yet remains to save the afflicted state.
He rose, and first he cast his mantle round,
Next on his feet the shining sandals bound;
A lion's yellow spoils his back conceal'd;
His warlike hand a pointed javelin held.
Meanwhile his brother, press'd with equal woes,
Alike denied the gifts of soft repose,
Laments for Greece, that in his cause before
So much had suffer'd and must suffer more.
A leopard's spotted hide his shoulders spread:
A brazen helmet glitter'd on his head:
Thus (with a javelin in his hand) he went
To wake Atrides in the royal tent.
Already waked, Atrides he descried,
His armour buckling at his vessel's side.
Joyful they met; the Spartan thus begun:
"Why puts my brother his bright armour on?
Sends he some spy, amidst these silent hours,
To try yon camp, and watch the Trojan powers?
But say, what hero shall sustain that task?
Such bold exploits uncommon courage ask;
Guideless, alone, through night's dark shade to go,
And midst a hostile camp explore the foe."
To whom the king: "In such distress we stand,
No vulgar counsel our affairs demand;
Greece to preserve, is now no easy part,
But asks high wisdom, deep design, and art.
For Jove, averse, our humble prayer denies,
And bows his head to Hector's sacrifice.
What eye has witness'd, or what ear believed,

In one great day, by one great arm achieved,
Such wondrous deeds as Hector's hand has done,
And we beheld, the last revolving sun?
What honours the beloved of Jove adorn!
Sprung from no god, and of no goddess born;
Yet such his acts, as Greeks unborn shall tell,
And curse the battle where their fathers fell.
"Now speed thy hasty course along the fleet,
There call great Ajax, and the prince of Crete;
Ourself to hoary Nestor will repair;
To keep the guards on duty be his care,
(For Nestor's influence best that quarter guides,
Whose son with Merion, o'er the watch presides.")
To whom the Spartan: "These thy orders borne,
Say, shall I stay, or with despatch return?"
"There shall thou stay, (the king of men replied,)
Else may we miss to meet, without a guide,
The paths so many, and the camp so wide.
Still, with your voice the slothful soldiers raise,
Urge by their fathers' fame their future praise.
Forget we now our state and lofty birth;
Not titles here, but works, must prove our worth.
To labour is the lot of man below;
And when Jove gave us life, he gave us woe."
This said, each parted to his several cares:
The king to Nestor's sable ship repairs;
The sage protector of the Greeks he found
Stretch'd in his bed with all his arms around;
The various-colour'd scarf, the shield he rears,
The shining helmet, and the pointed spears;
The dreadful weapons of the warrior's rage,
That, old in arms, disdain'd the peace of age.
Then, leaning on his hand his watchful head,
The hoary monarch raised his eyes and said:
"What art thou, speak, that on designs unknown,
While others sleep, thus range the camp alone;
Seek'st thou some friend or nightly sentinel?
Stand off, approach not, but thy purpose tell."
"O son of Neleus, (thus the king rejoin'd,)
Pride of the Greeks, and glory of thy kind!
Lo, here the wretched Agamemnon stands,
The unhappy general of the Grecian bands,
Whom Jove decrees with daily cares to bend,
And woes, that only with his life shall end!
Scarce can my knees these trembling limbs sustain,
And scarce my heart support its load of pain.

No taste of sleep these heavy eyes have known,
Confused, and sad, I wander thus alone,
With fears distracted, with no fix'd design;
And all my people's miseries are mine.
If aught of use thy waking thoughts suggest,
(Since cares, like mine, deprive thy soul of rest,)
Impart thy counsel, and assist thy friend;
Now let us jointly to the trench descend,
At every gate the fainting guard excite,
Tired with the toils of day and watch of night;
Else may the sudden foe our works invade,
So near, and favour'd by the gloomy shade."
To him thus Nestor: "Trust the powers above,
Nor think proud Hector's hopes confirm'd by Jove:
How ill agree the views of vain mankind,
And the wise counsels of the eternal mind!
Audacious Hector, if the gods ordain
That great Achilles rise and rage again,
What toils attend thee, and what woes remain!
Lo, faithful Nestor thy command obeys;
The care is next our other chiefs to raise:
Ulysses, Diomed, we chiefly need;
Meges for strength, Oïleus famed for speed.
Some other be despatch'd of nimbler feet,
To those tall ships, remotest of the fleet,
Where lie great Ajax and the king of Crete.
To rouse the Spartan I myself decree;
Dear as he is to us, and dear to thee,
Yet must I tax his sloth, that claims no share
With his great brother in his martial care:
Him it behoved to every chief to sue,
Preventing every part perform'd by you;
For strong necessity our toils demands,
Claims all our hearts, and urges all our hands."
To whom the king: "With reverence we allow
Thy just rebukes, yet learn to spare them now:
My generous brother is of gentle kind,
He seems remiss, but bears a valiant mind;
Through too much deference to our sovereign sway,
Content to follow when we lead the way:
But now, our ills industrious to prevent,
Long ere the rest he rose, and sought my tent.
The chiefs you named, already at his call,
Prepare to meet us near the navy-wall;
Assembling there, between the trench and gates,
Near the night-guards, our chosen council waits."

"Then none (said Nestor) shall his rule withstand,
For great examples justify command."
With that, the venerable warrior rose;
The shining greaves his manly legs enclose;
His purple mantle golden buckles join'd,
Warm with the softest wool, and doubly lined.
Then rushing from his tent, he snatch'd in haste
His steely lance, that lighten'd as he pass'd.
The camp he traversed through the sleeping crowd,
Stopp'd at Ulysses' tent, and call'd aloud.
Ulysses, sudden as the voice was sent,
Awakes, starts up, and issues from his tent.
"What new distress, what sudden cause of fright,
Thus leads you wandering in the silent night?"
"O prudent chief! (the Pylian sage replied)
Wise as thou art, be now thy wisdom tried:
Whatever means of safety can be sought,
Whatever counsels can inspire our thought,
Whatever methods, or to fly or fight;
All, all depend on this important night!"
He heard, return'd, and took his painted shield;
Then join'd the chiefs, and follow'd through the field.
Without his tent, bold Diomed they found,
All sheathed in arms, his brave companions round:
Each sunk in sleep, extended on the field,
His head reclining on his bossy shield.
A wood of spears stood by, that, fix'd upright,
Shot from their flashing points a quivering light.
A bull's black hide composed the hero's bed;
A splendid carpet roll'd beneath his head.
Then, with his foot, old Nestor gently shakes
The slumbering chief, and in these words awakes:
"Rise, son of Tydeus! to the brave and strong
Rest seems inglorious, and the night too long.
But sleep'st thou now, when from yon hill the foe
Hangs o'er the fleet, and shades our walls below?"
At this, soft slumber from his eyelids fled;
The warrior saw the hoary chief, and said:
"Wondrous old man! whose soul no respite knows,
Though years and honours bid thee seek repose,
Let younger Greeks our sleeping warriors wake;
Ill fits thy age these toils to undertake."
"My friend, (he answered,) generous is thy care;
These toils, my subjects and my sons might bear;
Their loyal thoughts and pious love conspire
To ease a sovereign and relieve a sire:

But now the last despair surrounds our host;
No hour must pass, no moment must be lost;
Each single Greek, in this conclusive strife,
Stands on the sharpest edge of death or life:
Yet, if my years thy kind regard engage,
Employ thy youth as I employ my age;
Succeed to these my cares, and rouse the rest;
He serves me most, who serves his country best."
This said, the hero o'er his shoulders flung
A lion's spoils, that to his ankles hung;
Then seized his ponderous lance, and strode along.
Meges the bold, with Ajax famed for speed,
The warrior roused, and to the entrenchments lead.
And now the chiefs approach the nightly guard;
A wakeful squadron, each in arms prepared:
The unwearied watch their listening leaders keep,
And, couching close, repel invading sleep.
So faithful dogs their fleecy charge maintain,
With toil protected from the prowling train;
When the gaunt lioness, with hunger bold,
Springs from the mountains toward the guarded fold:
Through breaking woods her rustling course they hear;
Loud, and more loud, the clamours strike their ear
Of hounds and men: they start, they gaze around,
Watch every side, and turn to every sound.
Thus watch'd the Grecians, cautious of surprise,
Each voice, each motion, drew their ears and eyes:
Each step of passing feet increased the affright;
And hostile Troy was ever full in sight.
Nestor with joy the wakeful band survey'd,
And thus accosted through the gloomy shade.
"'Tis well, my sons! your nightly cares employ;
Else must our host become the scorn of Troy.
Watch thus, and Greece shall live." The hero said;
Then o'er the trench the following chieftains led.
His son, and godlike Merion, march'd behind
(For these the princes to their council join'd).
The trenches pass'd, the assembled kings around
In silent state the consistory crown'd.
A place there was, yet undefiled with gore,
The spot where Hector stopp'd his rage before;
When night descending, from his vengeful hand
Reprieved the relics of the Grecian band:
(The plain beside with mangled corps was spread,
And all his progress mark'd by heaps of dead:)
There sat the mournful kings: when Neleus' son,

The council opening, in these words begun:
"Is there (said he) a chief so greatly brave,
His life to hazard, and his country save?
Lives there a man, who singly dares to go
To yonder camp, or seize some straggling foe?
Or favour'd by the night approach so near,
Their speech, their counsels, and designs to hear?
If to besiege our navies they prepare,
Or Troy once more must be the seat of war?
This could he learn, and to our peers recite,
And pass unharm'd the dangers of the night;
What fame were his through all succeeding days,
While Phœbus shines, or men have tongues to praise!
What gifts his grateful country would bestow!
What must not Greece to her deliverer owe?
A sable ewe each leader should provide,
With each a sable lambkin by her side;
At every rite his share should be increased,
And his the foremost honours of the feast."
Fear held them mute: alone, untaught to fear,
Tydides spoke—"The man you seek is here.
Through yon black camps to bend my dangerous way,
Some god within commands, and I obey.
But let some other chosen warrior join,
To raise my hopes, and second my design.
By mutual confidence and mutual aid,
Great deeds are done, and great discoveries made;
The wise new prudence from the wise acquire,
And one brave hero fans another's fire."
Contending leaders at the word arose;
Each generous breast with emulation glows;
So brave a task each Ajax strove to share,
Bold Merion strove, and Nestor's valiant heir;
The Spartan wish'd the second place to gain,
And great Ulysses wish'd, nor wish'd in vain.
Then thus the king of men the contest ends:
"Thou first of warriors, and thou best of friends,
Undaunted Diomed! what chief to join
In this great enterprise, is only thine.
Just be thy choice, without affection made;
To birth, or office, no respect be paid;
Let worth determine here." The monarch spake,
And inly trembled for his brother's sake.
"Then thus (the godlike Diomed rejoin'd)
My choice declares the impulse of my mind.
How can I doubt, while great Ulysses stands

To lend his counsels and assist our hands?
A chief, whose safety is Minerva's care;
So famed, so dreadful, in the works of war:
Bless'd in his conduct, I no aid require;
Wisdom like his might pass through flames of fire."
"It fits thee not, before these chiefs of fame,
(Replied the sage,) to praise me, or to blame:
Praise from a friend, or censure from a foe,
Are lost on hearers that our merits know.
But let us haste—Night rolls the hours away,
The reddening orient shows the coming day,
The stars shine fainter on the ethereal plains,
And of night's empire but a third remains."
Thus having spoke, with generous ardour press'd,
In arms terrific their huge limbs they dress'd.
A two-edged falchion Thrasymed the brave,
And ample buckler, to Tydides gave:
Then in a leathern helm he cased his head,
Short of its crest, and with no plume o'erspread:
(Such as by youths unused to arms are worn:)
No spoils enrich it, and no studs adorn.
Next him Ulysses took a shining sword,
A bow and quiver, with bright arrows stored:
A well-proved casque, with leather braces bound,
(Thy gift, Meriones,) his temples crown'd;
Soft wool within; without, in order spread,
A boar's white teeth grinn'd horrid o'er his head.
This from Amyntor, rich Ormenus' son,
Autolycus by fraudful rapine won,
And gave Amphidamas; from him the prize
Molus received, the pledge of social ties;
The helmet next by Merion was possess'd,
And now Ulysses' thoughtful temples press'd.
Thus sheathed in arms, the council they forsake,
And dark through paths oblique their progress take.
Just then, in sign she favour'd their intent,
A long-wing'd heron great Minerva sent:
This, though surrounding shades obscured their view,
By the shrill clang and whistling wings they knew.
As from the right she soar'd, Ulysses pray'd,
Hail'd the glad omen, and address'd the maid:
"O daughter of that god whose arm can wield
The avenging bolt, and shake the saber shield!
O thou! for ever present in my way,
Who all my motions, all my toils survey!
Safe may we pass beneath the gloomy shade,

Safe by thy succour to our ships convey'd,
And let some deed this signal night adorn,
To claim the tears of Trojans yet unborn."
Then godlike Diomed preferr'd his prayer:
"Daughter of Jove, unconquer'd Pallas! hear.
Great queen of arms, whose favour Tydeus won,
As thou defend'st the sire, defend the son.
When on Æsopus' banks the banded powers
Of Greece he left, and sought the Theban towers,
Peace was his charge; received with peaceful show,
He went a legate, but return'd a foe:
Then help'd by thee, and cover'd by thy shield,
He fought with numbers, and made numbers yield.
So now be present, O celestial maid!
So still continue to the race thine aid!
A youthful steer shall fall beneath the stroke,
Untamed, unconscious of the galling yoke,
With ample forehead, and with spreading horns,
Whose taper tops refulgent gold adorns."
The heroes pray'd, and Pallas from the skies
Accords their vow, succeeds their enterprise.
Now, like two lions panting for the prey,
With dreadful thoughts they trace the dreary way,
Through the black horrors of the ensanguined plain,
Through dust, through blood, o'er arms, and hills of slain.
Nor less bold Hector, and the sons of Troy,
On high designs the wakeful hours employ;
The assembled peers their lofty chief enclosed;
Who thus the counsels of his breast proposed:
"What glorious man, for high attempts prepared,
Dares greatly venture for a rich reward?
Of yonder fleet a bold discovery make,
What watch they keep, and what resolves they take?
If now subdued they meditate their flight,
And, spent with toil, neglect the watch of night?
His be the chariot that shall please him most,
Of all the plunder of the vanquish'd host;
His the fair steeds that all the rest excel,
And his the glory to have served so well."
A youth there was among the tribes of Troy,
Dolon his name, Eumedes' only boy,
(Five girls beside the reverend herald told.)
Rich was the son in brass, and rich in gold;
Not bless'd by nature with the charms of face,
But swift of foot, and matchless in the race.
"Hector! (he said) my courage bids me meet

This high achievement, and explore the fleet:
But first exalt thy sceptre to the skies,
And swear to grant me the demanded prize;
The immortal coursers, and the glittering car,
That bear Pelides through the ranks of war.
Encouraged thus, no idle scout I go,
Fulfil thy wish, their whole intention know,
Even to the royal tent pursue my way,
And all their counsels, all their aims betray."
The chief then heaved the golden sceptre high,
Attesting thus the monarch of the sky:
"Be witness thou! immortal lord of all!
Whose thunder shakes the dark aerial hall:
By none but Dolon shall this prize be borne,
And him alone the immortal steeds adorn."
Thus Hector swore: the gods were call'd in vain,
But the rash youth prepares to scour the plain:
Across his back the bended bow he flung,
A wolf's grey hide around his shoulders hung,
A ferret's downy fur his helmet lined,
And in his hand a pointed javelin shined.
Then (never to return) he sought the shore,
And trod the path his feet must tread no more.
Scarce had he pass'd the steeds and Trojan throng,
(Still bending forward as he coursed along,)
When, on the hollow way, the approaching tread
Ulysses mark'd, and thus to Diomed;
"O friend! I hear some step of hostile feet,
Moving this way, or hastening to the fleet;
Some spy, perhaps, to lurk beside the main;
Or nightly pillager that strips the slain.
Yet let him pass, and win a little space;
Then rush behind him, and prevent his pace.
But if too swift of foot he flies before,
Confine his course along the fleet and shore,
Betwixt the camp and him our spears employ,
And intercept his hoped return to Troy."
With that they stepp'd aside, and stoop'd their head,
(As Dolon pass'd,) behind a heap of dead:
Along the path the spy unwary flew;
Soft, at just distance, both the chiefs pursue.
So distant they, and such the space between,
As when two teams of mules divide the green,
(To whom the hind like shares of land allows,)
When now new furrows part the approaching ploughs.
Now Dolon, listening, heard them as they pass'd;

Hector (he thought) had sent, and check'd his haste,
Till scarce at distance of a javelin's throw,
No voice succeeding, he perceived the foe.
As when two skilful hounds the leveret wind;
Or chase through woods obscure the trembling hind;
Now lost, now seen, they intercept his way,
And from the herd still turn the flying prey:
So fast, and with such fears, the Trojan flew;
So close, so constant, the bold Greeks pursue.
Now almost on the fleet the dastard falls,
And mingles with the guards that watch the walls;
When brave Tydides stopp'd; a gen'rous thought
(Inspired by Pallas) in his bosom wrought,
Lest on the foe some forward Greek advance,
And snatch the glory from his lifted lance.
Then thus aloud: "Whoe'er thou art, remain;
This javelin else shall fix thee to the plain."
He said, and high in air the weapon cast,
Which wilful err'd, and o'er his shoulder pass'd;
Then fix'd in earth. Against the trembling wood
The wretch stood propp'd, and quiver'd as he stood;
A sudden palsy seized his turning head;
His loose teeth chatter'd, and his colour fled;
The panting warriors seize him as he stands,
And with unmanly tears his life demands.
"O spare my youth, and for the breath I owe,
Large gifts of price my father shall bestow:
Vast heaps of brass shall in your ships be told,
And steel well-temper'd and refulgent gold."
To whom Ulysses made this wise reply:
"Whoe'er thou art, be bold, nor fear to die.
What moves thee, say, when sleep has closed the sight,
To roam the silent fields in dead of night?
Cam'st thou the secrets of our camp to find,
By Hector prompted, or thy daring mind?
Or art some wretch by hopes of plunder led,
Through heaps of carnage, to despoil the dead?"
Then thus pale Dolon, with a fearful look:
(Still, as he spoke, his limbs with horror shook:)
"Hither I came, by Hector's words deceived;
Much did he promise, rashly I believed:
No less a bribe than great Achilles' car,
And those swift steeds that sweep the ranks of war,
Urged me, unwilling, this attempt to make;
To learn what counsels, what resolves you take:
If now subdued, you fix your hopes on flight,

And, tired with toils, neglect the watch of night."
"Bold was thy aim, and glorious was the prize,
(Ulysses, with a scornful smile, replies,)
Far other rulers those proud steeds demand,
And scorn the guidance of a vulgar hand;
Even great Achilles scarce their rage can tame,
Achilles sprung from an immortal dame.
But say, be faithful, and the truth recite!
Where lies encamp'd the Trojan chief to-night?
Where stand his coursers? in what quarter sleep
Their other princes? tell what watch they keep:
Say, since this conquest, what their counsels are;
Or here to combat, from their city far,
Or back to Ilion's walls transfer the war?"
Ulysses thus, and thus Eumedes' son:
"What Dolon knows, his faithful tongue shall own.
Hector, the peers assembling in his tent,
A council holds at Ilus' monument.
No certain guards the nightly watch partake;
Where'er yon fires ascend, the Trojans wake:
Anxious for Troy, the guard the natives keep;
Safe in their cares, the auxiliar forces sleep,
Whose wives and infants, from the danger far,
Discharge their souls of half the fears of war."
"Then sleep those aids among the Trojan train,
(Inquired the chief,) or scattered o'er the plain?"
To whom the spy: "Their powers they thus dispose
The Paeons, dreadful with their bended bows,
The Carians, Caucons, the Pelasgian host,
And Leleges, encamp along the coast.
Not distant far, lie higher on the land
The Lycian, Mysian, and Mæonian band,
And Phrygia's horse, by Thymbras' ancient wall;
The Thracians utmost, and apart from all.
These Troy but lately to her succour won,
Led on by Rhesus, great Eioneus' son:
I saw his coursers in proud triumph go,
Swift as the wind, and white as winter-snow;
Rich silver plates his shining car infold;
His solid arms, refulgent, flame with gold;
No mortal shoulders suit the glorious load,
Celestial panoply, to grace a god!
Let me, unhappy, to your fleet be borne,
Or leave me here, a captive's fate to mourn,
In cruel chains, till your return reveal
The truth or falsehood of the news I tell."

To this Tydides, with a gloomy frown:
"Think not to live, though all the truth be shown:
Shall we dismiss thee, in some future strife
To risk more bravely thy now forfeit life?
Or that again our camps thou may'st explore?
No—once a traitor, thou betray'st no more."
Sternly he spoke, and as the wretch prepared
With humble blandishment to stroke his beard,
Like lightning swift the wrathful falchion flew,
Divides the neck, and cuts the nerves in two;
One instant snatch'd his trembling soul to hell,
The head, yet speaking, mutter'd as it fell.
The furry helmet from his brow they tear,
The wolf's grey hide, the unbended bow and spear;
These great Ulysses lifting to the skies,
To favouring Pallas dedicates the prize:
"Great queen of arms, receive this hostile spoil,
And let the Thracian steeds reward our toil;
Thee, first of all the heavenly host, we praise;
O speed our labours, and direct our ways!"
This said, the spoils, with dropping gore defaced,
High on a spreading tamarisk he placed;
Then heap'd with reeds and gathered boughs the plain,
To guide their footsteps to the place again.
Through the still night they cross the devious fields,
Slippery with blood, o'er arms and heaps of shields,
Arriving where the Thracian squadrons lay,
And eased in sleep the labours of the day.
Ranged in three lines they view the prostrate band:
The horses yoked beside each warrior stand.
Their arms in order on the ground reclined,
Through the brown shade the fulgid weapons shined:
Amidst lay Rhesus, stretch'd in sleep profound,
And the white steeds behind his chariot bound.
The welcome sight Ulysses first descries,
And points to Diomed the tempting prize.
"The man, the coursers, and the car behold!
Described by Dolon, with the arms of gold.
Now, brave Tydides! now thy courage try,
Approach the chariot, and the steeds untie;
Or if thy soul aspire to fiercer deeds,
Urge thou the slaughter, while I seize the steeds."
Pallas (this said) her hero's bosom warms,
Breathed in his heart, and strung his nervous arms;
Where'er he pass'd, a purple stream pursued
His thirsty falchion, fat with hostile blood,

Bathed all his footsteps, dyed the fields with gore,
And a low groan remurmur'd through the shore.
So the grim lion, from his nightly den,
O'erleaps the fences, and invades the pen,
On sheep or goats, resistless in his way,
He falls, and foaming rends the guardless prey;
Nor stopp'd the fury of his vengeful hand,
Till twelve lay breathless of the Thracian band.
Ulysses following, as his partner slew,
Back by the foot each slaughter'd warrior drew;
The milk-white coursers studious to convey
Safe to the ships, he wisely cleared the way:
Lest the fierce steeds, not yet to battles bred,
Should start, and tremble at the heaps of dead.
Now twelve despatch'd, the monarch last they found;
Tydides' falchion fix'd him to the ground.
Just then a deathful dream Minerva sent,
A warlike form appear'd before his tent,
Whose visionary steel his bosom tore:
So dream'd the monarch, and awaked no more.
Ulysses now the snowy steeds detains,
And leads them, fasten'd by the silver reins;
These, with his bow unbent, he lash'd along;
(The scourge forgot, on Rhesus' chariot hung;)
Then gave his friend the signal to retire;
But him, new dangers, new achievements fire;
Doubtful he stood, or with his reeking blade
To send more heroes to the infernal shade,
Drag off the car where Rhesus' armour lay,
Or heave with manly force, and lift away.
While unresolved the son of Tydeus stands,
Pallas appears, and thus her chief commands:
"Enough, my son; from further slaughter cease,
Regard thy safety, and depart in peace;
Haste to the ships, the gotten spoils enjoy,
Nor tempt too far the hostile gods of Troy."
The voice divine confess'd the martial maid;
In haste he mounted, and her word obey'd;
The coursers fly before Ulysses' bow,
Swift as the wind, and white as winter-snow.
Not unobserved they pass'd: the god of light
Had watch'd his Troy, and mark'd Minerva's flight,
Saw Tydeus' son with heavenly succour bless'd,
And vengeful anger fill'd his sacred breast.
Swift to the Trojan camp descends the power,
And wakes Hippocoon in the morning-hour;

(On Rhesus' side accustom'd to attend,
A faithful kinsman, and instructive friend;)
He rose, and saw the field deform'd with blood,
An empty space where late the coursers stood,
The yet-warm Thracians panting on the coast;
For each he wept, but for his Rhesus most:
Now while on Rhesus' name he calls in vain,
The gathering tumult spreads o'er all the plain;
On heaps the Trojans rush, with wild affright,
And wondering view the slaughters of the night.
Meanwhile the chiefs, arriving at the shade
Where late the spoils of Hector's spy were laid,
Ulysses stopp'd; to him Tydides bore
The trophy, dropping yet with Dolon's gore:
Then mounts again; again their nimbler feet
The coursers ply, and thunder towards the fleet.

Old Nestor first perceived the approaching sound,
Bespeaking thus the Grecian peers around:
"Methinks the noise of trampling steeds I hear,
Thickening this way, and gathering on my ear;
Perhaps some horses of the Trojan breed
(So may, ye gods! my pious hopes succeed)
The great Tydides and Ulysses bear,
Return'd triumphant with this prize of war.
Yet much I fear (ah, may that fear be vain!)
The chiefs outnumber'd by the Trojan train;
Perhaps, even now pursued, they seek the shore;
Or, oh! perhaps those heroes are no more."
Scarce had he spoke, when, lo! the chiefs appear,
And spring to earth; the Greeks dismiss their fear:
With words of friendship and extended hands
They greet the kings; and Nestor first demands:
"Say thou, whose praises all our host proclaim,
Thou living glory of the Grecian name!
Say whence these coursers? by what chance bestow'd,
The spoil of foes, or present of a god?
Not those fair steeds, so radiant and so gay,
That draw the burning chariot of the day.
Old as I am, to age I scorn to yield,
And daily mingle in the martial field;
But sure till now no coursers struck my sight
Like these, conspicuous through the ranks of fight.
Some god, I deem, conferred the glorious prize,
Bless'd as ye are, and favourites of the skies;
The care of him who bids the thunder roar,

And her, whose fury bathes the world with gore."
"Father! not so, (sage Ithacus rejoin'd,)
The gifts of heaven are of a nobler kind.
Of Thracian lineage are the steeds ye view,
Whose hostile king the brave Tydides slew;
Sleeping he died, with all his guards around,
And twelve beside lay gasping on the ground.
These other spoils from conquer'd Dolon came,
A wretch, whose swiftness was his only fame;
By Hector sent our forces to explore,
He now lies headless on the sandy shore."
Then o'er the trench the bounding coursers flew;
The joyful Greeks with loud acclaim pursue.
Straight to Tydides' high pavilion borne,
The matchless steeds his ample stalls adorn:
The neighing coursers their new fellows greet,
And the full racks are heap'd with generous wheat.
But Dolon's armour, to his ships convey'd,
High on the painted stern Ulysses laid,
A trophy destin'd to the blue-eyed maid.
Now from nocturnal sweat and sanguine stain
They cleanse their bodies in the neighb'ring main:
Then in the polished bath, refresh'd from toil,
Their joints they supple with dissolving oil,
In due repast indulge the genial hour,
And first to Pallas the libations pour:
They sit, rejoicing in her aid divine,
And the crown'd goblet foams with floods of wine.

BOOK XI.

THE THIRD BATTLE, AND THE ACTS OF AGAMEMNON.

The saffron morn, with early blushes spread,
Now rose refulgent from Tithonus' bed;
With new-born day to gladden mortal sight,
And gild the courts of heaven with sacred light:
When baleful Eris, sent by Jove's command,
The torch of discord blazing in her hand,
Through the red skies her bloody sign extends,
And, wrapt in tempests, o'er the fleet descends.
High on Ulysses' bark her horrid stand
She took, and thunder'd through the seas and land.
Even Ajax and Achilles heard the sound,

Whose ships, remote, the guarded navy bound,
Thence the black fury through the Grecian throng
With horror sounds the loud Orthian song:
The navy shakes, and at the dire alarms
Each bosom boils, each warrior starts to arms.
No more they sigh, inglorious to return,
But breathe revenge, and for the combat burn.

The king of men his hardy host inspires
With loud command, with great example fires!
Himself first rose, himself before the rest
His mighty limbs in radiant armour dress'd,
And first he cased his manly legs around
In shining greaves with silver buckles bound;
The beaming cuirass next adorn'd his breast,
The same which once king Cinyras possess'd:
(The fame of Greece and her assembled host
Had reach'd that monarch on the Cyprian coast;
'Twas then, the friendship of the chief to gain,
This glorious gift he sent, nor sent in vain:)
Ten rows of azure steel the work infold,
Twice ten of tin, and twelve of ductile gold;
Three glittering dragons to the gorget rise,
Whose imitated scales against the skies
Reflected various light, and arching bow'd,
Like colour'd rainbows o'er a showery cloud
(Jove's wondrous bow, of three celestial dies,
Placed as a sign to man amidst the skies).
A radiant baldric, o'er his shoulder tied,
Sustain'd the sword that glitter'd at his side:
Gold was the hilt, a silver sheath encased
The shining blade, and golden hangers graced.
His buckler's mighty orb was next display'd,
That round the warrior cast a dreadful shade;
Ten zones of brass its ample brim surround,
And twice ten bosses the bright convex crown'd:
Tremendous Gorgon frown'd upon its field,
And circling terrors fill'd the expressive shield:
Within its concave hung a silver thong,
On which a mimic serpent creeps along,
His azure length in easy waves extends,
Till in three heads the embroider'd monster ends.
Last o'er his brows his fourfold helm he placed,
With nodding horse-hair formidably graced;
And in his hands two steely javelins wields,
That blaze to heaven, and lighten all the fields.

That instant Juno, and the martial maid,
In happy thunders promised Greece their aid;
High o'er the chief they clash'd their arms in air,
And, leaning from the clouds, expect the war.
Close to the limits of the trench and mound,
The fiery coursers to their chariots bound
The squires restrain'd: the foot, with those who wield
The lighter arms, rush forward to the field.
To second these, in close array combined,
The squadrons spread their sable wings behind.
Now shouts and tumults wake the tardy sun,
As with the light the warriors' toils begun.
Even Jove, whose thunder spoke his wrath, distill'd
Red drops of blood o'er all the fatal field;
The woes of men unwilling to survey,
And all the slaughters that must stain the day.
Near Ilus' tomb, in order ranged around,
The Trojan lines possess'd the rising ground:
There wise Polydamas and Hector stood;
Æneas, honour'd as a guardian god;
Bold Polybus, Agenor the divine;
The brother-warriors of Antenor's line:
With youthful Acamas, whose beauteous face
And fair proportion match'd the ethereal race.
Great Hector, cover'd with his spacious shield,
Plies all the troops, and orders all the field.
As the red star now shows his sanguine fires
Through the dark clouds, and now in night retires,
Thus through the ranks appear'd the godlike man,
Plunged in the rear, or blazing in the van;
While streamy sparkles, restless as he flies,
Flash from his arms, as lightning from the skies.
As sweating reapers in some wealthy field,
Ranged in two bands, their crooked weapons wield,
Bear down the furrows, till their labours meet;
Thick fall the heapy harvests at their feet:
So Greece and Troy the field of war divide,
And falling ranks are strow'd on every side.
None stoop'd a thought to base inglorious flight;
But horse to horse, and man to man they fight,
Not rabid wolves more fierce contest their prey;
Each wounds, each bleeds, but none resign the day.
Discord with joy the scene of death descries,
And drinks large slaughter at her sanguine eyes:
Discord alone, of all the immortal train,
Swells the red horrors of this direful plain:

The gods in peace their golden mansions fill,
Ranged in bright order on the Olympian hill:
But general murmurs told their griefs above,
And each accused the partial will of Jove.
Meanwhile apart, superior, and alone,
The eternal Monarch, on his awful throne,
Wrapt in the blaze of boundless glory sate;
And fix'd, fulfill'd the just decrees of fate.
On earth he turn'd his all-considering eyes,
And mark'd the spot where Ilion's towers arise;
The sea with ships, the fields with armies spread,
The victor's rage, the dying, and the dead.
Thus while the morning-beams, increasing bright,
O'er heaven's pure azure spread the glowing light,
Commutual death the fate of war confounds,
Each adverse battle gored with equal wounds.
But now (what time in some sequester'd vale
The weary woodman spreads his sparing meal,
When his tired arms refuse the axe to rear,
And claim a respite from the sylvan war;
But not till half the prostrate forests lay
Stretch'd in long ruin, and exposed to day)
Then, nor till then, the Greeks' impulsive might
Pierced the black phalanx, and let in the light.
Great Agamemnon then the slaughter led,
And slew Bienor at his people's head:
Whose squire Oïleus, with a sudden spring,
Leap'd from the chariot to revenge his king;
But in his front he felt the fatal wound,
Which pierced his brain, and stretch'd him on the ground.
Atrides spoil'd, and left them on the plain:
Vain was their youth, their glittering armour vain:
Now soil'd with dust, and naked to the sky,
Their snowy limbs and beauteous bodies lie.
Two sons of Priam next to battle move,
The product, one of marriage, one of love:
In the same car the brother-warriors ride;
This took the charge to combat, that to guide:
Far other task, than when they wont to keep,
On Ida's tops, their father's fleecy sheep.
These on the mountains once Achilles found,
And captive led, with pliant osiers bound;
Then to their sire for ample sums restored;
But now to perish by Atrides' sword:
Pierced in the breast the base-born Isus bleeds:
Cleft through the head his brother's fate succeeds,

Swift to the spoil the hasty victor falls,
And, stript, their features to his mind recalls.
The Trojans see the youths untimely die,
But helpless tremble for themselves, and fly.
So when a lion ranging o'er the lawns,
Finds, on some grassy lair, the couching fawns,
Their bones he cracks, their reeking vitals draws,
And grinds the quivering flesh with bloody jaws;
The frighted hind beholds, and dares not stay,
But swift through rustling thickets bursts her way;
All drown'd in sweat, the panting mother flies,
And the big tears roll trickling from her eyes.
Amidst the tumult of the routed train,
The sons of false Antimachus were slain;
He who for bribes his faithless counsels sold,
And voted Helen's stay for Paris' gold.
Atrides mark'd, as these their safety sought,
And slew the children for the father's fault;
Their headstrong horse unable to restrain,
They shook with fear, and dropp'd the silken rein;
Then in the chariot on their knees they fall,
And thus with lifted hands for mercy call:
"O spare our youth, and for the life we owe,
Antimachus shall copious gifts bestow:
Soon as he hears, that, not in battle slain,
The Grecian ships his captive sons detain,
Large heaps of brass in ransom shall be told,
And steel well-tempered, and persuasive gold."
These words, attended with the flood of tears,
The youths address'd to unrelenting ears:
The vengeful monarch gave this stern reply:
"If from Antimachus ye spring, ye die;
The daring wretch who once in council stood
To shed Ulysses' and my brother's blood,
For proffer'd peace! and sues his seed for grace?
No, die, and pay the forfeit of your race."
This said, Pisander from the car he cast,
And pierced his breast: supine he breathed his last.
His brother leap'd to earth; but, as he lay,
The trenchant falchion lopp'd his hands away;
His sever'd head was toss'd among the throng,
And, rolling, drew a bloody train along.
Then, where the thickest fought, the victor flew;
The king's example all his Greeks pursue.
Now by the foot the flying foot were slain,
Horse trod by horse, lay foaming on the plain.

From the dry fields thick clouds of dust arise,
Shade the black host, and intercept the skies.
The brass-hoof'd steeds tumultuous plunge and bound,
And the thick thunder beats the labouring ground,
Still slaughtering on, the king of men proceeds;
The distanced army wonders at his deeds,
As when the winds with raging flames conspire,
And o'er the forests roll the flood of fire,
In blazing heaps the grove's old honours fall,
And one refulgent ruin levels all:
Before Atrides' rage so sinks the foe,
Whole squadrons vanish, and proud heads lie low.
The steeds fly trembling from his waving sword,
And many a car, now lighted of its lord,
Wide o'er the field with guideless fury rolls,
Breaking their ranks, and crushing out their souls;
While his keen falchion drinks the warriors' lives;
More grateful, now, to vultures than their wives!
Perhaps great Hector then had found his fate,
But Jove and destiny prolong'd his date.
Safe from the darts, the care of heaven he stood,
Amidst alarms, and death, and dust, and blood.
Now past the tomb where ancient Ilus lay,
Through the mid field the routed urge their way:
Where the wild figs the adjoining summit crown,
The path they take, and speed to reach the town.
As swift, Atrides with loud shouts pursued,
Hot with his toil, and bathed in hostile blood.
Now near the beech-tree, and the Scæan gates,
The hero halts, and his associates waits.
Meanwhile on every side around the plain,
Dispersed, disorder'd, fly the Trojan train.
So flies a herd of beeves, that hear dismay'd
The lion's roaring through the midnight shade;
On heaps they tumble with successless haste;
The savage seizes, draws, and rends the last.
Not with less fury stern Atrides flew,
Still press'd the rout, and still the hindmost slew;
Hurl'd from their cars the bravest chiefs are kill'd,
And rage, and death, and carnage load the field.
Now storms the victor at the Trojan wall;
Surveys the towers, and meditates their fall.
But Jove descending shook the Idaean hills,
And down their summits pour'd a hundred rills:
The unkindled lightning in his hand he took,
And thus the many-coloured maid bespoke:

"Iris, with haste thy golden wings display,
To godlike Hector this our word convey—
While Agamemnon wastes the ranks around,
Fights in the front, and bathes with blood the ground,
Bid him give way; but issue forth commands,
And trust the war to less important hands:
But when, or wounded by the spear or dart,
That chief shall mount his chariot, and depart,
Then Jove shall string his arm, and fire his breast,
Then to her ships shall flying Greece be press'd,
Till to the main the burning sun descend,
And sacred night her awful shade extend."
He spoke, and Iris at his word obey'd;
On wings of winds descends the various maid.
The chief she found amidst the ranks of war,
Close to the bulwarks, on his glittering car.
The goddess then: "O son of Priam, hear!
From Jove I come, and his high mandate bear.
While Agamemnon wastes the ranks around,
Fights in the front, and bathes with blood the ground,
Abstain from fight; yet issue forth commands,
And trust the war to less important hands:
But when, or wounded by the spear or dart,
The chief shall mount his chariot, and depart,
Then Jove shall string thy arm, and fire thy breast,
Then to her ships shall flying Greece be press'd,
Till to the main the burning sun descend,
And sacred night her awful shade extend."
She said, and vanish'd. Hector, with a bound,
Springs from his chariot on the trembling ground,
In clanging arms: he grasps in either hand
A pointed lance, and speeds from band to band;
Revives their ardour, turns their steps from flight,
And wakes anew the dying flames of fight.
They stand to arms: the Greeks their onset dare,
Condense their powers, and wait the coming war.
New force, new spirit, to each breast returns;
The fight renew'd with fiercer fury burns:
The king leads on: all fix on him their eye,
And learn from him to conquer, or to die.
Ye sacred nine! celestial Muses! tell,
Who faced him first, and by his prowess fell?
The great Iphidamas, the bold and young,
From sage Antenor and Theano sprung;
Whom from his youth his grandsire Cisseus bred,
And nursed in Thrace where snowy flocks are fed.

Scarce did the down his rosy cheeks invest,
And early honour warm his generous breast,
When the kind sire consign'd his daughter's charms
(Theano's sister) to his youthful arms.
But call'd by glory to the wars of Troy,
He leaves untasted the first fruits of joy;
From his loved bride departs with melting eyes,
And swift to aid his dearer country flies.
With twelve black ships he reach'd Percope's strand,
Thence took the long laborious march by land.
Now fierce for fame, before the ranks he springs,
Towering in arms, and braves the king of kings.
Atrides first discharged the missive spear;
The Trojan stoop'd, the javelin pass'd in air.
Then near the corslet, at the monarch's heart,
With all his strength, the youth directs his dart:
But the broad belt, with plates of silver bound,
The point rebated, and repell'd the wound.
Encumber'd with the dart, Atrides stands,
Till, grasp'd with force, he wrench'd it from his hands;
At once his weighty sword discharged a wound
Full on his neck, that fell'd him to the ground.
Stretch'd in the dust the unhappy warrior lies,
And sleep eternal seals his swimming eyes.
Oh worthy better fate! oh early slain!
Thy country's friend; and virtuous, though in vain!
No more the youth shall join his consort's side,
At once a virgin, and at once a bride!
No more with presents her embraces meet,
Or lay the spoils of conquest at her feet,
On whom his passion, lavish of his store,
Bestow'd so much, and vainly promised more!
Unwept, uncover'd, on the plain he lay,
While the proud victor bore his arms away.
Coon, Antenor's eldest hope, was nigh:
Tears, at the sight, came starting from his eye,
While pierced with grief the much-loved youth he view'd,
And the pale features now deform'd with blood.
Then, with his spear, unseen, his time he took,
Aim'd at the king, and near his elbow strook.
The thrilling steel transpierced the brawny part,
And through his arm stood forth the barbed dart.
Surprised the monarch feels, yet void of fear
On Coon rushes with his lifted spear:
His brother's corpse the pious Trojan draws,
And calls his country to assert his cause;

Defends him breathless on the sanguine field,
And o'er the body spreads his ample shield.
Atrides, marking an unguarded part,
Transfix'd the warrior with his brazen dart;
Prone on his brother's bleeding breast he lay,
The monarch's falchion lopp'd his head away:
The social shades the same dark journey go,
And join each other in the realms below.
The vengeful victor rages round the fields,
With every weapon art or fury yields:
By the long lance, the sword, or ponderous stone,
Whole ranks are broken, and whole troops o'erthrown.
This, while yet warm distill'd the purple flood;
But when the wound grew stiff with clotted blood,
Then grinding tortures his strong bosom rend,
Less keen those darts the fierce Ilythiae send:
(The powers that cause the teeming matron's throes,
Sad mothers of unutterable woes!)
Stung with the smart, all-panting with the pain,
He mounts the car, and gives his squire the rein;
Then with a voice which fury made more strong,
And pain augmented, thus exhorts the throng:
"O friends! O Greeks! assert your honours won;
Proceed, and finish what this arm begun:
Lo! angry Jove forbids your chief to stay,
And envies half the glories of the day."
He said: the driver whirls his lengthful thong;
The horses fly; the chariot smokes along.
Clouds from their nostrils the fierce coursers blow,
And from their sides the foam descends in snow;
Shot through the battle in a moment's space,
The wounded monarch at his tent they place.
No sooner Hector saw the king retired,
But thus his Trojans and his aids he fired:
"Hear, all ye Dardan, all ye Lycian race!
Famed in close fight, and dreadful face to face:
Now call to mind your ancient trophies won,
Your great forefathers' virtues, and your own.
Behold, the general flies! deserts his powers!
Lo, Jove himself declares the conquest ours!
Now on yon ranks impel your foaming steeds;
And, sure of glory, dare immortal deeds."
With words like these the fiery chief alarms
His fainting host, and every bosom warms.
As the bold hunter cheers his hounds to tear
The brindled lion, or the tusky bear:

With voice and hand provokes their doubting heart,
And springs the foremost with his lifted dart:
So godlike Hector prompts his troops to dare;
Nor prompts alone, but leads himself the war.
On the black body of the foe he pours;
As from the cloud's deep bosom, swell'd with showers,
A sudden storm the purple ocean sweeps,
Drives the wild waves, and tosses all the deeps.
Say, Muse! when Jove the Trojan's glory crown'd,
Beneath his arm what heroes bit the ground?
Assaeus, Dolops, and Autonous died,
Opites next was added to their side;
Then brave Hipponous, famed in many a fight,
Opheltius, Orus, sunk to endless night;
Æsymnus, Agelaus; all chiefs of name;
The rest were vulgar deaths unknown to fame.
As when a western whirlwind, charged with storms,
Dispels the gather'd clouds that Notus forms:
The gust continued, violent and strong,
Rolls sable clouds in heaps on heaps along;
Now to the skies the foaming billows rears,
Now breaks the surge, and wide the bottom bares:
Thus, raging Hector, with resistless hands,
O'erturns, confounds, and scatters all their bands.
Now the last ruin the whole host appals;
Now Greece had trembled in her wooden walls;
But wise Ulysses call'd Tydides forth,
His soul rekindled, and awaked his worth.
"And stand we deedless, O eternal shame!
Till Hector's arm involve the ships in flame?
Haste, let us join, and combat side by side."
The warrior thus, and thus the friend replied:
"No martial toil I shun, no danger fear;
Let Hector come; I wait his fury here.
But Jove with conquest crowns the Trojan train:
And, Jove our foe, all human force is vain."
He sigh'd; but, sighing, raised his vengeful steel,
And from his car the proud Thymbraeus fell:
Molion, the charioteer, pursued his lord,
His death ennobled by Ulysses' sword.
There slain, they left them in eternal night,
Then plunged amidst the thickest ranks of fight.
So two wild boars outstrip the following hounds,
Then swift revert, and wounds return for wounds.
Stern Hector's conquests in the middle plain
Stood check'd awhile, and Greece respired again.

The sons of Merops shone amidst the war;
Towering they rode in one refulgent car:
In deep prophetic arts their father skill'd,
Had warn'd his children from the Trojan field.
Fate urged them on: the father warn'd in vain;
They rush'd to fight, and perish'd on the plain;
Their breasts no more the vital spirit warms;
The stern Tydides strips their shining arms.
Hypirochus by great Ulysses dies,
And rich Hippodamus becomes his prize.
Great Jove from Ide with slaughter fills his sight,
And level hangs the doubtful scale of fight.
By Tydeus' lance Agastrophus was slain,
The far-famed hero of Pæonian strain;
Wing'd with his fears, on foot he strove to fly,
His steeds too distant, and the foe too nigh:
Through broken orders, swifter than the wind,
He fled, but flying left his life behind.
This Hector sees, as his experienced eyes
Traverse the files, and to the rescue flies;
Shouts, as he pass'd, the crystal regions rend,
And moving armies on his march attend.
Great Diomed himself was seized with fear,
And thus bespoke his brother of the war:
"Mark how this way yon bending squadrons yield!
The storm rolls on, and Hector rules the field:
Here stand his utmost force."—The warrior said;
Swift at the word his ponderous javelin fled;
Nor miss'd its aim, but where the plumage danced
Razed the smooth cone, and thence obliquely glanced.
Safe in his helm (the gift of Phœbus' hands)
Without a wound the Trojan hero stands;
But yet so stunn'd, that, staggering on the plain.
His arm and knee his sinking bulk sustain;
O'er his dim sight the misty vapours rise,
And a short darkness shades his swimming eyes.
Tydides followed to regain his lance;
While Hector rose, recover'd from the trance,
Remounts his car, and herds amidst the crowd:
The Greek pursues him, and exults aloud:
"Once more thank Phœbus for thy forfeit breath,
Or thank that swiftness which outstrips the death.
Well by Apollo are thy prayers repaid,
And oft that partial power has lent his aid.
Thou shall not long the death deserved withstand,
If any god assist Tydides' hand.

Fly then, inglorious! but thy flight, this day,
Whole hecatombs of Trojan ghosts shall pay,"
Him, while he triumph'd, Paris eyed from far,
(The spouse of Helen, the fair cause of war;)
Around the fields his feather'd shafts he sent,
From ancient Ilus' ruin'd monument:
Behind the column placed, he bent his bow,
And wing'd an arrow at the unwary foe;
Just as he stoop'd, Agastrophus's crest
To seize, and drew the corslet from his breast,
The bowstring twang'd; nor flew the shaft in vain,
But pierced his foot, and nail'd it to the plain.
The laughing Trojan, with a joyful spring.
Leaps from his ambush, and insults the king.
"He bleeds! (he cries) some god has sped my dart!
Would the same god had fix'd it in his heart!
So Troy, relieved from that wide-wasting hand,
Should breathe from slaughter and in combat stand:
Whose sons now tremble at his darted spear,
As scatter'd lambs the rushing lion fear."
He dauntless thus: "Thou conqueror of the fair,
Thou woman-warrior with the curling hair;
Vain archer! trusting to the distant dart,
Unskill'd in arms to act a manly part!
Thou hast but done what boys or women can;
Such hands may wound, but not incense a man.
Nor boast the scratch thy feeble arrow gave,
A coward's weapon never hurts the brave.
Not so this dart, which thou may'st one day feel;
Fate wings its flight, and death is on the steel:
Where this but lights, some noble life expires;
Its touch makes orphans, bathes the cheeks of sires,
Steeps earth in purple, gluts the birds of air,
And leaves such objects as distract the fair."
Ulysses hastens with a trembling heart,
Before him steps, and bending draws the dart:
Forth flows the blood; an eager pang succeeds;
Tydides mounts, and to the navy speeds.
Now on the field Ulysses stands alone,
The Greeks all fled, the Trojans pouring on;
But stands collected in himself, and whole,
And questions thus his own unconquer'd soul:
"What further subterfuge, what hopes remain?
What shame, inglorious if I quit the plain?
What danger, singly if I stand the ground,
My friends all scatter'd, all the foes around?

Yet wherefore doubtful? let this truth suffice,
The brave meets danger, and the coward flies.
To die or conquer, proves a hero's heart;
And, knowing this, I know a soldier's part."
Such thoughts revolving in his careful breast,
Near, and more near, the shady cohorts press'd;
These, in the warrior, their own fate enclose;
And round him deep the steely circle grows.
So fares a boar whom all the troop surrounds
Of shouting huntsmen and of clamorous hounds;
He grinds his ivory tusks; he foams with ire;
His sanguine eye-balls glare with living fire;
By these, by those, on every part is plied;
And the red slaughter spreads on every side.
Pierced through the shoulder, first Deiopis fell;
Next Ennomus and Thoon sank to hell;
Chersidamas, beneath the navel thrust,
Falls prone to earth, and grasps the bloody dust.
Charops, the son of Hippasus, was near;
Ulysses reach'd him with the fatal spear;
But to his aid his brother Socus flies,
Socus the brave, the generous, and the wise.
Near as he drew, the warrior thus began:
"O great Ulysses! much-enduring man!
Not deeper skill'd in every martial sleight,
Than worn to toils, and active in the fight!
This day two brothers shall thy conquest grace,
And end at once the great Hippasian race,
Or thou beneath this lance must press the field."
He said, and forceful pierced his spacious shield:
Through the strong brass the ringing javelin thrown,
Plough'd half his side, and bared it to the bone.
By Pallas' care, the spear, though deep infix'd,
Stopp'd short of life, nor with his entrails mix'd.
The wound not mortal wise Ulysses knew,
Then furious thus (but first some steps withdrew):
"Unhappy man! whose death our hands shall grace,
Fate calls thee hence and finish'd is thy race.
Nor longer check my conquests on the foe;
But, pierced by this, to endless darkness go,
And add one spectre to the realms below!"
He spoke, while Socus, seized with sudden fright,
Trembling gave way, and turn'd his back to flight;
Between his shoulders pierced the following dart,
And held its passage through the panting heart:
Wide in his breast appear'd the grisly wound;

He falls; his armour rings against the ground.
Then thus Ulysses, gazing on the slain:
"Famed son of Hippasus! there press the plain;
There ends thy narrow span assign'd by fate,
Heaven owes Ulysses yet a longer date.
Ah, wretch! no father shall thy corpse compose;
Thy dying eyes no tender mother close;
But hungry birds shall tear those balls away,
And hovering vultures scream around their prey.
Me Greece shall honour, when I meet my doom,
With solemn funerals and a lasting tomb."
Then raging with intolerable smart,
He writhes his body, and extracts the dart.
The dart a tide of spouting gore pursued,
And gladden'd Troy with sight of hostile blood.
Now troops on troops the fainting chief invade,
Forced he recedes, and loudly calls for aid.
Thrice to its pitch his lofty voice he rears;
The well-known voice thrice Menelaus hears:
Alarm'd, to Ajax Telamon he cried,
Who shares his labours, and defends his side:
"O friend! Ulysses' shouts invade my ear;
Distressed he seems, and no assistance near;
Strong as he is, yet one opposed to all,
Oppress'd by multitudes, the best may fall.
Greece robb'd of him must bid her host despair,
And feel a loss not ages can repair."
Then, where the cry directs, his course he bends;
Great Ajax, like the god of war, attends,
The prudent chief in sore distress they found,
With bands of furious Trojans compass'd round.
As when some huntsman, with a flying spear,
From the blind thicket wounds a stately deer;
Down his cleft side, while fresh the blood distils,
He bounds aloft, and scuds from hills to hills,
Till life's warm vapour issuing through the wound,
Wild mountain-wolves the fainting beast surround:
Just as their jaws his prostrate limbs invade,
The lion rushes through the woodland shade,
The wolves, though hungry, scour dispersed away;
The lordly savage vindicates his prey.
Ulysses thus, unconquer'd by his pains,
A single warrior half a host sustains:
But soon as Ajax leaves his tower-like shield,
The scattered crowds fly frighted o'er the field;
Atrides' arm the sinking hero stays,

And, saved from numbers, to his car conveys.
Victorious Ajax plies the routed crew;
And first Doryclus, Priam's son, he slew,
On strong Pandocus next inflicts a wound,
And lays Lysander bleeding on the ground.
As when a torrent, swell'd with wintry rains,
Pours from the mountains o'er the deluged plains,
And pines and oaks, from their foundations torn,
A country's ruins! to the seas are borne:
Fierce Ajax thus o'erwhelms the yielding throng;
Men, steeds, and chariots, roll in heaps along.
But Hector, from this scene of slaughter far,
Raged on the left, and ruled the tide of war:
Loud groans proclaim his progress through the plain,
And deep Scamander swells with heaps of slain.
There Nestor and Idomeneus oppose
The warrior's fury; there the battle glows;
There fierce on foot, or from the chariot's height,
His sword deforms the beauteous ranks of fight.
The spouse of Helen, dealing darts around,
Had pierced Machaon with a distant wound:
In his right shoulder the broad shaft appear'd,
And trembling Greece for her physician fear'd.
To Nestor then Idomeneus begun:
"Glory of Greece, old Neleus' valiant son!
Ascend thy chariot, haste with speed away,
And great Machaon to the ships convey;
A wise physician skill'd our wounds to heal,
Is more than armies to the public weal."
Old Nestor mounts the seat; beside him rode
The wounded offspring of the healing god.
He lends the lash; the steeds with sounding feet
Shake the dry field, and thunder toward the fleet.
But now Cebriones, from Hector's car,
Survey'd the various fortune of the war:
"While here (he cried) the flying Greeks are slain,
Trojans on Trojans yonder load the plain.
Before great Ajax see the mingled throng
Of men and chariots driven in heaps along!
I know him well, distinguish'd o'er the field
By the broad glittering of the sevenfold shield.
Thither, O Hector, thither urge thy steeds,
There danger calls, and there the combat bleeds;
There horse and foot in mingled deaths unite,
And groans of slaughter mix with shouts of fight."
Thus having spoke, the driver's lash resounds;

Swift through the ranks the rapid chariot bounds;
Stung by the stroke, the coursers scour the fields,
O'er heaps of carcases, and hills of shields.
The horses' hoofs are bathed in heroes' gore,
And, dashing, purple all the car before;
The groaning axle sable drops distils,
And mangled carnage clogs the rapid wheels.
Here Hector, plunging through the thickest fight,
Broke the dark phalanx, and let in the light:
(By the long lance, the sword, or ponderous stone,
The ranks he scatter'd and the troops o'erthrown:)
Ajax he shuns, through all the dire debate,
And fears that arm whose force he felt so late.
But partial Jove, espousing Hector's part,
Shot heaven-bred horror through the Grecian's heart;
Confused, unnerved in Hector's presence grown,
Amazed he stood, with terrors not his own.
O'er his broad back his moony shield he threw,
And, glaring round, by tardy steps withdrew.
Thus the grim lion his retreat maintains,
Beset with watchful dogs, and shouting swains;
Repulsed by numbers from the nightly stalls,
Though rage impels him, and though hunger calls,
Long stands the showering darts, and missile fires;
Then sourly slow the indignant beast retires:
So turn'd stern Ajax, by whole hosts repell'd,
While his swoln heart at every step rebell'd.
As the slow beast, with heavy strength endued,
In some wide field by troops of boys pursued,
Though round his sides a wooden tempest rain,
Crops the tall harvest, and lays waste the plain;
Thick on his hide the hollow blows resound,
The patient animal maintains his ground,
Scarce from the field with all their efforts chased,
And stirs but slowly when he stirs at last:
On Ajax thus a weight of Trojans hung,
The strokes redoubled on his buckler rung;
Confiding now in bulky strength he stands,
Now turns, and backward bears the yielding bands;
Now stiff recedes, yet hardly seems to fly,
And threats his followers with retorted eye.
Fix'd as the bar between two warring powers,
While hissing darts descend in iron showers:
In his broad buckler many a weapon stood,
Its surface bristled with a quivering wood;
And many a javelin, guiltless on the plain,

Marks the dry dust, and thirsts for blood in vain.
But bold Eurypylus his aid imparts,
And dauntless springs beneath a cloud of darts;
Whose eager javelin launch'd against the foe,
Great Apisaon felt the fatal blow;
From his torn liver the red current flow'd,
And his slack knees desert their dying load.
The victor rushing to despoil the dead,
From Paris' bow a vengeful arrow fled;
Fix'd in his nervous thigh the weapon stood,
Fix'd was the point, but broken was the wood.
Back to the lines the wounded Greek retired,
Yet thus retreating, his associates fired:
"What god, O Grecians! has your hearts dismay'd?
Oh, turn to arms; 'tis Ajax claims your aid.
This hour he stands the mark of hostile rage,
And this the last brave battle he shall wage:
Haste, join your forces; from the gloomy grave
The warrior rescue, and your country save."
Thus urged the chief: a generous troop appears,
Who spread their bucklers, and advance their spears,
To guard their wounded friend: while thus they stand
With pious care, great Ajax joins the band:
Each takes new courage at the hero's sight;
The hero rallies, and renews the fight.
Thus raged both armies like conflicting fires,
While Nestor's chariot far from fight retires:
His coursers steep'd in sweat, and stain'd with gore,
The Greeks' preserver, great Machaon, bore.
That hour Achilles, from the topmost height
Of his proud fleet, o'erlook'd the fields of fight;
His feasted eyes beheld around the plain
The Grecian rout, the slaying, and the slain.
His friend Machaon singled from the rest,
A transient pity touch'd his vengeful breast.
Straight to Menoetius' much-loved son he sent:
Graceful as Mars, Patroclus quits his tent;
In evil hour! Then fate decreed his doom,
And fix'd the date of all his woes to come.
"Why calls my friend? thy loved injunctions lay;
Whate'er thy will, Patroclus shall obey."
"O first of friends! (Pelides thus replied)
Still at my heart, and ever at my side!
The time is come, when yon despairing host
Shall learn the value of the man they lost:
Now at my knees the Greeks shall pour their moan,

And proud Atrides tremble on his throne.
Go now to Nestor, and from him be taught
What wounded warrior late his chariot brought:
For, seen at distance, and but seen behind,
His form recall'd Machaon to my mind;
Nor could I, through yon cloud, discern his face,
The coursers pass'd me with so swift a pace."
The hero said. His friend obey'd with haste,
Through intermingled ships and tents he pass'd;
The chiefs descending from their car he found:
The panting steeds Eurymedon unbound.
The warriors standing on the breezy shore,
To dry their sweat, and wash away the gore,
Here paused a moment, while the gentle gale
Convey'd that freshness the cool seas exhale;
Then to consult on farther methods went,
And took their seats beneath the shady tent.
The draught prescribed, fair Hecamede prepares,
Arsinous' daughter, graced with golden hairs:
(Whom to his aged arms, a royal slave,
Greece, as the prize of Nestor's wisdom gave:)
A table first with azure feet she placed;
Whose ample orb a brazen charger graced;
Honey new-press'd, the sacred flour of wheat,
And wholesome garlic, crown'd the savoury treat,
Next her white hand an antique goblet brings,
A goblet sacred to the Pylian kings
From eldest times: emboss'd with studs of gold,
Two feet support it, and four handles hold;
On each bright handle, bending o'er the brink,
In sculptured gold, two turtles seem to drink:
A massy weight, yet heaved with ease by him,
When the brisk nectar overlook'd the brim.
Temper'd in this, the nymph of form divine
Pours a large portion of the Pramnian wine;
With goat's-milk cheese a flavourous taste bestows,
And last with flour the smiling surface strows:
This for the wounded prince the dame prepares:
The cordial beverage reverend Nestor shares:
Salubrious draughts the warriors' thirst allay,
And pleasing conference beguiles the day.
Meantime Patroclus, by Achilles sent,
Unheard approached, and stood before the tent.
Old Nestor, rising then, the hero led
To his high seat: the chief refused and said:
"'Tis now no season for these kind delays;

The great Achilles with impatience stays.
To great Achilles this respect I owe;
Who asks, what hero, wounded by the foe,
Was borne from combat by thy foaming steeds?
With grief I see the great Machaon bleeds.
This to report, my hasty course I bend;
Thou know'st the fiery temper of my friend."
"Can then the sons of Greece (the sage rejoin'd)
Excite compassion in Achilles' mind?
Seeks he the sorrows of our host to know?
This is not half the story of our woe.
Tell him, not great Machaon bleeds alone,
Our bravest heroes in the navy groan,
Ulysses, Agamemnon, Diomed,
And stern Eurypylus, already bleed.
But, ah! what flattering hopes I entertain!
Achilles heeds not, but derides our pain:
Even till the flames consume our fleet he stays,
And waits the rising of the fatal blaze.
Chief after chief the raging foe destroys;
Calm he looks on, and every death enjoys.
Now the slow course of all-impairing time
Unstrings my nerves, and ends my manly prime;
Oh! had I still that strength my youth possess'd,
When this bold arm the Epeian powers oppress'd,
The bulls of Elis in glad triumph led,
And stretch'd the great Itymonaeus dead!
Then from my fury fled the trembling swains,
And ours was all the plunder of the plains:
Fifty white flocks, full fifty herds of swine,
As many goats, as many lowing kine:
And thrice the number of unrivall'd steeds,
All teeming females, and of generous breeds.
These, as my first essay of arms, I won;
Old Neleus gloried in his conquering son.
Thus Elis forced, her long arrears restored,
And shares were parted to each Pylian lord.
The state of Pyle was sunk to last despair,
When the proud Elians first commenced the war:
For Neleus' sons Alcides' rage had slain;
Of twelve bold brothers, I alone remain!
Oppress'd, we arm'd; and now this conquest gain'd,
My sire three hundred chosen sheep obtain'd.
(That large reprisal he might justly claim,
For prize defrauded, and insulted fame,
When Elis' monarch, at the public course,

Detain'd his chariot, and victorious horse.)
The rest the people shared; myself survey'd
The just partition, and due victims paid.
Three days were past, when Elis rose to war,
With many a courser, and with many a car;
The sons of Actor at their army's head
(Young as they were) the vengeful squadrons led.
High on the rock fair Thryoessa stands,
Our utmost frontier on the Pylian lands:
Not far the streams of famed Alphaeus flow:
The stream they pass'd, and pitch'd their tents below.
Pallas, descending in the shades of night,
Alarms the Pylians and commands the fight.
Each burns for fame, and swells with martial pride,
Myself the foremost; but my sire denied;
Fear'd for my youth, exposed to stern alarms;
And stopp'd my chariot, and detain'd my arms.
My sire denied in vain: on foot I fled
Amidst our chariots; for the goddess led.
"Along fair Arene's delightful plain
Soft Minyas rolls his waters to the main:
There, horse and foot, the Pylian troops unite,
And sheathed in arms, expect the dawning light.
Thence, ere the sun advanced his noon-day flame,
To great Alphaeus' sacred source we came.
There first to Jove our solemn rites were paid;
An untamed heifer pleased the blue-eyed maid;
A bull, Alphaeus; and a bull was slain
To the blue monarch of the watery main.
In arms we slept, beside the winding flood,
While round the town the fierce Epeians stood.
Soon as the sun, with all-revealing ray,
Flamed in the front of Heaven, and gave the day.
Bright scenes of arms, and works of war appear;
The nations meet; there Pylos, Elis here.
The first who fell, beneath my javelin bled;
King Augias' son, and spouse of Agamede:
(She that all simples' healing virtues knew,
And every herb that drinks the morning dew:)
I seized his car, the van of battle led;
The Epeians saw, they trembled, and they fled.
The foe dispersed, their bravest warrior kill'd,
Fierce as the whirlwind now I swept the field:
Full fifty captive chariots graced my train;
Two chiefs from each fell breathless to the plain.
Then Actor's sons had died, but Neptune shrouds

The youthful heroes in a veil of clouds.
O'er heapy shields, and o'er the prostrate throng,
Collecting spoils, and slaughtering all along,
Through wide Buprasian fields we forced the foes,
Where o'er the vales the Olenian rocks arose;
Till Pallas stopp'd us where Alisium flows.
Even there the hindmost of the rear I slay,
And the same arm that led concludes the day;
Then back to Pyle triumphant take my way.
There to high Jove were public thanks assign'd,
As first of gods; to Nestor, of mankind.
Such then I was, impell'd by youthful blood;
So proved my valour for my country's good.
"Achilles with unactive fury glows,
And gives to passion what to Greece he owes.
How shall he grieve, when to the eternal shade
Her hosts shall sink, nor his the power to aid!
O friend! my memory recalls the day,
When, gathering aids along the Grecian sea,
I, and Ulysses, touch'd at Phthia's port,
And entered Peleus' hospitable court.
A bull to Jove he slew in sacrifice,
And pour'd libations on the flaming thighs.
Thyself, Achilles, and thy reverend sire
Menoetius, turn'd the fragments on the fire.
Achilles sees us, to the feast invites;
Social we sit, and share the genial rites.
We then explained the cause on which we came,
Urged you to arms, and found you fierce for fame.
Your ancient fathers generous precepts gave;
Peleus said only this:—'My son! be brave.'
Menoetius thus: 'Though great Achilles shine
In strength superior, and of race divine,
Yet cooler thoughts thy elder years attend;
Let thy just counsels aid, and rule thy friend.'
Thus spoke your father at Thessalia's court:
Words now forgot, though now of vast import.
Ah! try the utmost that a friend can say:
Such gentle force the fiercest minds obey;
Some favouring god Achilles' heart may move;
Though deaf to glory, he may yield to love.
If some dire oracle his breast alarm,
If aught from Heaven withhold his saving arm,
Some beam of comfort yet on Greece may shine,
If thou but lead the Myrmidonian line;
Clad in Achilles' arms, if thou appear,

Proud Troy may tremble, and desist from war;
Press'd by fresh forces, her o'er-labour'd train
Shall seek their walls, and Greece respire again."
This touch'd his generous heart, and from the tent
Along the shore with hasty strides he went;
Soon as he came, where, on the crowded strand,
The public mart and courts of justice stand,
Where the tall fleet of great Ulysses lies,
And altars to the guardian gods arise;
There, sad, he met the brave Euaemon's son,
Large painful drops from all his members run;
An arrow's head yet rooted in his wound,
The sable blood in circles mark'd the ground.
As faintly reeling he confess'd the smart,
Weak was his pace, but dauntless was his heart.
Divine compassion touch'd Patroclus' breast,
Who, sighing, thus his bleeding friend address'd:
"Ah, hapless leaders of the Grecian host!
Thus must ye perish on a barbarous coast?
Is this your fate, to glut the dogs with gore,
Far from your friends, and from your native shore?
Say, great Eurypylus! shall Greece yet stand?
Resists she yet the raging Hector's hand?
Or are her heroes doom'd to die with shame,
And this the period of our wars and fame?"
Eurypylus replies: "No more, my friend;
Greece is no more! this day her glories end;
Even to the ships victorious Troy pursues,
Her force increasing as her toil renews.
Those chiefs, that used her utmost rage to meet,
Lie pierced with wounds, and bleeding in the fleet.
But, thou, Patroclus! act a friendly part,
Lead to my ships, and draw this deadly dart;
With lukewarm water wash the gore away;
With healing balms the raging smart allay,
Such as sage Chiron, sire of pharmacy,
Once taught Achilles, and Achilles thee.
Of two famed surgeons, Podalirius stands
This hour surrounded by the Trojan bands;
And great Machaon, wounded in his tent,
Now wants that succour which so oft he lent."
To him the chief: "What then remains to do?
The event of things the gods alone can view.
Charged by Achilles' great command I fly,
And bear with haste the Pylian king's reply:
But thy distress this instant claims relief."

He said, and in his arms upheld the chief.
The slaves their master's slow approach survey'd,
And hides of oxen on the floor display'd:
There stretch'd at length the wounded hero lay;
Patroclus cut the forky steel away:
Then in his hands a bitter root he bruised;
The wound he wash'd, the styptic juice infused.
The closing flesh that instant ceased to glow,
The wound to torture, and the blood to flow.

BOOK XII.

THE BATTLE AT THE GRECIAN WALL.

While thus the hero's pious cares attend
The cure and safety of his wounded friend,
Trojans and Greeks with clashing shields engage,
And mutual deaths are dealt with mutual rage.
Nor long the trench or lofty walls oppose;
With gods averse the ill-fated works arose;
Their powers neglected, and no victim slain,
The walls were raised, the trenches sunk in vain.
Without the gods, how short a period stands
The proudest monument of mortal hands!
This stood while Hector and Achilles raged,
While sacred Troy the warring hosts engaged;
But when her sons were slain, her city burn'd,
And what survived of Greece to Greece return'd;
Then Neptune and Apollo shook the shore,
Then Ida's summits pour'd their watery store;
Rhesus and Rhodius then unite their rills,
Caresus roaring down the stony hills,
Æsepus, Granicus, with mingled force,
And Xanthus foaming from his fruitful source;
And gulfy Simois, rolling to the main
Helmets, and shields, and godlike heroes slain:
These, turn'd by Phœbus from their wonted ways,
Deluged the rampire nine continual days;
The weight of waters saps the yielding wall,
And to the sea the floating bulwarks fall.

Incessant cataracts the Thunderer pours,
And half the skies descend in sluicy showers.
The god of ocean, marching stern before,
With his huge trident wounds the trembling shore,
Vast stones and piles from their foundation heaves,
And whelms the smoky ruin in the waves.
Now smooth'd with sand, and levell'd by the flood,
No fragment tells where once the wonder stood;
In their old bounds the rivers roll again,
Shine 'twixt the hills, or wander o'er the plain.
But this the gods in later times perform;
As yet the bulwark stood, and braved the storm;
The strokes yet echoed of contending powers;
War thunder'd at the gates, and blood distain'd the towers.
Smote by the arm of Jove with dire dismay,
Close by their hollow ships the Grecians lay:
Hector's approach in every wind they hear,
And Hector's fury every moment fear.
He, like a whirlwind, toss'd the scattering throng,
Mingled the troops, and drove the field along.
So 'midst the dogs and hunters' daring bands,
Fierce of his might, a boar or lion stands;
Arm'd foes around a dreadful circle form,
And hissing javelins rain an iron storm:
His powers untamed, their bold assault defy,
And where he turns the rout disperse or die:
He foams, he glares, he bounds against them all,
And if he falls, his courage makes him fall.
With equal rage encompass'd Hector glows;
Exhorts his armies, and the trenches shows.
The panting steeds impatient fury breathe,
And snort and tremble at the gulf beneath;
Just at the brink they neigh, and paw the ground,
And the turf trembles, and the skies resound.
Eager they view'd the prospect dark and deep,
Vast was the leap, and headlong hung the steep;
The bottom bare, (a formidable show!)
And bristled thick with sharpen'd stakes below.
The foot alone this strong defence could force,
And try the pass impervious to the horse.
This saw Polydamas; who, wisely brave,
Restrain'd great Hector, and this counsel gave:
"O thou, bold leader of the Trojan bands!
And you, confederate chiefs from foreign lands!
What entrance here can cumbrous chariots find,
The stakes beneath, the Grecian walls behind?

No pass through those, without a thousand wounds,
No space for combat in yon narrow bounds.
Proud of the favours mighty Jove has shown,
On certain dangers we too rashly run:
If 'tis his will our haughty foes to tame,
Oh may this instant end the Grecian name!
Here, far from Argos, let their heroes fall,
And one great day destroy and bury all!
But should they turn, and here oppress our train,
What hopes, what methods of retreat remain?
Wedged in the trench, by our own troops confused,
In one promiscuous carnage crush'd and bruised,
All Troy must perish, if their arms prevail,
Nor shall a Trojan live to tell the tale.
Hear then, ye warriors! and obey with speed;
Back from the trenches let your steeds be led;
Then all alighting, wedged in firm array,
Proceed on foot, and Hector lead the way.
So Greece shall stoop before our conquering power,
And this (if Jove consent) her fatal hour."

This counsel pleased: the godlike Hector sprung
Swift from his seat; his clanging armour rung.
The chief's example follow'd by his train,
Each quits his car, and issues on the plain,
By orders strict the charioteers enjoin'd
Compel the coursers to their ranks behind.
The forces part in five distinguish'd bands,
And all obey their several chiefs' commands.
The best and bravest in the first conspire,
Pant for the fight, and threat the fleet with fire:
Great Hector glorious in the van of these,
Polydamas, and brave Cebriones.
Before the next the graceful Paris shines,
And bold Alcathous, and Agenor joins.
The sons of Priam with the third appear,
Deiphobus, and Helenas the seer;
In arms with these the mighty Asius stood,
Who drew from Hyrtacus his noble blood,
And whom Arisba's yellow coursers bore,
The coursers fed on Sellè's winding shore.
Antenor's sons the fourth battalion guide,
And great Æneas, born on fountful Ide.
Divine Sarpedon the last band obey'd,
Whom Glaucus and Asteropaeus aid.
Next him, the bravest, at their army's head,

But he more brave than all the hosts he led.
Now with compacted shields in close array,
The moving legions speed their headlong way:
Already in their hopes they fire the fleet,
And see the Grecians gasping at their feet.
While every Trojan thus, and every aid,
The advice of wise Polydamas obey'd,
Asius alone, confiding in his car,
His vaunted coursers urged to meet the war.
Unhappy hero! and advised in vain;
Those wheels returning ne'er shall mark the plain;
No more those coursers with triumphant joy
Restore their master to the gates of Troy!
Black death attends behind the Grecian wall,
And great Idomeneus shall boast thy fall!
Fierce to the left he drives, where from the plain
The flying Grecians strove their ships to gain;
Swift through the wall their horse and chariots pass'd,
The gates half-open'd to receive the last.
Thither, exulting in his force, he flies:
His following host with clamours rend the skies:
To plunge the Grecians headlong in the main,
Such their proud hopes; but all their hopes were vain!
To guard the gates, two mighty chiefs attend,
Who from the Lapiths' warlike race descend;
This Polypœtes, great Perithous' heir,
And that Leonteus, like the god of war.
As two tall oaks, before the wall they rise;
Their roots in earth, their heads amidst the skies:
Whose spreading arms with leafy honours crown'd,
Forbid the tempest, and protect the ground;
High on the hills appears their stately form,
And their deep roots for ever brave the storm.
So graceful these, and so the shock they stand
Of raging Asius, and his furious band.
Orestes, Acamas, in front appear,
And Œnomaus and Thoon close the rear:
In vain their clamours shake the ambient fields,
In vain around them beat their hollow shields;
The fearless brothers on the Grecians call,
To guard their navies, and defend the wall.
Even when they saw Troy's sable troops impend,
And Greece tumultuous from her towers descend,
Forth from the portals rush'd the intrepid pair,
Opposed their breasts, and stood themselves the war.
So two wild boars spring furious from their den,

Roused with the cries of dogs and voice of men;
On every side the crackling trees they tear,
And root the shrubs, and lay the forest bare;
They gnash their tusks, with fire their eye-balls roll,
Till some wide wound lets out their mighty soul.
Around their heads the whistling javelins sung,
With sounding strokes their brazen targets rung;
Fierce was the fight, while yet the Grecian powers
Maintain'd the walls, and mann'd the lofty towers:
To save their fleet their last efforts they try,
And stones and darts in mingled tempests fly.
As when sharp Boreas blows abroad, and brings
The dreary winter on his frozen wings;
Beneath the low-hung clouds the sheets of snow
Descend, and whiten all the fields below:
So fast the darts on either army pour,
So down the rampires rolls the rocky shower:
Heavy, and thick, resound the batter'd shields,
And the deaf echo rattles round the fields.
With shame repulsed, with grief and fury driven,
The frantic Asius thus accuses Heaven:
"In powers immortal who shall now believe?
Can those too flatter, and can Jove deceive?
What man could doubt but Troy's victorious power
Should humble Greece, and this her fatal hour?
But like when wasps from hollow crannies drive,
To guard the entrance of their common hive,
Darkening the rock, while with unwearied wings
They strike the assailants, and infix their stings;
A race determined, that to death contend:
So fierce these Greeks their last retreats defend.
Gods! shall two warriors only guard their gates,
Repel an army, and defraud the fates?"
These empty accents mingled with the wind,
Nor moved great Jove's unalterable mind;
To godlike Hector and his matchless might
Was owed the glory of the destined fight.
Like deeds of arms through all the forts were tried,
And all the gates sustain'd an equal tide;
Through the long walls the stony showers were heard,
The blaze of flames, the flash of arms appear'd.
The spirit of a god my breast inspire,
To raise each act to life, and sing with fire!
While Greece unconquer'd kept alive the war,
Secure of death, confiding in despair;
And all her guardian gods, in deep dismay,

With unassisting arms deplored the day.
Even yet the dauntless Lapithae maintain
The dreadful pass, and round them heap the slain.
First Damasus, by Polypœtes' steel,
Pierced through his helmet's brazen visor, fell;
The weapon drank the mingled brains and gore!
The warrior sinks, tremendous now no more!
Next Ormenus and Pylon yield their breath:
Nor less Leonteus strews the field with death;
First through the belt Hippomachus he gored,
Then sudden waved his unresisted sword:
Antiphates, as through the ranks he broke,
The falchion struck, and fate pursued the stroke:
Iamenus, Orestes, Menon, bled;
And round him rose a monument of dead.
Meantime, the bravest of the Trojan crew,
Bold Hector and Polydamas, pursue;
Fierce with impatience on the works to fall,
And wrap in rolling flames the fleet and wall.
These on the farther bank now stood and gazed,
By Heaven alarm'd, by prodigies amazed:
A signal omen stopp'd the passing host,
Their martial fury in their wonder lost.
Jove's bird on sounding pinions beat the skies;
A bleeding serpent of enormous size,
His talons truss'd; alive, and curling round,
He stung the bird, whose throat received the wound:
Mad with the smart, he drops the fatal prey,
In airy circles wings his painful way,
Floats on the winds, and rends the heaven with cries:
Amidst the host the fallen serpent lies.
They, pale with terror, mark its spires unroll'd,
And Jove's portent with beating hearts behold.
Then first Polydamas the silence broke,
Long weigh'd the signal, and to Hector spoke:
"How oft, my brother, thy reproach I bear,
For words well meant, and sentiments sincere?
True to those counsels which I judge the best,
I tell the faithful dictates of my breast.
To speak his thoughts is every freeman's right,
In peace, in war, in council, and in fight;
And all I move, deferring to thy sway,
But tends to raise that power which I obey.
Then hear my words, nor may my words be vain!
Seek not this day the Grecian ships to gain;
For sure, to warn us, Jove his omen sent,

And thus my mind explains its clear event:
The victor eagle, whose sinister flight
Retards our host, and fills our hearts with fright,
Dismiss'd his conquest in the middle skies,
Allow'd to seize, but not possess the prize;
Thus, though we gird with fires the Grecian fleet,
Though these proud bulwalks tumble at our feet,
Toils unforeseen, and fiercer, are decreed;
More woes shall follow, and more heroes bleed.
So bodes my soul, and bids me thus advise;
For thus a skilful seer would read the skies."
To him then Hector with disdain return'd:
(Fierce as he spoke, his eyes with fury burn'd:)
"Are these the faithful counsels of thy tongue?
Thy will is partial, not thy reason wrong:
Or if the purpose of thy heart thou vent,
Sure heaven resumes the little sense it lent.
What coward counsels would thy madness move
Against the word, the will reveal'd of Jove?
The leading sign, the irrevocable nod,
And happy thunders of the favouring god,
These shall I slight, and guide my wavering mind
By wandering birds that flit with every wind?
Ye vagrants of the sky! your wings extend,
Or where the suns arise, or where descend;
To right, to left, unheeded take your way,
While I the dictates of high heaven obey.
Without a sign his sword the brave man draws,
And asks no omen but his country's cause.
But why should'st thou suspect the war's success?
None fears it more, as none promotes it less:
Though all our chiefs amidst yon ships expire,
Trust thy own cowardice to escape their fire.
Troy and her sons may find a general grave,
But thou canst live, for thou canst be a slave.
Yet should the fears that wary mind suggests
Spread their cold poison through our soldiers' breasts,
My javelin can revenge so base a part,
And free the soul that quivers in thy heart."
Furious he spoke, and, rushing to the wall,
Calls on his host; his host obey the call;
With ardour follow where their leader flies:
Redoubling clamours thunder in the skies.
Jove breathes a whirlwind from the hills of Ide,
And drifts of dust the clouded navy hide;
He fills the Greeks with terror and dismay,

And gives great Hector the predestined day.
Strong in themselves, but stronger in his aid,
Close to the works their rigid siege they laid.
In vain the mounds and massy beams defend,
While these they undermine, and those they rend;
Upheaved the piles that prop the solid wall;
And heaps on heaps the smoky ruins fall.
Greece on her ramparts stands the fierce alarms;
The crowded bulwarks blaze with waving arms,
Shield touching shield, a long refulgent row;
Whence hissing darts, incessant, rain below.
The bold Ajaces fly from tower to tower,
And rouse, with flame divine, the Grecian power.
The generous impulse every Greek obeys;
Threats urge the fearful; and the valiant, praise.
"Fellows in arms! whose deeds are known to fame,
And you, whose ardour hopes an equal name!
Since not alike endued with force or art;
Behold a day when each may act his part!
A day to fire the brave, and warm the cold,
To gain new glories, or augment the old.
Urge those who stand, and those who faint, excite;
Drown Hector's vaunts in loud exhorts of fight;
Conquest, not safety, fill the thoughts of all;
Seek not your fleet, but sally from the wall;
So Jove once more may drive their routed train,
And Troy lie trembling in her walls again."
Their ardour kindles all the Grecian powers;
And now the stones descend in heavier showers.
As when high Jove his sharp artillery forms,
And opes his cloudy magazine of storms;
In winter's bleak uncomfortable reign,
A snowy inundation hides the plain;
He stills the winds, and bids the skies to sleep;
Then pours the silent tempest thick and deep;
And first the mountain-tops are cover'd o'er,
Then the green fields, and then the sandy shore;
Bent with the weight, the nodding woods are seen,
And one bright waste hides all the works of men:
The circling seas, alone absorbing all,
Drink the dissolving fleeces as they fall:
So from each side increased the stony rain,
And the white ruin rises o'er the plain.
Thus godlike Hector and his troops contend
To force the ramparts, and the gates to rend:
Nor Troy could conquer, nor the Greeks would yield,

Till great Sarpedon tower'd amid the field;
For mighty Jove inspired with martial flame
His matchless son, and urged him on to fame.
In arms he shines, conspicuous from afar,
And bears aloft his ample shield in air;
Within whose orb the thick bull-hides were roll'd,
Ponderous with brass, and bound with ductile gold:
And while two pointed javelins arm his hands,
Majestic moves along, and leads his Lycian bands.
So press'd with hunger, from the mountain's brow
Descends a lion on the flocks below;
So stalks the lordly savage o'er the plain,
In sullen majesty, and stern disdain:
In vain loud mastiffs bay him from afar,
And shepherds gall him with an iron war;
Regardless, furious, he pursues his way;
He foams, he roars, he rends the panting prey.
Resolved alike, divine Sarpedon glows
With generous rage that drives him on the foes.
He views the towers, and meditates their fall,
To sure destruction dooms the aspiring wall;
Then casting on his friend an ardent look,
Fired with the thirst of glory, thus he spoke:
"Why boast we, Glaucus! our extended reign,
Where Xanthus' streams enrich the Lycian plain,
Our numerous herds that range the fruitful field,
And hills where vines their purple harvest yield,
Our foaming bowls with purer nectar crown'd,
Our feasts enhanced with music's sprightly sound?
Why on those shores are we with joy survey'd,
Admired as heroes, and as gods obey'd,
Unless great acts superior merit prove,
And vindicate the bounteous powers above?
'Tis ours, the dignity they give to grace;
The first in valour, as the first in place;
That when with wondering eyes our martial bands
Behold our deeds transcending our commands,
Such, they may cry, deserve the sovereign state,
Whom those that envy dare not imitate!
Could all our care elude the gloomy grave,
Which claims no less the fearful and the brave,
For lust of fame I should not vainly dare
In fighting fields, nor urge thy soul to war.
But since, alas! ignoble age must come,
Disease, and death's inexorable doom,
The life, which others pay, let us bestow,

And give to fame what we to nature owe;
Brave though we fall, and honour'd if we live,
Or let us glory gain, or glory give!"
He said; his words the listening chief inspire
With equal warmth, and rouse the warrior's fire;
The troops pursue their leaders with delight,
Rush to the foe, and claim the promised fight.
Menestheus from on high the storm beheld
Threatening the fort, and blackening in the field:
Around the walls he gazed, to view from far
What aid appear'd to avert the approaching war,
And saw where Teucer with the Ajaces stood,
Of fight insatiate, prodigal of blood.
In vain he calls; the din of helms and shields
Rings to the skies, and echoes through the fields,
The brazen hinges fly, the walls resound,
Heaven trembles, roar the mountains, thunders all the
ground.
Then thus to Thoos: "Hence with speed (he said),
And urge the bold Ajaces to our aid;
Their strength, united, best may help to bear
The bloody labours of the doubtful war:
Hither the Lycian princes bend their course,
The best and bravest of the hostile force.
But if too fiercely there the foes contend,
Let Telamon, at least, our towers defend,
And Teucer haste with his unerring bow
To share the danger, and repel the foe."
Swift, at the word, the herald speeds along
The lofty ramparts, through the martial throng,
And finds the heroes bathed in sweat and gore,
Opposed in combat on the dusty shore.
"Ye valiant leaders of our warlike bands!
Your aid (said Thoos) Peteus' son demands;
Your strength, united, best may help to bear
The bloody labours of the doubtful war:
Thither the Lycian princes bend their course,
The best and bravest of the hostile force.
But if too fiercely, here, the foes contend,
At least, let Telamon those towers defend,
And Teucer haste with his unerring bow
To share the danger, and repel the foe."
Straight to the fort great Ajax turn'd his care,
And thus bespoke his brothers of the war:
"Now, valiant Lycomede! exert your might,
And, brave Oïleus, prove your force in fight;

To you I trust the fortune of the field,
Till by this arm the foe shall be repell'd:
That done, expect me to complete the day.
Then with his sevenfold shield he strode away."
With equal steps bold Teucer press'd the shore,
Whose fatal bow the strong Pandion bore.
High on the walls appear'd the Lycian powers,
Like some black tempest gathering round the towers:
The Greeks, oppress'd, their utmost force unite,
Prepared to labour in the unequal fight:
The war renews, mix'd shouts and groans arise;
Tumultuous clamour mounts, and thickens in the skies.
Fierce Ajax first the advancing host invades,
And sends the brave Epicles to the shades,
Sarpedon's friend. Across the warrior's way,
Rent from the walls, a rocky fragment lay;
In modern ages not the strongest swain
Could heave the unwieldy burden from the plain:
He poised, and swung it round; then toss'd on high,
It flew with force, and labour'd up the sky;
Full on the Lycian's helmet thundering down,
The ponderous ruin crush'd his batter'd crown.
As skilful divers from some airy steep
Headlong descend, and shoot into the deep,
So falls Epicles; then in groans expires,
And murmuring to the shades the soul retires.
While to the ramparts daring Glaucus drew,
From Teucer's hand a winged arrow flew;
The bearded shaft the destined passage found,
And on his naked arm inflicts a wound.
The chief, who fear'd some foe's insulting boast
Might stop the progress of his warlike host,
Conceal'd the wound, and, leaping from his height
Retired reluctant from the unfinish'd fight.
Divine Sarpedon with regret beheld
Disabled Glaucus slowly quit the field;
His beating breast with generous ardour glows,
He springs to fight, and flies upon the foes.
Alcmaon first was doom'd his force to feel;
Deep in his breast he plunged the pointed steel;
Then from the yawning wound with fury tore
The spear, pursued by gushing streams of gore:
Down sinks the warrior with a thundering sound,
His brazen armour rings against the ground.
Swift to the battlement the victor flies,
Tugs with full force, and every nerve applies:

It shakes; the ponderous stones disjointed yield;
The rolling ruins smoke along the field.
A mighty breach appears; the walls lie bare;
And, like a deluge, rushes in the war.
At once bold Teucer draws the twanging bow,
And Ajax sends his javelin at the foe;
Fix'd in his belt the feather'd weapon stood,
And through his buckler drove the trembling wood;
But Jove was present in the dire debate,
To shield his offspring, and avert his fate.
The prince gave back, not meditating flight,
But urging vengeance, and severer fight;
Then raised with hope, and fired with glory's charms,
His fainting squadrons to new fury warms.
"O where, ye Lycians, is the strength you boast?
Your former fame and ancient virtue lost!
The breach lies open, but your chief in vain
Attempts alone the guarded pass to gain:
Unite, and soon that hostile fleet shall fall:
The force of powerful union conquers all."
This just rebuke inflamed the Lycian crew;
They join, they thicken, and the assault renew:
Unmoved the embodied Greeks their fury dare,
And fix'd support the weight of all the war;
Nor could the Greeks repel the Lycian powers,
Nor the bold Lycians force the Grecian towers.
As on the confines of adjoining grounds,
Two stubborn swains with blows dispute their bounds;
They tug, they sweat; but neither gain, nor yield,
One foot, one inch, of the contended field;
Thus obstinate to death, they fight, they fall;
Nor these can keep, nor those can win the wall.
Their manly breasts are pierced with many a wound,
Loud strokes are heard, and rattling arms resound;
The copious slaughter covers all the shore,
And the high ramparts drip with human gore.
As when two scales are charged with doubtful loads,
From side to side the trembling balance nods,
(While some laborious matron, just and poor,
With nice exactness weighs her woolly store,)
Till poised aloft, the resting beam suspends
Each equal weight; nor this, nor that, descends:
So stood the war, till Hector's matchless might,
With fates prevailing, turn'd the scale of fight.
Fierce as a whirlwind up the walls he flies,
And fires his host with loud repeated cries.

"Advance, ye Trojans! lend your valiant hands,
Haste to the fleet, and toss the blazing brands!"
They hear, they run; and, gathering at his call,
Raise scaling engines, and ascend the wall:
Around the works a wood of glittering spears
Shoots up, and all the rising host appears.
A ponderous stone bold Hector heaved to throw,
Pointed above, and rough and gross below:
Not two strong men the enormous weight could raise,
Such men as live in these degenerate days:
Yet this, as easy as a swain could bear
The snowy fleece, he toss'd, and shook in air;
For Jove upheld, and lighten'd of its load
The unwieldy rock, the labour of a god.
Thus arm'd, before the folded gates he came,
Of massy substance, and stupendous frame;
With iron bars and brazen hinges strong,
On lofty beams of solid timber hung:
Then thundering through the planks with forceful sway,
Drives the sharp rock; the solid beams give way,
The folds are shatter'd; from the crackling door
Leap the resounding bars, the flying hinges roar.
Now rushing in, the furious chief appears,
Gloomy as night! and shakes two shining spears:
A dreadful gleam from his bright armour came,
And from his eye-balls flash'd the living flame.
He moves a god, resistless in his course,
And seems a match for more than mortal force.
Then pouring after, through the gaping space,
A tide of Trojans flows, and fills the place;
The Greeks behold, they tremble, and they fly;
The shore is heap'd with death, and tumult rends the sky.

More Lifkowitz editions, each hand-picked by Roland!

Find on Amazon, Barnes & Noble or Lifkowitz.com.

www.ingramcontent.com/pod-product-compliance
Lightning Source LLC
Chambersburg PA
CBHW022005090426
42741CB00007B/907